WHO'S REALLY DRIVING YOUR BUS TODAY

James O. Henman, Ph.D.

Copyright © 2022 James O. Henman, Ph.D.

All rights reserved. No part of this book may be reproduced, stored, or transmitted by any means—whether auditory, graphic, mechanical, or electronic—without written permission of both publisher and author, except in the case of brief excerpts used in critical articles and reviews. Unauthorized reproduction of any part of this work is illegal and is punishable by law.

The ideas, procedures, and suggestions contained in this book are not intended as a ubstitute for consulting with a mental health professional. All names and identities of clients have been altered to protect their confidentiality.

Scripture references in this volume are from The Layman's Parallel Bible, copyright 1991 by The Zondervan Corporation.

ISBN: 979-8-88640-001-4 (sc)
ISBN: 979-8-88640-002-1 (hc)
ISBN: 979-8-88640-003-8 (e)

Because of the dynamic nature of the Internet, any web addresses or links contained in this book may have changed since publication and may no longer be valid. The views expressed in this work are solely those of the author and do not necessarily reflect the views of the publisher, and the publisher hereby disclaims any responsibility for them.

One Galleria Blvd., Suite 1900, Metairie, LA 70001
1-888-421-2397

Little Girl Lost

She lived in shadows behind the doors
Hidden in silence
Afraid to be seen or heard.
Her existence was a nuisance
Especially to the adults, and
It threatened the child's safety.
Isn't she precious?
Can't she get the love she needs?
Not then, Not now.
How do I acknowledge that part of me
I have forsaken?
Put my arm around her and
Let her know my love?
She needs to know she's special,
I need to know I love her.
Acknowledge all her weakness
And let her feel loved.

Christina W. 1992

CONTENTS

Dedication vii
Preface xi

Chapter 1. Introduction to Drivers Training 1
Fundamental Principles of Healthy Change A New Program For Living 4
Meeting Your Coach 5
A Peek At Drivers Training 8
Getting To Know Your Drivers Manual For Change 16

Chapter 2. Seeing Clearly Through Your Windshield 22
Nugget: You Experience Reality Through Perceptual Filters! 24
Power Of Mind Distortions 25

Chapter 3. A Look Inside Your Perceptual Bus 46
The Adult Child Concept 47
A Personal Look Inside 56
The Concept of Therapeutic Life Coaching 65
The Twelve-Step Concept Of Healing 70
The Concept Of Spirituality 71
The Concept Of Self-Esteem 73

Chapter 4. Driver's Training-Learning To Read The Signs 77
ABC's Of Observation 78
Additional Observation Tools Constructive Problem Solving 81
Movie Check 83
Role Reversal Check 83
Five-Step Deep Sharing Exercise 84

Chapter 5. Inside A Drivers Training Session 86
Introduction from Emma 86
Emma's Therapeutic Life Coaching Session
    (Read out loud-Experiencing the dialogue) 88

Introduction From Bill 107
Bill's Therapeutic Life Coaching Session
    (Read out loud-Experiencing the dialogue) 108

Chapter 6. Core Elements Of Drivers Training 127
Nugget: Truth Transcends Our Perceptions Of Reality! 127
Nugget: We Become Addicted To The Familiar! 134
Nugget: Change Is Possible In The Present! 151
Nugget: Personal Change Is An Active Participation Process! 155
Nugget: Freedom Is The Willingness To Accept The Consequences
    Of Your Choices! 156

Chapter 7. The Power Of Identity In Drivers Training 162
Nugget: I Am Not My Story, And My Story Affects Where
    I Am Starting Today! 163
Nugget: Identity Leads To Perceptions! 169
Nugget: I Am The Chooser In My Life 176
Nugget: There Is An Economy In Your Giving! 181

Chapter 8. Advanced Driving Tips For Healthy Change 184
Nugget: Believing Is Seeing! 184
Nugget: Judging and Defending Prevent Change! 192
Nugget: It Is Wise To See Your Glass Half Full Rather Than Half Empty! 204
Nugget: Forgiveness Is Letting Go Of Holding On! 207
Final Thoughts From Your Coach 209

Epilogue 211
Additional "Nuggets of Wisdom" For Further Reflection 216
Cognitive / Perceptual Reconstruction: Applied Mindfulness 218
The Journey Series Podcasts 219
The Grace Series Podcasts 221
About the Author 223

DEDICATION

T his book is dedicated to the core belief that deep, profound changes are possible for you in the present! This belief is the culmination of 40+ years of experience as a Therapeutic Life Coach and 40 years of experiencing my own personal recovery as an Adult Child. I want to thank the thousands of clients, who have shown such courage in facing their difficulties and growing through them. I have learned so much from sharing their lives. From the feedback of countless members of CAIR and CAIRing Grace Support Groups, I have learned to appreciate the ability of people to help each other in the healing process-all that is required is a safe place to learn and practice powerful tools, and concepts about how to approach healthy change. I have found that when I embrace these healthy resources in my personal life, they really help, when I slip into automatic pilot, my life does not work as well. I am pleased to be sharing these experiences with you as you begin reading *"Who's REALLY Driving Your Bus Today?" It works when you work it!*

   I have had wonderful support in writing this book. To all of those who read version after version of the book drafts, giving feedback and suggestions that allowed the drafts to evolve into its current form-THANK YOU FROM THE BOTTOM OF MY HEART! I could not have done it without your support and encouragement. I want to give a special thanks to Amelia Pinkus, Tony Dias, Michael Douglas, Ed Schroeder, and Lynn Breshears for conceptual and editing contributions. To my nephew Lance, THANKS! My mom has been a support in more ways than I can ever describe-believing in me before I could believe in myself, helping with editing and feedback, and just being herself.

   I want to thank my sons, Jesse and Nathan, for teaching me so much about life and living. They have been very patient during this long writing process. To my wife, Sonia, who is my best friend and partner for 50 years-I love you! Finally, I want to thank my Big Brother Jesus, who made this all possible.

Be Still And Know Me

I look upon your heart and see your sadness.
I search your soul and know its despair.
You turn to me but cannot find the words to pray.
You look to me but cannot find the song to sing.
Do not worry, child of mine.
I know all that is within you, and I understand.
For now, your silence will be a prayer to me,
And your tears, an offering.
I do not wish for you to act a part.
I do not require a spiritual charade.
But bring me, instead, your true feelings,
Your brokenness is what I wait for.
And I will meet you in the silence.
There I will stay with you and heal your heart.
And later, when the music has returned to your life,
You will look back in love and recall this silent song
We sang together.
God

Author Unknown

How Do You Approach Your Goals?

Do you demand instant results?

Do you allow small steps to build?

PREFACE

Pillars Supporting A Prayer of Serenity

The 21st Century has been a time of profound challenge to cultural and personal peace in America. These challenges have impacted our core sense of reality in significant ways. Political polarization has left the two extremes in mortal combat, leaving moderation to be attacked by both sides. Each side presents different "Truth". There has been a growing intolerant demand for "Political Correctness" that leads to superficial sound bites.

A growing movement of 'cancel culture' that can rupture relationships due to a single difference of opinion is prevalent. Economic uncertainty has continued to grow, while restricted freedom of movement and interpersonal connection with others has become more confusing, due to the pandemic. Riots across the country have often been met with ignoring the rule of law, at the cost of protection and prosecution. An explosion of social media has fed comparison, leading to a false sense of connection and expectations.

All of this has added to a general feeling of powerlessness and frustration/resentment/ entitlement. It has produced stress/tension which often triggers our Survival Software without us even being aware of the shift. We will explore Survival Software as the essay unfolds.

Briefly, Survival Software comes from the reflection we receive as children growing up, as to who we should be, in order to receive love, acceptance and safety from our key parental figures. **From a child's perspective, their parents are their higher power.** The parents are usually not conscious of sending their own Survival Software to their child, and the child is not aware of receiving. We all learn a core sense of self in that process. We also learn to hide parts of self and put on a mask that helps us survive. Masks prevent us from believing reactions from others - **Is it about me or my masks?** There are subtle but profound differences between Survival Software and Living Software. This essay will explore both deeply.

One of those changes is an increasing general sense that we deserve to be happy and life should be easy. Ironically when happiness becomes a goal, we can never seem to reach it, or maintain it over time. The reason is that **happiness is actually a byproduct of deep, meaningful experience.** When we feel that we are entitled to get what we want, when we want it, and how we want it, we try to control everything and become very self-centered. We tend to become "Right fighters", where it's more important to win than learn and grow. The more self-centered, the more empty and lonely we feel. We can't seem to ever feel full enough. **It is not possible to fill a sieve with liquid!** We judge ourselves and others with a toxic flashlight that looks for problems and whose fault it is. In this atmosphere the hunger for Serenity becomes an impossible challenge.

We all need core acceptance from a higher power committed to accuracy and honesty, given with love and acceptance. It is a normal part of how we're made. **This higher power can become the core of your own inner coach who can guide you through this essay.**

We expect others to make us feel loved, and if they can't/don't we often move on to someone or something else. The paradox is that the more we demand/expect something, the harder it is to actually appreciate it and feel a sense of gratitude for it. **Without genuine gratitude, we can not experience the wanted feelings.**

This is partly the results of the misunderstood concept of "Self-Esteem" that swept our schools and homes in the seventy's and eighty's. The goal of self-esteem became the goal of each child/person feeling like a winner and good about themselves, no matter what they did or didn't do or say. Effort and reward became very blurred. Every paper gets a star! Homes became much more child centered at the same time more families had both parents working, and divorce became more the norm. Protecting a child from anything challenging prevents them from developing healthy resiliency. Without resilience, anxiety and depression are the natural result. Parents wanting their children to have what they didn't have growing up fed this toxic circle. Things often ended up replacing relationships as a primary focus. Increased instability mixed with very high expectations creates pressure and stress. This is the opposite of serenity.

I did my Dissertation on Self-Esteem and the Affect On Personality. In that study I used the definition adopted by the California Task Force on Self-Esteem: "The process of appreciating our own worth and importance, having the character to be accountable for ourselves, and to act responsibly toward others." This definition reflects mutual respect and valuing. Notice the difference between that definition and the general definition of feeling good about yourself independent of character and action.

The Task Force definition was shown in my research to produce noticeable healthy changes in areas of personality for those who attended a weekly group with a focus on tools to support healthy esteem, in an environment of nonjudgmental openness and honesty. The focus on mindful accuracy as a starting point in the present moment was very different than most of the participants had experienced before. They learned to put down their flashlight and pick up a lantern of mutual respect and valuing. The result was often healthy change.

Let's start with an expanded Prayer of Serenity:

Grant me the Serenity to change what I can change;
The freedom to release to You what I can't change;
And a growing wisdom to know the difference,
Imperfectly experiencing a life of learning and growing,
As I live in the present, BECOMING ME.

We are going to look deeply into the experience of Serenity and the process of healthy change. Serenity is the state of experiencing a sense of peace and calm, even in challenging times. I will be sharing many nuggets of wisdom throughout this essay. These nuggets come from over 40 years experience as a Psychologist focusing on Therapeutic Life Coaching, and a lifetime of learning and growing in my personal life - never arriving! I developed Cognitive/Perceptual Reconstruction as a way of approaching Life Coaching to support healthy change, and wrote "Changing Attitudes In Recovery - A Handbook On Esteem", and "Who's Really Driving Your Bus Today?"

While you may be able to take in intellectual information and knowledge at a high speed, wisdom requires time to digest at an experiential level, **"realizing that with new perception comes new choices."** The more unfamiliar or confusing the perspective feels as you read, the slower you need to proceed, **to experience the resistance as a step in the adventure**. Respecting and learning from the resistance helps make deep, healthy change possible.

Accuracy is key, and a mindful response to what you experience is what allows accuracy to continue developing. The truth is that the more often you practice digesting wisdom accurately through nonjudgmental mindfulness, the better chance that wisdom can come alive in the present. Many of these nuggets may seem obvious, or insignificant. I have found them to be deep truth that helps make accuracy and Serenity possible. They are Pillars of Serenity.

We can't have more healthy power in dealing with challenging situations than freely applying the Prayer of Serenity. When we demand ourselves to do more than we actually can, ironically we end up reducing our ability in the present. We steal our own healthy power. We use our judging and defending to stay trapped in our Survival Software, rather than learning and growing through the challenging situations.

There is an antidote to this toxic habit of using a harsh, judgmental flashlight. **The antidote is consciously choosing to actively embrace a mindful Lantern of Mutual Respect and Valuing (Inside and Out).** Choosing to learn and grow through applied mindfulness - Feeling good about noticing (as accurately as possible), with a growing attitude of grateful humility, where we are starting in the present moment. The truth is that we are all becoming, none of us will arrive! The core question is are you willing to start where your starting today? Take a moment to explore all the different reactions you notice. **This is actually the first step in healthy change. This accuracy in the present allows us to choose differently (imperfectly).**

Notice the difference between feeling good about noticing as accurately as possible, something you don't like or want, compared to feeling good about that unwanted thing! A common pattern I often notice in new clients is their tendency for feeling my badly about noticing unwanted issues, judging what they're noticing. This judging makes it painful to notice accurately, causing less accuracy in the present. Another common pattern is getting trapped in a past experience, with a huge flashlight sucking the life out of everyone.

Mindfulness helps produce accuracy. **Accuracy allows meaningful choice in the present.** Using a nurturing light of mindfulness helps create an experience of Serenity - It doesn't mean you won't have challenges, only that you are more free to make a desired choice with your next step in the present. We will all have these valleys. It is normal and healthy to feel sad about sad things. That is not depression. This essay is about how we can approach our valleys with as much healthy power as possible. **It is about healthy influence, not control.** When we go for control, it's at the expense of healthy influence. It doesn't get better than that!! There is a profound difference between forcing and allowing. **The natural reaction to forcing is RESISTANCE, while the natural reaction to non-judgmental mindfulness is feeling DRAWN TOWARD.**

This is not an intellectual process, but rather a relational (spiritual) experience we imperfectly embrace, as we relax into our becoming. Serenity is only possible in the present moment, as we experience having the freedom to start where we are starting in that present. We can experience our lanterns as they shine in all directions with a light of grateful humility, nurturing ourselves on an amazing/challenging journey called life. **The self-nurturing is an essential aspect of healthy change and Serenity.** These nuggets of wisdom often seem abstract at first. As we continue exploring them deeply, they can come alive as sources of Serenity. Nuggets require active digesting to become powerful tools for healthy change.

Our goal can be a developing sense of nonjudgmental openness and accuracy as we reflect on the nuggets in the essay. **Healthy change comes from practicing mindful accuracy, reflecting and experiencing what it's like to approach life differently. Accuracy is what gives choice real meaning. Hear a loving voice reading the essay to you.** Experience the words as perceptions/perspective, rather than as intellectual information.

This goal of growing Serenity is absolutely possible if we believe we are capable of imperfectly learning and growing spiritually. **We must start with a desire to live consciously and purposefully in the present, with nonjudgmental openness and accuracy, inside and out.** How we talk to ourselves and others, the tone, attitude, and perceptions we bring into the present moment, all affect Serenity and accuracy.

We will explore four Pillars supporting Serenity and healthy change. Each adds significantly to our ability to successfully experience growing Serenity: 1) Identity; 2) Mindfulness; 3) A Lantern perspective of Accuracy; 4) Protecting others from hurting us. Let's explore each of these Pillars briefly. The key is appreciating that the dynamics of each Pillar interacts with all of the dynamics of the other three Pillars. The whole is greater than sum of the parts. **Serenity comes from embracing all four Pillars imperfectly, in the present moment. It is not following rules, rather it's experiencing becoming. It is a spiritual experience.**

Identity

John came into his first coaching session in his late 50's. He had sought therapy several times earlier in his life for depression, anxiety and insecurity. Each time he would focus on getting rid of the problems, and as soon as the problems would improve somewhat, he would terminate sessions. He was very driven/impatient, judgmental and perfectionistic. He was demanding of himself and those around him. His personal relationships were quite strained and often a source of disappointment and pain.

He had come to believe that "it's just the way I am! I've been this way my whole life, and tried to change, but it never lasted". He had proof to back it up. Every time he would begin to notice any of these unwanted feelings, he would become relentless in beating himself up, thus noticing itself was painful and he would begin to stuff/ignore noticing before long.

John grew up with a father that could never be pleased. If he got 5 "A's" and 1 "B", his father would focus on the B. His mother was chronically depressed and unavailable to nurture John. He learned to ignore his feelings (stuff them) and focus on trying to be good enough. He had two marriages, both dysfunctional and ended in divorce.

He had a difficult time in Coaching, resisting feeling good about noticing accurately where he was starting at any given moment with a mindful lantern. **It took a lot of confronting/ encouraging for him to slowly begin to embrace the pillars of serenity. By focusing on the underlying pillars, appreciating that the toxic results of Survival Software made perfect sense, he slowly began to take "baby steps" of self-nurturing.** He would work with the podcasts (listed at the end of this essay), and joined a CAIR Self-Help Group to practice between sessions. Little by little John began to embrace the wisdom of the pillars for himself personally. He would come back for an "oil and lube" from time to time to support his growth. He learned that how he approached healthy change made a profound difference.

Nurturing himself for small steps forward, and allowing it to be an adventure rather than a test made imperfect change possible.

1) Identity - Who we believe ourselves to be at the core (our true self). How do you feel about this core perception of yourself? Most of us assume that "how we have been up until now" must mean "who we

really are", and therefore "how we will be in the future". **Does "That's just the way I am!" feel familiar? It is ironic that there is actually a healthy resistance to making yourself try to be someone you don't believe yourself to be.**

2) The truth is that **"I am not my story and my story affects where I'm starting today."** To be perfectly accurate, who I am is becoming! Who you are is becoming too! The reality is we are all becoming! **When we believe the lie - "that it's just the way We are", we actually make that lie effectively true.** When we try to make changes by hating/resenting ourselves and/or others, by blaming and defending, by demanding perfect change immediately, we "prove" that we can't change. **All we actually "prove" is that our approach can't produce healthy change.**

3) If we choose to live in the past or future, we actually sacrifice our ability to have choice in the present. If we don't change (update) our identity (who we believe ourselves to be at our core) as we learn and grow, there will be a healthy resistance to those healthy changes. **Have you unintentionally proven the lie that change is not possible for you?** How have you approached making changes up until now?

4) Each of us need to face the deeply spiritual question "Who am I at my core, when all my masks and defenses are removed with loving grace and caring? Most of us fill our core with our wounded inner kids, feeling shame and a deep need to hide them from the outer world. All of our defense mechanisms have their roots in this self rejection process.

5) **Learning to develop our own Inner Coach, committed to accuracy and truth, is a key step in gaining Serenity and healthy change.** Imagine an Inner Coach lovingly guiding us into the present with grace and respect. **Giving ourselves conscious acknowledgment for small steps forward, and Learning from steps backward, help build that Inner Coach.**

6) We all see imperfectly through Perceptual Filters. As we grow up in an imperfect world, **we all develop Survival Software, without realizing it.** Rather than accuracy, this survival software helped cope with our biggest challenges. They helped us survive. **The problem comes when we use this software to try to create healthy living.** Survival Software violates many of the pillars that can produce Serenity and Healthy Change. To make it worse, survival software has the most toxic impact

when we slip into Automatic Pilot, judging and blaming/defending rather than seeking mindful accuracy.

7) Two common filters are "What If" and "If Only". The "What If" filter actively feeds anxiety, as **we enter our Time Machine into the future, experiencing endless unwanted possibilities, as if they are actually happening. Our body absorbs the stress from the "What If" experience, which compounds the toxic circle.** It is an exhausting habit. The **"If Only" filter feeds depression, as we are drawn into the past, reliving unwanted experiences, as if they were happening in the present. It is truly self torture.** You cannot go to the party I gave yesterday!!! Our goal can be to feel good about noticing, as accurately as we can, in the present moment, when we realize we're going an unwanted direction. **When we slip into our TimeMachine, we can learn to gently bring ourselves back to the present - where true choice exists.** We can use our nonjudgmental lantern to see ourselves and others with mindful accuracy. We can learn from these times or let them define who we are as we look through a judgmental flashlight. Good to have choices. **Life can become an adventure of looking for opportunities to learn and grow, to practice becoming.**

8) **When we consciously embrace the mundane in our day to day life, we begin to experience the profound. Living each day as if it could be our last, AND living each day as if we are going to live a long, long time, allows us to experience a life of abundance.**

The Role Of Spiritually In Identity

9) We all need a power greater than self to begin healing our core identity. We need to see ourselves deeply through a reflection that is committed to nonjudgmental, loving accuracy in the present. **As a child, our parents tend to be our higher power.** We learn "who we are" through these reflections of our parents' survival software. We often see God having the qualities of our parents. If our parents are demanding and frequently angry, we tend to assume God has these qualities. If we can never seem to please our parents, never good enough to celebrate, we will tend to approach God with this expectation.

10) This core perception of self can not be altered through intellectual challenging, but rather from experiencing self through a power greater than self. A loving higher power, committed to mindful accuracy

makes it possible to transform our core sense of self. This loving Inner Coach can draw you toward healthy becoming. We call this process Spirituality. Spirituality has three different levels of relationship: 1. Relationship between ourselves in the present and our wounded core (we all have a wounded core); 2. Relationship between ourselves and others; and 3. Relationship between ourselves and a sense of something greater than self that can give us meaning and purpose. This is not intellectual, but rather experiential.

11) There is a difference between religion and spirituality. They can work wonderfully together, but they are not the same. Recovery is about Spirituality/Relationship transforming at all three levels: with self, with others, and our sense of meaning and purpose. In the same way that each pillar is interconnected with each other pillar, each level of spirituality interacts with each other level.

12) **I strongly encourage you to reflect deeply on what gives you meaning and purpose in your life.** Purpose provides a rudder as you go through life. Without purpose it is accurate that we have little power to influence the direction our lives unfold. Without purpose the vacuum of purpose creates depression and anxiety. I will share my spirituality as an example. We each must develop our own personal spirituality. It is a deeply personal relationship

13) For me personally, Who I am at my core is becoming in my Big Brother Jesus. His loving accuracy, given in grace and kindness, is my own personal Inner Coach, letting me see myself and others (imperfectly) through His Eyes and responding through His Nature, in the present. I am free to accept His guidance or not. His loving relationship is unconditional. I can not earn His love because He gives it freely. When I allow Him to draw me lovingly forward, toward healthy accuracy in the present, things tend to go well. When I ignore His coaching, not so much ☹. It is an active allowing, not a passive finding.

14) The truth is We all choose throughout our day. Unfortunately much of the time we slip into Automatic Pilot and forget to consciously choose, which is also a choice. **It is important to choose to live consciously and purposefully in the present.** Often we slip into our Time Machine, going into the past or future, and miss the present moment (often totally unaware we left the present).

15) I believe that I am a deeply loved child of God; and I choose to be becoming His ambassador (imperfectly reflecting His Nature and

Style), as I practice living consciously and purposefully in the present moment, with my lantern of grace shining inside and out, allowing Him through me, to maximize my healthy power for good.

16) I believe that I am not my successes or failures; who I am is becoming in God. How I feel and how well I'm doing at any given time is just that - how I feel or do. Nothing defines my core self except becoming in Him. My Big Brother Jesus draws me lovingly toward Him, toward my becoming, toward true health.

17) It can be an amazing adventure, once we realize change is naturally an awkward and clumsy process. The reality is that it becomes easier with practice. **It does require being conscious and purposeful, with mindfulness shining through our lanterns in the present.** If we believe life should be easy, or things don't turn out the way they "should", we tend to react strongly to difficult challenges. Our Survival Software becomes activated, and we react. There is a subtle, profound difference between reacting in automatic pilot, and responding with mindful accuracy in the present - Living Software.

18) **The deeper the valleys (challenges) we go through, the more abundant the nuggets of wisdom we can experience. These nuggets come from our Serenity. Serenity comes when we allow ourselves to imperfectly embrace the Pillars that support Serenity. This is not an intellectual, conceptual process. It is an intentional, conscious experience of imperfectly believing "who I am is becoming". I personally don't particularly like valleys, but if I am going through a valley, I want my nuggets!!!**

Mindfulness

Judy came to coaching at 32, very frustrated and confused. Tearfully she shared, **"I have everything going for me and yet I'm irritated that I feel like I'm failing somehow. My work life is solid, I have lots of friends, including a wonderful boyfriend. I have plenty of money. What's wrong with me?"**

As we began to explore where she was starting, it became clear that she had strong perfectionistic expectations and was extremely demanding and judgmental toward herself. She was so used to it that she was actually surprised when I pointed it out. She was not that way with others, just herself. Growing up as an only child with a single mom who made Judy her life, she was given everything. Mom would give freely to Judy, but not to herself. Mom was demanding and judgmental toward herself, while being nurturing and accepting toward Judy.

She really struggled with feeling good about noticing unwanted things without judging. As she began to recognize her Survival Software, and how it made sense of where she was starting, she slowly began to put down her flashlight and pick up a lantern. As she embraced the pillars, it slowly became an adventure. She drops me am email every once in a while, letting me know she still hears me in her head saying "feel good about noticing" and it makes her smile. Her inner coach continues to help her grow in her becoming.

1) **Mindfulness boils down to an attitude/perception of feeling good about noticing unwanted things as accurately as possible, realizing that it is the first step of healthy change.** A common pattern is to feel bad about "What" is being noticed. This reaction actually punishes us for noticing. The common result is we stop noticing. Research has shown that bringing Mindfulness into a situation greatly increases accuracy - a Pillar of Serenity.

2) Mindfulness affects the words and tone we use in thinking about approaching a situation. Notice what it's like for you, at a feeling level, to want to do something, verses having to or should do that same thing (In a demanding voice). Take a moment to actually notice the differences. **Without realizing or consciously choosing the words that automatically come, our Perceptual Filters are actually coloring our perceptions as we think or talk.**

3) **We may think we are describing, but actually we are creating our experiences.** If you like what you notice, feel good about noticing it accurately. If you don't like what you notice, feel good about noticing it accurately as the first step in making changes in the present.

4) By feeling good about noticing, with a focus on nonjudgmental openness and accuracy, our becoming is supported. We can enjoy the adventure of becoming more accurate, looking for opportunities to practice.

5) Our expectation that life should be fair often triggers our judgmental Flashlight, working against the Pillar of Mindfulness. Expectations can feed resentment and bitterness.

6) The truth is we will never arrive. We can never do it perfectly. Perfect change is not possible, imperfect change is absolutely possible. How we approach the process of healthy change makes a profound difference. Judging, blaming, defending, feeling shame, all prevent healthy change. **Healthy regret is an important aspect of healing and growing. Regret is a feeling of sadness about something that leads to a desire to change it in the present.**

7) When we slip into Automatic Pilot, we forfeit our ability to choose, as our Survival Software chooses for us. What we consciously want to accomplish is often overpowered by our Survival Software. **This Survival Software actually worked earlier in our lives, but can be very destructive in the present. It is intended to support survival, not healthy living.**

8) Trying Not to get angry, hurt, scared, be like a hurtful parent, etc., actually helps produce the unwanted thing. Try as hard as you can, not to think of the color purple. What do you notice? It's just how the brain works. **The "Not" model does not work. Without realizing it, the harder we try "not" to …, the more likely we will creat the unwanted result. It is important to focus on what you are wanting rather than what you are not wanting. It really makes a difference.**

A Lantern Perspective Of Accuracy

Fred and Sharon came to coaching as a last resort before divorce. They had been married 26 years and neither of them could stand the other one. Years of toxic "right fighting" had taken its toll. The first few sessions felt like being a referee of a boxing match. I am a very active coach, and would interrupt the circle as quickly as possible. Both knew they were right, and the other one was wrong!!! They both couldn't understand why I couldn't see it.

Slowly we began to shift from the black or white filter, armed with a judgmental flashlight attitude, to a lantern view of "and", making room for both of them to be right and wrong. As they came to realize they both had created their toxic relationship, forgiveness and openness became possible. They sent me a note that they were celebrating their 32nd anniversary and still going strong.

1) **A lantern of mutual respect and valuing has no double standards - what's true for one is true for all.** The lantern shines a gentle light

of grace and mindfulness in all directions. Accuracy comes from acknowledging there will be a number of different perspectives that may have value. This supports an attitude of openness and curiosity. It shows what is and what can be possible. The focus is on feeling good about noticing accurately as a first step in healthy change. It is the opposite of demanding to be right, and attacking differences.

2) A more common light source is the flashlight. Unlike the lantern, **the flashlight shines a harsh, judgmental light that only shines in one direction, with a polarized light that only lets in what builds the anticipated case.** The result of the judgmental light is defensiveness and resistance. It only sees a portion of what it shines on, and none of the other direction. The flashlight can not be very accurate. It's polarized light only sees what's wrong or what should be, not what is possible and attacks differences judgmentally - whether towards self or others.

Protecting Others From Hurting Us

Carol and Bill came to coaching because of Carol's "depression" and Bill wanting to make sure he knew what was going on in the coaching sessions. Bill was extremely controlling and was often very hurtful toward Carol without intending it or even realizing it. Carol would absorb it, stuff it, and blame herself for upsetting Bill. This naturally fed into depression, which fueled the toxic circles.

I would acknowledge Bill's intentions and also share the effect it was having. It was a delicate process at first, because Bill was very defensive. I spent a lot of time making a distinction between intent and effect. I would repeatedly share that by Bill defending his intention, he was actually expecting Carol not to feel the effect she would often have. After building some healthy momentum in the relationship the other pillars could be introduced. Carol began to honor her feelings with Bill, using her lantern (inside and out), and Bill learned to use his lantern inside and out too. Their marriage was not perfect after the coaching, but as they both continued learning and growing as a team, the marriage became a place for them both to practice healthy becoming.

1) **Loving can be significantly different than being nice.** It is loving to focus mindfully on deep truth and accuracy in our relationships.

There is a profound difference between giving freely, and giving begrudgingly. The saying, "It is more blessed to give than receive", is referring to freely giving.

2) When we can't say no, we are not free to say yes. When we feel we must give, it costs us double retail, while the receiver experiences it at a fraction of wholesale. If we give $5 begrudgingly, it effectively costs us emotionally $10. If we give $5 freely, it emotionally gives us a $20 rebate. The more we give freely, the more we have! It is loving to be able to say no respectfully, because it allows us the freedom to say yes.

3) If it is wrong to be hurtful to others, is it not also wrong to absorb hurtfulness from others, without doing what you can to make it as healthy as possible for both of you? The key is bringing your mindful lantern shining inside and out with a attitude of curiosity and openness toward both of you. Realizing that each of you will have a unique perspective that is usually different for each person. The need to be "right" assumes your view is correct/understandable/reasonable compared to your partner.

4) When most folks think of areas in their marriage that cause hurt/anger/anxiety/withdrawal reactions, they tend to experience judgmental flashlights - shining either toward themselves or each other. Internal dialogue is often ignored by many people. Notice the difference between saying inside with a frustrating/resentful tone that "I have to … vs. I want to…, or I choose to …. When you see it as an adventure in your healthy becoming, it draws you forward rather than pushing yourself or demanding yourself. The suggestion may seem strange: How can something that may have been a problem for years become an adventure for both of you? The other Pillars help make that possible.

5) An important fact about human beings is that we all have a deep need to be loved and appreciated, to feel free to let your partner know you deeply and to know your partner deeply. **When we hide significant parts of ourselves, we can not really know it we are being accepted or our mask is being accepted. This feeds our anxiety and insecurity, which feeds our defensiveness, that steals our ability to develop healthy power for ourselves and others.**

6) By bringing healthy tools from the other three Pillars, we can introduce curiosity and confusion into the process. These are actually very

powerful tools when dealing with challenging relationships with our lantern. The lantern is actually more powerful than a flashlight. **Powerful Vulnerability comes when it's more important to learn and grow than being right. The only way to actually win in a relational conflict is when both participants learn and grow in the exchange. Focus on the process, not just the content.**

7) Would you really want others to stuff their feelings regarding issues they have with you, harboring hurt and resentment toward you without sharing these issues with you in a constructive, respectful way? **Serenity calls for nonjudgmental openness and accuracy.** There are no double standards with a lantern, and therefore no double standards in our Serenity. The flashlight regularly assumes double standards. The

8) How we approach interactions teaches others how we will treat them, and what we'll accept from others. How do you feel about how you have been teaching others up until now? **Remember in a relationship, both parties help co-create the existing patterns in the present. It is extremely difficult for a "victim" to see themselves as "perpetrators". The Black/White Filter creates labels that are not accurate! It's not about blame, but rather mindful accuracy leading to healthy change. Labels prevent healthy change.**

9) **Mindfulness allows a growing, healthy relationship with our inner resistance to change.** We can embrace that resistance, listening respectfully with our lantern, to what the resistance is trying to say. What is it trying to defend. Which part or parts of us are most triggered by the issue? Fighting resistance usually strengthens it. Listening respectfully and accurately to our resistance generates the most healthy changes.

10) **If I try to approach others with nonjudgmental, mindful accuracy, while using a flashlight on myself, it can not work!! The in-congruency causes resistance for the sender and the receiver.** "Addiction to the familiar" builds over time. Like any addiction, we build tolerance, and experience withdrawals when it's not present. We often don't like our addictions. Appreciating this addictive process allows us to approach these natural reactions differently.

11) Change can only happen in the present, although we often want to start where we want to end up. Unfortunately that is not possible. It's

important to nurture ourselves for noticing small steps forward and noticing unwanted steps backwards.

12) We can focus on shame and blame, using our flashlights to judge and defend - and stay stuck; or we can use our lanterns to see mindfully as accurately as possible - allowing healthy change. There are a number of podcasts presented at the end of this essay, that are filled with tools and nuggets supporting your growth and Serenity. Let them support your becoming. It's great to have a choice!! Which do you choose?

It seems hard to believe that the original Bus Book was written almost 20 years ago. At that time I invited the readers to experience sitting across from me in coaching sessions.

During that time I've gotten a lot of feedback from people who found it valuable to build their own inner coach through using the tools, nuggets and examples from the book.

I have decided to retain most of the original material in the new addition, adding things that have come up between then and now.

The goal is to help people realize that deep significant change is possible when approached in the way described in the book, applying Therapeutic Life Coaching.

As I am in the process of publishing "Who's REALLY Driving Your Bus Today?" I realize, as usual, God has again given me a special gift (a nugget) to celebrate the occasion. While going through a routine medical exam (which I tend to put off way too long) I learned that I had multiple myeloma. I did not have any symptoms, nor reason to suspect there was any problems. The news was a big shock, and when I came home I set trying to let this news sink in. What came was profound. An overwhelming feeling of curiosity and peace. I began to wonder how we would go through this challenging valley in a way that would give meaning and value to it. How would my Big Brother Jesus and I use this to touch my life and others in a meaningful way. I had never felt more alive and loved by Him than at that moment. I didn't like the valley that I had just learned about, but if I'm going to go through it, we will make it an adventure of learning and growing. This book is a part of that adventure. The valley sucks but the nuggets are priceless.

INTRODUCTION TO DRIVERS TRAINING

As you pick up this book, take a moment to consider what motivated you to start reading. Allow yourself to feel good about noticing where you are starting in the present. Are you the kind of person who loves to learn and grapple with deeper meanings in life? Have you made significant changes in your life and want to continue growing? Would you like a guide/coach to accompany you as we explore together the process of making healthy changes in your life?

Are you currently in therapy or considering starting? Is there a vague sense of something missing, a hunger that you can't put into words? When you think of your childhood and how you were parented, is it important for you to raise your own children differently? Do you want to break the cycle?

Are you dealing with areas of your life you have tried to change-and somehow it hasn't worked? These problem areas may be causing you considerable pain. The harder you have tried to make healthy changes in these areas, the more hopeless and trapped you may have felt. I call that **NORMAL!**

You may be drowning in some addictive patterns, dying in a toxic marriage or work situation, or fighting off the "nothingness" of depression. Each new day may loom for you as a minefield to travel through, anxiety and self-doubt beating you down each step of the way. You want to go north but a part of you grabs the steering wheel of your life's bus and you head south, hating yourself the entire time.

Are you doing what you don't want to do and not doing the things you really want to do? Do you find yourself surviving from day to day? Is your life feeling out of control? Do you need/ want a coach to help you learn to drive differently, so you can enjoy your life? Would you like to gain skills and tools to handle difficult stretches of road differently? Would you like to have life become an adventure, a journey into health rather than an ordeal to survive?

How would you like to find out who has REALLY been driving your emotional bus on these treacherous roads? I will show you how to recognize who is really driving and how to become a healthy driver today. **Perception is the key to healthy driving.** Recognizing filters that distort your perceptions and replacing them with more accurate filters, makes healthy driving much easier. Imagine driving into the sun in the late afternoon, your windshield streaked and dirty. The sun's light reflects off the grime and makes it almost impossible for you to see what is ahead of you. You can continue driving; feeling anxious about the poor visibility, or you can pull over, clean the windshield and continue driving, able to see much more clearly and accurately.

Most of the distortions seen through the windshield of your perceptual bus come from learning to survive the pains of life up until now. I will show you how to shift from surviving to living, and help you understand the differences between these two perspectives.

The more you learned to adopt "survival" coping skills growing up, the more likely you will unconsciously (or consciously) bring these survival filters into your present circumstances. Survival is the process of blocking painful experiences and learning to deny parts of self in order to avoid pain. The pain can come in many different forms, at different ages, causing different decisions and reactions.

Survival always has a core element of scarcity. Scarcity is the fear of not getting enough of what you need. Scarcity and abundance are incompatible. The more you gain the paradox of abundance, the less you feel scarcity.

Survival mode is present when one of your significant considerations is how to make sure others don't get upset with you, that they won't reject you, that they won't hurt you too badly. When you illuminate your experiences with judgmental flashlights rather than respectful lanterns, you are probably filtering your perceptions with survival mode. When making sure that it's not your fault is more important than coming to a healthy outcome, you can bet you are in survival mode. There is a core self-rejection/self-protection at the heart of survival mode that filters everything you experience. Are there certain areas of your life that activate your survival mode?

There is always a cost attached to survival. Survival mode is at odds with the *Fundamental Principles of Healthy Change* that will be explored deeply in this book. Violating these fundamental principles makes happiness and intimacy difficult to experience over time. I will share many "Nuggets of Wisdom" reflecting the Fundamental Principles of Healthy Change throughout the book. *These fundamental principles form a New Program perspective to change.*

You can learn to listen more deeply both to yourself and others. You can learn to see patterns in behavior and the underlying assumptions that drive toxic patterns. *You can gain the ability to have real choices in the difficult areas of your life.*

In the same way that there are fundamental principles of physics such as gravity, which allow predictability in life; there are *Fundamental Principles of Healthy Change* that can help predict your success in making desired changes in your life. If you jump off your roof, you can predict from the fundamental principles of physics that you will fall down, and not up. This predictability is also true about your ability to make healthy changes in your life.

When you try to hate yourself into positive changes, there will be an impasse between the vector of energy pushing for change, and the vector of resistance to conditional demands. Trying *not* to think or do something actually increases the desire to think or do that thing. *Certain attitudes and perceptions prevent healthy change, while others help make change possible.*

The problem for most people is learning how to make healthy changes. After many unsuccessful attempts at trying to make changes in such areas as addictions, relationship issues, and depression and anxiety, how would you like to have a personal coach who would help you learn how to relax into difficult areas of your life today? I will give you the tools you need to make healthy changes in the present.

My many years of experience as a Therapeutic Life Coach (TLC) in peoples' lives has given me a chance to watch the Fundamental Principles of Healthy Change unfold, both within the same client, and within different clients over time. I have seen the effects when clients chose to resist and ignore these fundamental principles.

Since these principles are integrated, when you violate one principle, it affects all aspects of New Program. An example would be learning to see more accurately, but insisting on judging and feeling bad about what you see. It is predictable that this strategy will result in a growing resistance to seeing accurately. ***Judging will cause you not to notice the very things that are being judged-what a great paradox.***

I have formed eight of these Fundamental Principles of Healthy Change into an esteeming New Program for recovery and growth. I have found them particularly useful in coaching and in the free CAIR Self-Help and CAIRing Grace Groups. These principles can guide you on your journey:

Fundamental Principles of Healthy Change
A New Program For Living

1. A growing commitment to being non-judgmental, open and accurate.
2. A growing commitment to believing that we are all Fallible Human Beings.
3. A growing understanding that we react through our perceptual filters rather than directly to "reality."
4. A growing commitment to the acceptance (acknowledgement) of Reality in the present.
5. A growing commitment to Mutual Respect and Valuing.
6. A growing commitment to a healthy parenting relationship with the "wounded parts of yourself."
7. A commitment to a growing relationship with a Loving Higher Power.
8. A realization that Recovery is an ongoing process of growth and change-a way of life.

These eight Fundamental Principles of Healthy Change are the heart of an esteeming New Program that allows you to nurture your ability to bring healthy perceptions into your life. When I refer to New Program, I am including the beliefs, attitudes, perceptions and tools presented throughout this book that reflect the Fundamental Principles of Healthy Change. New Program is an integrated perspective that has a direct affect at the level of perception. It is a process of developing healthy attitudes affecting your perceptions, not a set of rules. It is a way to approach your life.

Meeting Your Coach

I have spent the past 40+ years successfully coaching/guiding people in my clinical psychology practice. As a Therapeutic Life Coach, it is my job to help you make healthy change the path of least resistance. As you go through this book, I will provide the tools you need and show you how to apply these tools in your life so you can make the healthy changes you desire today. I will provide you with "Nuggets of Wisdom" about the change process. I will show you a New Program with powerful tools for growth.

You can learn to recognize your Old Program patterns and the cost/benefit of unconsciously choosing those patterns. ***Old Program is what comes naturally when you are not consciously aware of what you are choosing.*** Awareness is not the same as analyzing. It is an ability to be conscious in the present. I can help you develop this powerful skill. ***You provide the willingness to invest the time and thought that makes the "Nuggets" in this book come alive in a healthy New Program for living your life.*** You get to feel the awkwardness of putting your learning into action; I provide the faith in your ability to succeed. We can be a team! You don't have to make the journey alone.

In this book we will be facing deep issues of meaning and spirituality. ***I make a significant distinction between religion and spirituality.*** It is for you to choose what religious path you travel. Our coaching relationship will focus deeply on your assumptions about your spirituality and how it affects your life. I will help you explore the qualities within your Higher Power relationship that support your recovery.

Normally my clients can share directly with me regarding their spirituality. I work within the frame of my client's spirituality in Therapeutic Life Coaching; being open with them when they want me to share my spirituality in sessions. Imposing my beliefs would go against everything I believe.

In this book I will share how I make sense of my own personal spirituality as a relational Christian. I consider myself a "liberal fundamentalist." I understand that this sounds like anoxymoron at first glance. Let's look deeper.

"Liberal," refers to my freedom to relax into becoming a new creation in Christ, *"Fundamentalist,"* refers to the depth of my relationship with God. I believe in His Perfect Plan of Grace and accept personal responsibility to desire and allow His Holy Spirit to transform me, as a new creation, through a deeper, growing relationship with Him. My grateful humility for His free, unearned gift helps create the emotional and perceptual ecology necessary for His Spirit to transform my life.

This "No-Fault" attitude toward noticing and changing helps make my growth the path of least resistance. I am free to make changes in my life. I am free to want to want to make changes. I am free to accept myself right where I'm starting in the present, as I continue to be becoming in His Nature. It takes a lifetime to learn to believe this core truth of my identity, and I'll never live it perfectly.

I welcome Him to use as much of me for His Purposes as I am able to make available at any given moment. It is exciting to me to be on an amazing team with my Big Brother, who is my own wonderful coach. What is so amazing to me as a coach is that His Plan is so powerful that you don't even have to believe in the Author-Jesus-for His Plan to help your recovery.

It is important that the relationship you have with your own Higher Power has the following qualities: (1) unearned grace and valuing, (2) unchanging consistency about Truth, (3) loving, accurate feedback given non-judgmentally, and (4) absolute faith in your ability to continue moving forward in your recovery. **These four qualities help create the perfect ecology for healthy change.**

To the extent any of these qualities are missing in your Higher Power relationship, you need to find a way to add the missing dimensions. **I am talking spirituality in recovery, not religious issues of salvation! Please recognize the difference.** Alcoholics Anonymous meets these four dimensions in their process of recovery. I have had clients who utilized A.A. as their Higher Power. They developed deep relational connections with the fellowship as they continued to work the steps, and grow in the program. Reflect on your own Higher Power in light of these needed qualities. Are there areas that need attention?

Grace is a key to healthy change. *In recovery, grace is freely embracing an attitude of grateful humility, which grows out of the unearned, unconditional love from your Higher Power.* This grace is then given imperfectly to yourself and others in an attitude of unearned mutual respect and valuing. It leads to increasing honesty and transparency.

People often think of honesty as being brutally frank and direct. When you deliver honesty in this tone, the natural reaction is defending and blocking against that honesty. *Honesty without grace distorts the truth and harms relationships. This is true whether you are being honest with yourself or others.* Many Christians try to share His Truth without His Nature and Style, distorting His Truths in the process.

I believe that life is precious and that we all have the right to live it abundantly. Consider the following paradox: *To live life most abundantly you must live as if it may be your last day; while living as if you will live a very long time.* Imagine that you've suddenly learned that this may be your last day alive. What would you be feeling and how would you experience your last 24 hours?

A healthy response would be to live it very consciously and deliberately, savoring each moment to the fullest, seeing the sunrise as if for the first time, hearing birds differently, smelling familiar things deeply, taking in the sunset with the ones you love, sharing things with the important people in your life that you had always meant to say. Interactions would be experienced from a very different perspective, priorities suddenly coming into clear focus.

You would begin getting to know people in your life again for the first time, as you experience yourself and them differently-as becoming in the precious time remaining. You would begin living life manually; consciously noticing the various "Nuggets" that are present in any given situation.

I have been going through some serious medical issues in the past few years and this attitude that I'm describing is very real for me as I write this book. You can decide to live your life with meaning and purpose today! You can deliberately choose to relax into New Program principles and attitudes consciously, imperfectly. *This allows you the greatest chance of making healthy changes in your life. It also allows you the most pleasure and enjoyment possible at any given time.* If you are willing to invest the time and thought necessary, you can learn to live this way. It's nice to have a choice! Reflect deeply on this truth, it is a key to freedom and growth.

At the same time you are living each day as if it might be your last, imagine living your life as if you are going to be around a long, long time. What do you notice as you look from this long range perspective? ***Living life as a long-term investment has a significant impact on your perspective.*** When I was first married to my wife, Sonia, 50 years ago, we both made the conscious decision that "since we are going to be married for a very long time, we may as well make it as good and enjoyable as possible." That commitment has been very helpful over the years when deciding whether or not to invest energy in dealing with problem situations.

As a long-term investment, my marriage pays the best dividends and interest if I deal with things as quickly as possible, so we have the longest time to enjoy the rewards of our efforts. This long-term perspective helps you own the fact that you are chooser in your life, that you live out the long-term consequences of your choices-whether you are conscious of choosing or not. ***How do you like your consequences up until now?***

Compare this sense of permanency with one of constantly wondering if your relationship is going to end today or maybe tomorrow. ***There is a high price for avoiding commitment in important relationships.*** The Fundamental Principles of Healthy Change reflected throughout this book help you live your life to the fullest by embracing the paradox of abundance.

God has always given me a precious "Nugget" to share with my audience when I am preparing a major presentation. That is true in writing this book too. Over the years the "Nuggets" have come in many different forms.

As I said above, I am currently going through a medical challenge - cancer. I don't like or want it but that is not my choice. My choice is how I approach this valley. I have learned a lot of wonderful nuggets by experiencing it as an adventure rather than asking "why me?" I've never felt more alive than going through this valley. I don't like valleys, but if I'm going to have to go through one, I want all the nuggets I can gain.

A Peek At Drivers Training

To me, the beauty of Therapeutic Life Coaching is that it (1) takes judgmental, defensive, flashlight perspectives and turns them into lantern perspectives that shine nonjudgmentally from all directions, (2) encourages an attitude of curiosity, openness and accuracy, (3) provides New Program tools and resources from the Fundamental Principles of Healthy Change, (4) brings a desire to learn and grow into the situation, and (5) brings absolute faith in your ability to apply New Program in your life today.

Confusion and curiosity are strong, positive feelings in New Program. "I don't know" is a great start. Therapeutic Life Coaching confronts common survival responses, and addresses them deeply and accurately, with a respectful, "No-Fault" attitude. New Program tools can give you the best chance of making healthy changes in your life, over the long haul. I believe God wants us all to be a healthy influence, a healing light in our world.

Over the years that CAIR Self-Help and CAIRing Grace Groups have been going, I have heard many wonderful stores of people who learned to accept themselves, and apply New Program in their lives. I have known of others who worked very hard on their recovery, attending often 2-3 groups a week for years, who seemed to be stuck in their Old Program toxic patterns. They would make some progress, only to slide back into their familiar pain.

Les was a member of the original Steering Committee of CAIR Self-help Groups. Members came together from a variety of different problem backgrounds, giving me feedback to help develop The CAIR Handbook. It became the format and structure for a new generation of support groups of people wanting to learn and practice building healthy esteem. The CAIR Handbook provided the needed tools and resources; the CAIR Group provided a safe place to practice an esteeming New Program way of living. Les shared her story in the CAIR Handbook, describing her life in her own words. Two examples of patterns that came out of my sharing with Les appear in the CAIR Handbook as the "Success Trap" and the "OK'ness Trap."

The OK'ness Trap is a common vicious circle that leads to feelings of hopelessness and despair: The harder you try to prove that you are OK, the more overpowering the question of your OK'ness becomes. The greater the question becomes, the more insecure you feel about yourself, leading to increasing self-consciousness. As your self-consciousness grows, your performance becomes impaired, feeding you proof that you are really not OK. There is no way out of this debilitating circle as long as you believe that you must prove your value. Does this pattern feel familiar to you? Allow yourself to reflect deeply into the patterns in your life.

Those CAIR members who seemed to blossom allowed themselves to imperfectly believe in New Program attitudes and perceptions, believing and applying healthy tools and concepts to themselves personally in their daily lives. They were very clumsy and awkward at first, but they would let it be an adventure of "becoming."

Those who seemed to struggle so hard, and suffer such pain in the change process, would acknowledge that New Program is a powerful set of tools for change. They would often share it with their friends, helping their friends make changes in their lives, but having difficulty applying it in their own lives. They would hold on to the truth of New Program, believing it intellectually, but refusing to allow themselves the grace, the No-Fault learning that makes New Program come alive at a level of personal experience.

You can learn in our coaching relationship to recognize *"Perceptual Filters"* that make it difficult for you to see accurately. *You experience through your beliefs, attitudes and assumptions that color what you see, and you can learn to replace faulty filters with more accurate lenses.* I will take you through many of the common "Perceptual Filters" that rob you of desired choices in the present. It is imperative that you realize the truth of the statement: *"You experience your world through filters that have a profound effect on how you feel and what you believe possible."* This book is all about perceptual filters that affect your *experience of reality,* and I will explain the meaning of these words in great depth through the course of the book.

These perceptual filters are made up of your underlying assumptions about reality, your attitudes toward yourself and others, your experiences from the past, your current expectations, and how you process all of this information. *If you look at life through a pair of eyeglasses that have dirty lenses or a faulty prescription, you cannot see clearly. If you want to see accurately, you would choose glasses that create 20/20 vision.*

I will help you see your process of change more clearly and accurately. As you learn to live more consciously, you can exercise more real choice in your life. Notice what you are feeling as you consider some of the ways your perceptions are being filtered without your conscious awareness.

By contrast to consciously choosing New Program, Old Program is what comes naturally when you are functioning on automatic pilot, unaware of your choices. Not all of your Old Program patterns are dysfunctional in your present situation. It is just that when your programming is working at a subliminal level, you give up consciously noticing what you believe to be true in Introductions to Drivers Training the present moment. You give up any quality control in your life.

It is important to be aware of the limitations of your current Old Program software toward achieving your present goals. *Software designed for surviving does not work well for living. There are many "bugs" in the survival software that make living much more difficult.* We can work together learning to apply new software in the form of a New Program that will help you make your desired changes into healthy living.

If you are currently in a wounded relationship, it would be very helpful to ask your partner if they are interested in improving your relationship in a way that can be fun, and personally enriching. The investment can have a healthy impact on your relationship in the present. You can go through the book together, sharing with each other your reactions to my questions and observations. It can be amazing what happens when you care enough about each other to invest time and thought in healing your relationship. Anything is possible when you begin to share openly with grateful humility.

You can enjoy chewing together on the "Nuggets of Wisdom" in this book. *One fundamental principle of New Program is that deep change is possible in the present.* What better gift than sharing the process of learning how to live consciously, growing in New Program with the important people in your life? Reflect deeply on your key relationships. Is there someone you would want to share this learning process with as you start your adventure of change?

Relationships can be like wood stoves. When you wake up in the morning and touch the side of the stove it may feel cool. When you open the door, the ashes may feel cool. Only after digging around in the ashes can you find out if there are any embers protected by the cool ash. If you try to put a big oak log on the embers, it helps kill them. If you are willing to add dry pine needles and oxygen, and slowly build up to small twigs and pieces of wood, you can finally add that big log. Don't give up too quickly.

Deep change is possible. Sometimes embers survive in the cool ash of our Old Programs, and can be brought back to a flame through applying New Program resources. What is the cost of finding out? The only real cost is "Hope!" Have you let your fear of being disappointed keep you from moving forward in your recovery?

Think of a battery terminal that has corrosion built up on it. You try to start your engine and it won't respond. It doesn't mean that the battery is defective, only that the juice can't get through the corrosion. Pouring baking soda dissolved in water or soda on the terminal causes it to bubble and fizz, and after it is rinsed off the engine may start just fine. Without some healthy means of conflict, relationships get corrosion built up to such an extent that the juices of the relationship can no longer flow. It doesn't mean the relationship is dead! ***Cleaning the terminals in your relationship can be messy and scary at first. Like any important skill, this takes practice, practice, and more practice. I will be happy to coach.***

Spending a few hours "getting real" with Sonia regarding some issue that is affecting us is rewarding as it helps our marriage to be all that it can be. We have a whole future to reap the benefits of what grows out of our sharing time, no matter how uncomfortable it may be during parts of the exchange.

I know, I can almost hear you saying, "Sure, when it has a happy ending it's great, but how about when it turns out like s—? What then? Do I have to keep knocking my head against a brick wall, over and over? It's not fair if I have to always be the one who tries to make things better!" Often when you feel that you are always the one that has to reach out, the other person may have a very different perception. Check it out!

It's amazing how different each person's "movie" of a situation can be, without either person realizing it. It can be like one person watching "Gone With The Wind" and the other watching "The Music Man." If they both assume they went to the same movie, the following discussion would be very interesting. One person begins to discuss the wonderful staircases and beautiful gowns at the parties, while the other one is repeating the dangers of playing pool. Each assumes the other one is distorting things, and both may get quite defensive. They will each argue for their experience of "reality" and feel the other one is "doing" this to them. Does this pattern feel familiar? Learn how to break the circular nature of this interaction.

The truth is that because of the long-term nature of my relationship with Sonia, it doesn't matter which of us shines the lantern first; what matters is that at least one of us remembers to put down the flashlight and pick up the lantern. We both get the benefits of the effort if it goes well, and if it doesn't go well, that experience becomes useful information. We can use it to help us approach the situation differently in the future. **We can learn and grow from our "mistakes" (the only real mistake is not learning from an experience).** We can learn to approach each other in a way that makes us both feel better. We both want each other to be happy, and have the chance to approach each other in a way most likely to succeed. We can make healthy changes in the present.

We can use the experience of our relationship as an opportunity to practice our recovery. The long-term nature of the investment makes this possible. This perception allows the whole process to feel more relaxed, an adventure we can share rather than a test we must pass or die. ***Our rough spots become a facet of our intimacy.*** I believe that true intimacy involves loving someone with their flaws and shortcomings rather than demanding their perfection before we give our love. This attitude is important to have toward yourself too. Mutual respect and valuing are at the heart of New Program. Both Sonia and I have grown through the clashes and conflicts of 50 years together. Investing deeply in my marriage is a key part of my recovery.

That doesn't mean that Sonia and I have a perfect relationship. The first five years of our marriage we had a lot of conflict as we adjusted to each other. We both had significant emotional wounds that generated survival patterns in our relationship. These patterns collided frequently in those early years. I remember the first year of my doctoral program. Sonia was starting her R.N. program at the same time. We were both under incredible pressures.

One of the students from my program stayed with us overnight because her field placement was in Modesto. She gave Sonia and me a set of foam bats called "Batakas" to help when we had conflict (remember, it was the 70's). We laughed at the gift, and continued to allow our conflicts to be open and acknowledged. Looking back, of the 18 students starting in my doctoral program, I believe we are one of the only married couples still together. ***Healthy conflict that does not go below the belt helps release tensions before they can build up. Watch out when the gas pressure begins to build!***

As this book unfolds, we will explore attitudes, beliefs, and assumptions in many different aspects of your life. I will assist you in learning to experience believing more deeply and accurately, in ways that allow you to begin relaxing into the changes you want to make in your life. *This is not an intellectual exercise! It is a process of noticing the many different perceptions available in a given situation by learning to live consciously.*

As your coach, I want you to take the time to chew on each "Nugget of Wisdom" that we explore together. In the CAIR and CAIRing Grace Groups we talk about going *"faster than the speed of feelings."* In the groups, members may spend an hour sharing reactions and associations to a single paragraph from the CAIR Handbook. *You can learn information at a fast speed, but wisdom and truth take time to digest.*

Approaching change at this level of depth allows me to help you recognize patterns that work against your healthy growth. You will learn to recognize many perceptual patterns as we go through the book. One of the more invisible, but powerful, dynamic patterns is the "addiction to the familiar." As human beings, it is natural for us all to be drawn to what is known and familiar, whether we like that familiarity or not. The fact is that the more pervasive your survival mentality, the stronger will be the draw of familiar, toxic situations.

The pull toward these familiar situations does not mean that you want to feel that way, or like the feeling. It is because of this *addiction to the familiar* that you will experience natural withdrawal symptoms in the process of making positive changes in your life. If you don't realize that these feelings are a natural part of the healing process, you are likely to have strong reactions to the withdrawal feelings. You may have strong feelings about your strong reactions. I will share a way of minimizing these withdrawal symptoms that so often undermine your healthy change.

Another powerful pattern that often adds confusion is what I call *"Second-Order feelings."* It is normal for us all to have feelings about what we are feeling. For example, you may feel silly about feeling scared, or feel angry for feeling vulnerable. You may feel afraid of feeling happy. There may be feelings stacked on feelings, stacked on more feelings in complex relationships. These Second-Order feelings are often much more intense than the original feelings. If you are not aware of how these Second-Order feelings affect your emotions, the result can be confusing, leading to faulty conclusions and decisions. We will discuss this principle further in the book, and you can learn to recognize this pattern in your life.

If you are not consciously aware of the assumptions you bring to a present situation (what you believe to be true!), by default you are at the mercy of your Old Program. ***Old Program is like software on the computer. Different software has different qualities and characteristics. Do you like the results of following your Old Program software up until now?*** Were you aware that you have been following a program?

By not actively choosing to live consciously, you are effectively choosing to continue your Old Program. By not intentionally learning and applying New Program in your daily life, you will continue to get the same results you have gotten up until now. People often get defensive and say "I didn't mean to get into Old Program" and I will respond, ***"The important question for you to be asking yourself throughout every day of your life, from this point on is, 'Am I consciously, intentionally choosing to apply New Program tools and principles in my daily life?'"***

I will help you recognize the underlying presuppositions in the questions you ask. If I ask you whether or not you noticed the statue of the elephant in the waiting room of my office, you may suddenly feel self-conscious because you have often been told you never pay attention. You may feel that you are taking a test, make a quick mental review of the waiting room to see if you remember the statue, and may actually see the statue in your mind. The question of noticing is very different than a direct question regarding the existence of the statue. If I ask you whether or not there is a statue of an elephant in my waiting room, you are less likely to say that there is such a statue. The truth is that there is not an elephant statue in my waiting room.

Notice your feelings as you ask, "Why should I believe in a God when you can't prove He exists?" vs. "Why shouldn't I believe in a God when you can't prove He doesn't exist?" "What is the cost of believing in a loving God if it is not true?" vs. "What is the cost of believing in a loving God if it is true?" "Will believing in a loving God help me in my recovery?" What reactions do you notice as you ask these questions? Reflect deeply on the impact of questions on your life.

Notice the underlying assumptions when you ask, "Why are you mad at me?" (This question assumes the other person is feeling mad, while they may be having many different feelings; it also assumes that you are the cause of their mad feelings), "What did I do wrong?" (This question assumes that the problem is about something you did, while the truth may be that the real problem is something you are not doing), "Why do you keep rejecting me?" (This question assumes that it is their intent to reject you, while the truth may be that they are feeling so overwhelmed with fear of you leaving them that they put up a wall to protect themselves, causing you to feel rejected by their wall). Notice what it's like to begin recognizing the assumptions and presuppositions in the questions you ask, and the questions others ask you. Enjoy noticing.

Take a recent time when you felt bad about a situation. How did you deal with the experience? Reflect deeply on the example, taking the time to make it as vivid as possible. What attitudes, beliefs and assumptions were you having during and after the situation? **Notice what would happen if you were to (1) apply New Program resources to your situation, (2) use a "lantern" perspective of seeing deeply from all directions without judging, and (3) feel good about** noticing what you are seeing accurately-as the first step in the process of change?

I will coach you as you learn to develop the paradoxical perspective of living each day as if it might be your last, while living as if you will be around for a long, long time. The "Nuggets" in this book can work like pieces of a jigsaw puzzle, fitting together in different combinations to create different perspectives. The key is to appreciate the process of putting them together, and have fun on your adventure. These "Nuggets" are to be digested slowly, while you reflect deeply. Give yourself the freedom to be awkward as you apply these "Nuggets" in your daily life. Enjoy learning to drive!

Getting To Know Your Drivers Manual For Change

The first time through the book, you may want to get to the end before beginning to journal. You may want to open it randomly, applying your current situations to whatever you read. ***Respect your learning style as you approach our coaching experience.*** You may want to make marks in the book where you want to go back and spend special time reflecting more deeply. As you feel ready, share your experiences with me as you go through the book by keeping an ongoing journal of what you notice. Talk to me about what you are learning on your journey, and how you feel about what you are learning, just as my coaching clients do.

Have fun sharing with me both your *"Got Its"*-successes, and your *"Ain't Got Its"*-things you want to do differently. Draw from the material in the book to know how I would respond. I am very predictable. Journaling with me will help you slow down the process and allow you to be more conscious as we share your adventure. As you journal, applying my responses to problems you are writing about, you are actually building your own inner coach muscles. **This book is a resource to be used over and over as you build your own healthy coach inside.**

You need to also choose at least one other person to share this material with on a regular basis. This can be sharing in any form: face-to-face (this is usually the most powerful for most people), by telephone or e-mail, or by writing letters back and forth. What is important is that you both feel safe becoming more transparent with each other, as you share the experience of going through the book together.

If you do not have someone, make that one of your early goals, or explore to see if there are CAIR or CAIRing Grace Groups in your area or Twelve Step oriented groups where you can share. If there are no groups in your area presently, all the material needed to start one can be found for free on www.CAIRforYou.com.

All it takes is two or more people willing to help co-create a safe place to practice the tools you will be learning on your adventure through this book. The free groups are an opportunity to explore deep issues of the change process, and share your personal recovery experiences. In the groups you are practicing an esteeming New Program set of tools, principles and attitudes that develop healthy core self-esteem. You will be learning this New Program throughout this book.

I will be sharing with you as if you are sitting across from me in a Therapeutic Life Coaching session. It requires all your attention and thought to digest the deep truths we will be exploring together on your journey into change. It allows you to gain accurate perceptions that maximize your healthy power. We will be focusing on wisdom and truth, applying accuracy to difficult areas of your life, while learning to develop an esteeming New Program. Are you ready to get started on this adventure together?

In the *Second Chapter* we will explore *25 Power Of Mind Distortions,* which are common perceptual filters that rob you of accurate choice. You will probably find that several of them are frequently filtering your current perceptions. These Power Of Mind Distortions affect how you perceive yourself and others, and how you perceive the process of change. *Whether you are aware or not, you are constantly filtering what you see and hear. This is an example where what you don't know can hurt you!*

We will start by helping you perceive more accurately in your daily life. By allowing yourself to feel good about noticing any familiar distorted perceptual filters, you can put your energy into noticing and replacing distorted filters with more accurate perceptions. *It is important to experience "consciously believing" the new, more accurate replacement perceptions.* Practice, practice, and more practice.

The biggest danger of perceiving more accurately is the tendency to judge where you are starting, and confusing your starting point with "who you are at some unchanging level of identity." The first principle in New Program is a growing commitment to non-judgmental openness and accuracy. If you allow yourself to begin applying the eight Fundamental Principles of Healthy Change as a New Program in your learning, you can avoid much of the pain and resistance normally experienced in the recovery process.

Allowing yourself to accept yourself and others where you are starting, in the present, makes it possible for you to focus on learning and growing. Rather than putting your energy into judging and blaming others, or defending yourself against the judging process, you are free to put your energy into changing. We call this healthy perspective "Powerful Vulnerability." We have found that No-Fault learning allows the deepest changes in areas of personal identity in the shortest period of time, with the least pain and effort.

In the *Third Chapter* we will explore core concepts that help you understand your perceptual bus more deeply. It gives you a better understanding of the driving process. These core concepts serve as building blocks to help you successfully approach your journey into change. In this chapter we will explore the concept of an *Adult Child Character* and how this concept can help you understand your process of change differently. We will consider the concept of *Therapeutic Life Coaching* in the change process. We will look at the *Twelve-Step* process of recovery, focusing on

Step 2 and ***Step 3,*** how we can regain our sanity by turning our lives over to God, as we understand Him. We will explore the concept of ***Spirituality*** in recovery, and the distinction between religion and spirituality. We will study a definition of healthy ***Self-Esteem,*** and explore the common symptoms of people who are suffering from damaged esteem.

In the ***Fourth Chapter*** we will explore and practice using the ***ABC's of Observation*** and other tools that help you organize the many thoughts and feelings associated with areas of your life that you want to change. Learning how to organize what you are noticing allows you to spot dysfunctional patterns.

Chapter Five presents two examples of Therapeutic Life Coaching sessions so you can get a feeling of the process, and how it approaches change. In these two examples, you are able to sit in on the sessions, and experience the personal process first hand.

We will chew on and digest several ***"Nuggets of Wisdom,"*** which reflect the Fundamental Principles of Healthy Change. These perceptual "Nuggets" often function at a subliminal level of consciousness, reflecting patterns that impact your ability to make desired growth in your life today. These "Nuggets" of Wisdom allow you to see more accurately what you are actually choosing in the present.

In the ***Sixth Chapter*** we will look deeply into some core "Nuggets", elements necessary in order for healthy change to take place. Exploring these "Nuggets" allows you to become aware of their subliminal dynamics and gain choice in these areas.

Chapter Seven explores "Nuggets" regarding the role of identity in the change process. We will examine deeply your perceptions about who you truly believe yourself to be, and learn how to develop choices in this key area of identity. You will learn that you are not your story, and your story affects where you are starting today.

Chapter Eight examines attitudes about the change process, and the impact they have on your ability to make healthy changes in your life today. **This book is all about the process of "becoming," helping you learn to appreciate and apply the "Fundamental Principles of Healthy Change" in your life today.**

Throughout this book I will be repeating key concepts over and over because that is what is needed in Therapeutic Life Coaching. My clients often ask me if I get tired of repeating the same "Nuggets" over and over in different ways and coming up with new examples of old patterns. I honestly say that I don't get tired of finding different ways to say the same thing. I use whatever situations are going on in the present to illustrate repetitive patterns, until the client is able to connect at the level of believing-in-action with New Program principles, attitudes and tools. We all change in our own ways and in our own time. As a coach, it is my responsibility to continually help generate choices that allow you to see more deeply and accurately.

I believe that language affects our perceptions and also reflects our perceptions at the same time. It often takes time for clients to get accustomed to using language that reflects their identity as being a process "of becoming" in the present. Notice your reactions to how I communicate in this book/session we are sharing together. I often use word pictures to capture complex concepts in a way clients can experience at their deepest levels of perception.

There is a reason I put my words together in a particular way. Explore the underlying assumptions in the words and language patterns that feel most natural to you today. What patterns do you notice as we are starting? *It is important to read this book very slowly. Really reflect on what you are reading and feel what it is like to begin imagining yourself applying what you are reading in your daily life.* Shall we begin?

Are you ready to face the truth that you really can make fundamental changes in your life today? Notice any resistances to believing this truth. Feel good about noticing your resistances; they are the signals that allow you to make deep change. Ponder this paradox as we begin our journey together!

I Am Complete In Him

By His blood I am covered
And made perfect.
AND, I am a fallible Human Being,
Loved completely by God,
In my humanness.
When I use the faith He gives
And say "yes" to Him,
He, by His Grace, makes me
Perfect, complete.
Even when I go my own way,
When I, in effect, say "no,"
His Love and Grace are extended
To me to cover me
And bring me back.
In this wonderful relationship
I can live…Not a perfectionist,
But a fallible human, becoming by Grace.

Roberta K.

SEEING CLEARLY THROUGH YOUR WINDSHIELD

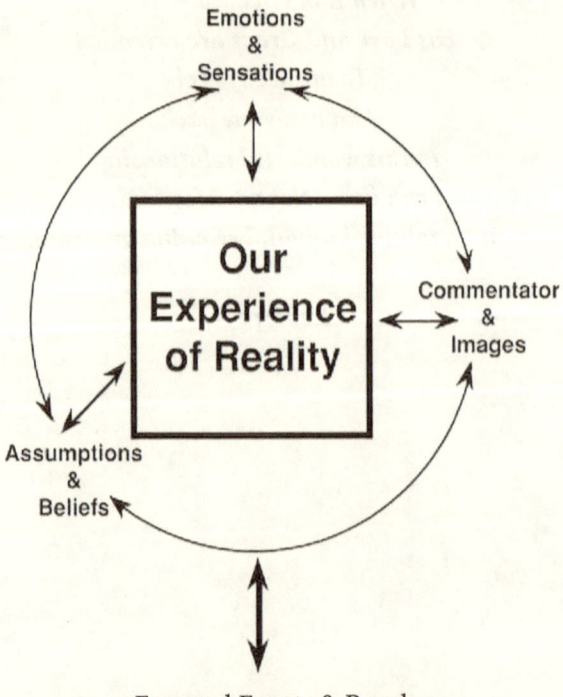

Your windshield filters what you see as you drive your bus. Imagine driving west into the sun in the afternoon, with bugs, grime, and dirt covering your windshield. What are you feeling as you drive along? What if you assumed that your poor vision was "just how you are" and there was nothing you could do about your poor visibility.

Someone sitting in the passenger seat would probably demand that you pull off at a gas station and clean your windshield, whether you thought it would help or not. They wouldn't want to risk their lives as you drive blindly.

Are you ready to begin cleaning your windshield of the many distortions and filters that color everything you perceive? You may enjoy driving a lot more when you can see clearly to choose healthy driving. This concept of perceptual filters is key in the recovery process.

The CAIR Handbook explains: "Our perceptions are filtered through our beliefs and assumptions, our internal dialogue (thoughts) and images, our physiological and behavioral responses, and our emotions. All of these interact to form a filter through which we experience the world. In the process of growing up in an unsafe environment, we make many decisions about ourselves, and the world outside of us. These decisions form the filter of our Old Program. Over time we become addicted to this way of looking at the world, and the decisions that underlie our filters become unconscious. If our filter sees us as inadequate and unlovable, positive feedback from those around us cannot get through. Keeping our internal view and rejecting the external information usually resolves the mismatch between how we see ourselves, and how others react to us. (Stop and discuss.)"

It is very helpful to keep a journal of our coaching adventure, taking the time to reflect and respond to what I am sharing with you. This is part of the "homework" that is always a key element of successful coaching. Over the years, one thing has been consistently true with coaching clients. Those who accept recovery as a process, a journey into healthy esteem, make the fastest and deepest gains in their lives. They have an attitude of grateful humility, where things that came up in their lives became an opportunity to practice "becoming" healthy. Their focus was practice, practice, and more practice, and they let themselves have fun with the practicing, choosing to live "consciously," with meaning and purpose.

Nugget: You Experience Reality Through Perceptual Filters!

Once you begin to appreciate the profound impact of this "Nugget", your life will never be the same. When you realize that your perceptions may be sending you inaccurate information, and that others may be having the same experience, it changes everything. Believing this truth helps create a humble attitude of openness and curiosity. I will help you learn how to apply "Nuggets" of truth to your perceptions, helping you develop a 20/20 perspective (knowing it will never be perfect). Truths are what you can base your faith/believing on, what you can count on to help provide new choices in difficult situations. We will be exploring 25 common perceptual filters that help create our *"Selective Movies."* We each have our own unique *"Selective Movie,"* although most of us are not aware consciously of how selective our movies really can be. Share in your journal what you notice as you reflect on your own movies.

We will review these perceptual filters and determine which ones are most familiar to you. These "Power Of Mind Distortions" can add, delete or distort significant aspects of your experience of choice. They can take a small part of the scene and enlarge it to fill the entire screen or they can leave out significant elements that change the meaning of an experience. These filters create **Selective Movies** that are unique and different for each person.

As you consider each of these "Power Of Mind Distortions," notice which ones feel most familiar in different situations. Do you use certain filters more with specific people or settings? What effect have these filters had on your experiences? Jot down examples in your journal. Take your time to reflect deeply on each filter. Feel good about noticing the filters that are causing you themost trouble, as this is the first step in the change process.

Begin to practice replacing old filters with accurate, healthy ones that allow you to move toward 20/20 perception (knowing that you'll never achieve it perfectly). Experience the different feelings, and the sense of choice when you replace dysfunctional filters with more accurate ones. Practice, practice, and more practice! Share what you are noticing with me in your journal.

Power Of Mind Distortions

1. Expectations create a powerful filtering of your experience of reality. We all have expectations, the question is your awareness of how your expectations affect and color your experience. *(1)* Do you have detailed pictures of how things should go, having spent a lot of time working out the specifics from every angle in your mind? *(2)* Are you only aware of vague feelings about what you want, unable to put into words or recognize it until it actually happens? *(3)* Are you only able to recognize what you don't want, without a clue about what you do want? Each of these patterns creates different styles of interaction. Are you aware of how you experience your inner thoughts and feelings?

The detailed pictures draw you into a process of trying to get your outside world to match your internal images. It can become a tremendous source of pressure and stress. If you recognize this pattern, realize that the tension and frustration you often feel comes from this expectation pattern.

By comparison, you may be aware of vague feelings that draw you forward without a clear direction or goal, only a sense of something wanted and not achieved, something missing. If you recognize this pattern, you can understand why you are so open to others leading, but why you probably would not be as good at making suggestions or taking the lead in situations yourself.

The third style of only having awareness of what you don't want, tends to keep you looking through the negative. We will explore the impact of this "Not" model in the "Addiction To The Familiar Nugget" later in this book. If you recognize this pattern, you can begin to appreciate some of your defensiveness and general lack of initiative.

When Sonia and I got together 50 years ago, she had very detailed pictures of how things should be. She was clear about who should do what. I had a vague sense of something missing, something pulling at me that I could not recognize. I didn't know what I wanted or what I liked, only what didn't fit. At the same time I have always had a very strong resistance to being told what to do. I have always hated being bossed.

Sonia grew up in a military home where orders would fly constantly. Her voice would often reflect this ordering tone. She would often be feeling frustrated that I wasn't seeing what "obviously" needed to be done, which added to the tone in her voice. We would go in circles with me defending and resisting, while she would feel frustrated and resentful at having to take all the responsibility to notice and make decisions. Does this feel familiar to you? Do you recognize these patterns in your relationships?

She would ask me what I wanted to eat or what show I wanted to see. She wanted me to be an active participant in our marriage and I didn't have a clue about what I liked. I had never really paid attention. *I had lived much of my life going "faster than the speed of feelings," not noticing what was going on inside.* She would get frustrated at my lack of input, which would reflect in her voice tone and attitude. This circle caused many fights and hurt feelings in the early years of our marriage. I saw myself as a "good guy" for letting Sonia make all the decisions and choices (as long as they weren't things I didn't like), while she felt lonely from the lack of interaction. It is another example of selective movies.

Notice what it feels like to connect the emotions you commonly experience with a perception that can be changed with practice. Each pattern described has some advantages and some disadvantages. If you want a different outcome, learn to notice which pattern you are functioning in, and begin to add elements of one of the other patterns. Practice allows you to begin feeling more natural with more flexibility in your expectations. Common words that signal expectations include "should," "have to," "must," "can't," "should not," etc. Share with me in your journal as you reflect on this subtle filter.

2. Self-fulfilling Prophesies reflects the fact that we often help create the very things we believe. When you expect/fear a situation will turn out a certain way, the belief itself helps to generate the resulting outcome. *You tend to look for signs that confirm your fears, and ignore anything that does not fit your expectations. This is not conscious or intentional; it helps form your Selective Movie.* Notice any patterns of fearful expectations that may be working against your goals. This pattern plays a significant role in depression and anxiety. Screening out anything that doesn't help build your case (whether you want/like it or not, does not matter) robs you of accuracy and therefore choice. ***Choice depends on accuracy.***

I have had a habit of being later than I predict with Sonia. It has been a repeated issue over the years. For years I would expect her to be mad when

I got home late, and would defensively react to that assumption as I came in the door. Many times I actually caused Sonia to have a negative reaction by the way I acted toward her as I came in. Do you recognize any patterns in your life where your fears have actually caused the unwanted events? Share with me in your journal what you notice.

Begin to practice noticing more accurately in these situations, focusing on how New Program tools can help you gain a healthy outcome. *Rather than fearing an unwanted outcome, practice focusing on what you do want to have happen.* This dynamic can work to your advantage in your recovery by believing the truth of your becoming in your chosen goal areas. *Believing that the core of your identity is based on your spirituality helps you approach yourself and others differently.* Share in your journal ways this filter has had an impact on your life up until now. What ways do you want to use this truth as a tool in your recovery?

3. Conditional Acceptance assumes that you must earn acceptance. This demand to earn acceptance may be directed toward self or others. Others may make conditional demands on their acceptance of you or their acceptance of themselves. It usually takes the form of "If/Then." If I can just get a good job, then I can feel good about myself. If I can keep my sobriety, then I can accept myself. If I can get her to love me, then I will know I am lovable. If I can lose 40 pounds, then I will be acceptable. If you would just change these behaviors, then I could love you. If you make me feel good all the time, then I will stay with you. If you loved me, you would see things my way. These, and many more forms of conditional acceptance create a dynamic tension that actually makes reaching your goals more difficult.

There is a tremendous difference between wanting healthy changes because you care, and demanding the changes be made in order for you to care. When you hold caring as a hostage to meeting the conditional demands, there is a healthy part of self that will resist conditional acceptance, in direct proportion to the intensity of the perceived demand for that condition. The stronger the perceived demand, the stronger the resistance will be.

Change is so much easier, with less effort and pain, when you allow yourself to accept yourself and others right where you are starting in any given area, and with that acceptance, allow yourself to begin relaxing into the desired changes. *This attitude allows the healthy power of New Program to be maximized. This acceptance does not assume you like where you are starting, only that you accept yourself and others where you are starting!* You cannot hate yourself or others into change!

4. Demanding Comfort in your recovery is not realistic. This is a common trap-"change should be easy and comfortable, or there is something terribly wrong." *First* of all, it is important for you to remember that the patterns you want to change are probably not that comfortable either. *Second,* the truth is that change requires thought and practice to become a new habit. *Third,* change cannot come through automatic pilot, it comes by living consciously, manually, intentionally accepting yourself and others as becoming. *Fourth,* the more you allow yourself to feel good about small steps towards your goals, the deeper your changes become. *New Program allows you to enjoy healthy steps forward and feel good about learning from steps backward.*

The opposite can also be a trap. I have seen many people come to Therapeutic Life Coaching with the assumption that "for change to be real, there must be a great deal of pain in the process." *You can't suffer your way into healthy esteem.* You can apply the Fundamental Principles of Healthy Change to your life in the present, by allowing yourself to bring accuracy into your current situations. This is not just intellectual knowing; it is the process of believing these truths at the level of applying (imperfectly) in your daily perceptions.

Not all pain is equal! When you are judging something, the pain from the condemning is added to the experience. The judging also accentuates negative elements in our Selective Movies. When you experience painful things with an attitude of grateful humility and the Prayer of Serenity, it becomes possible for you to relax into the pain, sharing it with your Higher Power, and with other safe people. Share your reflections on this filter in your journal. What do you notice and how can you apply this to your becoming?

5. Learned Helplessness is the self-perception of personal powerlessness. It is you believing you don't/can't have an impact on your world in the present. It usually comes from repeated experiences growing up where you were unable to make the changes you needed in order to feel safe and healthy. *Your inability to feel healthy power to impact your environment,* *over and over again, can lead to the decision and perception that your world is something you can not impact or influence, so why bother trying to change things?*

This attitude of giving up is often associated with depression and anxiety. This filter is like sitting on the fence, watching your life unfolding, wondering why things aren't changing, with no ownership in the change process. The truth is that you are chooser in your life and believing-this-in-action is key in your recovery.

The truth is that you can learn to exercise more healthy power in your relationships by gaining New Program Tools and perceptions. Your greatest source of healthy power is an attitude of grateful humility, applying the Prayer of Serenity in areas that feel overwhelming. *The Prayer of Serenity calls for the serenity to change what you can change, the freedom to release what you can't change, and a growing wisdom to know the difference.* It will feel strange at first, but practice, practice, practice. By starting where you are starting, and feeling good about noticing where you are starting, you can begin to apply healthy power as you gain it.

Remember that change is possible! The more you experience this book, applying what you are learning in your daily life, the more healthy power you can gain. Share your reactions with me in your journal. Do you notice any resistance to believing that you can learn to develop more healthy power? Allow those signals to help you connect with the wounded parts of you that fear getting their hopes up, only to be disappointed again. Respect this resistance and begin developing a healing, parenting relationship with those parts of you. You can be becoming your own personal coach as you grow.

6. *Control vs. Influence* is an important distinction in recovery. Controlling is a very different approach than influencing a situation. You may have a strong need to control circumstances, feelings, people, etc., and feel a heavy responsibility to do so. It invariably leads to your feeling unappreciated and drained by the pressures to control. You may feel the opposite, that it is someone else's responsibility to control you, and not your job to control yourself. You may rebel any time you feel someone else is trying to control you at all.

No matter what form the control takes, the more you control, the less influence you have in the situation. Control generates resistance and rigid control stimulates rebellion. This is true whether you are trying to control yourself or someone else. This is also true when someone else is trying to control you. Share your reactions to this whole issue of control in your life today.

An important paradox in control is that the more you believe you are succeeding in controlling the situation, the less you can believe the reactions of the others in that situation. Are their reactions how they really feel or are their reactions the result of your powerful control? **Therefore the more controlling you become, the more insecure and isolated you will naturally feel. Anxiety and depression are a natural result of strong control issues.**

By contrast, influence is a way of relating to others that causes them to consider your perspective. You are not in control, but you do have an impact on the situation. The problem is that if you go for control, you lose the ability to have healthy influence. You need to consider which pattern you want to be developing in your present relationships, regardless of what patterns you have used up until now. I believe there is no way to have more healthy influence than applying New Program with grateful humility. When you try to do more than that, I believe you lose healthy power.

If your current situations feel very stressful, start by noticing how you would like them to be. From what you know of each person involved, how can you begin to let others know of the healthy changes you want to begin in the present? What have you taught them to expect of you in the past? *I use the term "Powerful Vulnerability" to reflect healthy influence, where it is more important to you that you learn and grow, than to be right.* I find it helpful to use "confusion" and "curiosity" when beginning big changes in a situation. Starting with anger or defensiveness will draw you back into a control position. *It is important for you to use a lantern, which illuminates 360 degrees, so you can appreciate the different perspectives.* When you use a judgmental flashlight, you can only see one direction at a time, which reduces your healthy power for influence.

7. *Fairness* is a concept you developed as a child and you may have continued assuming that things should be fair in your adult life. The fact is that in reality good things happen to bad people, and unfair things happen to good people. Life is not fair or unfair; it simply is what it is. *Although it is often*

disappointing when things turn out unfair from your perspective, you can learn to challenge the assumption that you have to be totally undone by unfairness. Make sure you are using a lantern to see the whole picture, and not a flashlight that only sees one side of the situation. Fairness often varies widely depending on whose perspective you are using.

This filter often triggers a regression where one of your wounded inner kids grabs the wheel and tries to deal with the "unfair" situation. Notice who is driving your perceptual bus! The best you can do when the fairness issue comes up is to apply the Prayer of Serenity in the situation. Share in your journal times this filter has been active in your life. Do you see any patterns?

8. Fault and Blame assumes that if something is wrong, then someone must be at fault and should be blamed. You may put all your energy into blaming someone else, you may put your energy into blaming yourself, or defending yourself against blame from someone else. No matter what direction the blame comes from, you are not putting your energy into changing the situation.

The truth is that fault and blame interfere with healthy change. It is much more useful to put your energy into changing in the present. ***Remember that you can't defend and change at the same time.*** I think it is significant that there is not one example of Jesus defending Himself anywhere in Scripture. When you start to defend, you give up much of your healthy power. Share in your journal how this filter has affected your life up until now.

9. Needs vs. Wants is a concept many people have a hard time understanding. What you need to live a satisfying, meaningful life is often quite different than what you want to have in your life. Jot down some of the needs you believe are critical for your life to be satisfying. Needs tend to be fairly basic. Next include a list of wants that you have. Notice the difference between needs and wants for you personally.

I may need to have someone love me, but I want that someone to be my wife, Sonia. I need food and shelter; I may want certain kinds of foods and for my shelter to look a certain way. It is important for this distinction to be clear for you as you approach making changes in your life. **Respecting**

needs as needs, and wants as wants, allows you to make more accurate choices. Confusing these two concepts often leads to entitlement problems.

10. The Comparison Trap forgets that we are all unique individuals, and comparison has little or no real meaning. You can try to feel better about yourself by noticing others who seem lesser than you, or you may feel inadequate by seeing others who seem better than you. Either way, you lose! This trap assumes a contest, with a winner and loser. The comparison trap is a great source of depression and anxiety. If you feel "less-than," you feel depressed; if you feel "better-than," you feel anxious about who will come along to be better than you in the future.

This comparison process usually involves your "private" self and the other person's "public" self. ***The truth is that you can never really know another persons "private" self, and others can never really know your "private" self.*** The best you can hope for is an adventure learning to risk knowing and being known by others. The comparison trap turns the adventure into a test. The free CAIR Self-Help Groups and CAIRing Grace Groups provide a safe place to practice turning the test back into an adventure. Remember that it only takes two people interested in sharing and growing to begin a group. All the needed material is available free on our Web site www.CAIRforYou.com.

Over the years I have done many groups. In the first group meeting I always have each person share both their internal experience and their perceptions of the other group members who were in the waiting room with them while waiting for the first group to start. This one exercise brings an amazing amount of information to the surface about this trap. There is usually a significant difference between how group members describe their inner experiences, compared to how other members saw them. They also realized that their perceptions of others could be way off, too! Share in your journal times you have fallen for the comparison trap, and notice any patterns.

11. The Giant "Me" is a confusing filter. When you are feeling extremely self-conscious, it is usually accompanied by feelings of insecurity and inadequacy. The assumption that everyone is looking at you, or talking about you, or thinking about you to such a point that it makes you feel anxious self-consciousness, would mean that you must be an important person. This giant "me" makes you feel insecure by making you feel the focus of others-this paradox needs to be examined closely.

The truth is that others tend to be too preoccupied with themselves to focus on your shortcomings! Others have more going on in their lives than to make you the center of their attention. It is important to challenge this giant "me", replacing it with more accurate truth, and experience believing that truth more with practice. Are there certain situations that predictably bring your giant "me" filter into action? What patterns do you notice? Reflect and share with me in your journal times and situations where you have felt painful self-consciousness. Were you assuming that others were preoccupied with your flaws and shortcomings? What is it like to challenge this filter?

12. Why, Why, Why is a powerful question that can derail your recovery process! A client who was reading this filter in the CAIR Handbook told me that his first A.A. Sponsor taught him not to whine. Whenever George would ask his sponsor "why me" when bad things kept happening in his recovery, his sponsor would respond with "why not you?" George had never looked at it that way and found it helpful to gain this perspective. It is natural for you to want to understand what is happening in your life, but the questions you ask to achieve that understanding can have a powerful impact on the process. I encourage my clients to focus on questions like "Who," "What," "Where," "When," and "How." These questions can help lead to action, and action leads to changes.

By comparison, the question "Why" tends to generate a trance-like state, somewhat like a "black hole" in space, drawing you into the content and away from the truth. This filter becomes even more destructive when you demand to understand why before beginning to take action toward changes in your life. I tell my clients that they can want to understand why, as long as they are willing to find it in the process of becoming, and not wait to take action until after the "why" is clear. Jot down in your journal which questions seem most familiar.

The question "Why" also tends to hide powerful presuppositions that can feed your **Selective Movie.** Why am I so unlovable? Why doesn't anyone like me? Why am I so hopeless? Why is my life so hard? Each of these questions makes profound assumptions seem like facts. Fact-I'm unlovable! Fact-No one likes me! Fact-I am hopeless! Fact-My life is so unusually hard! When you present these *"facts" as part of a question, you tend to accept them without real thought. Begin to notice the assumptions you are making in your questions, particularly the question "Why."*

13. The Test is a perceptual filter that generates anxiety and self-consciousness at a subliminal level. Most of my clients are not aware that they have a choice in how they approach perceiving situations in their lives. They don't realize that they can approach situations as an adventure rather than as a test. When this "test" filter is active, the results of your activity will be perceived as determining whether you have a "right" to be happy and loved. This is a key element of "test anxiety," where passing a history exam measures your O.K'ness as a human being and not just how much you have learned about history.

Perfectionism also feeds into life being a test. Fear of doing less than perfect creates severe tension and leads to anxiety and depression, as well as a number of stress related physical problems and autoimmune responses. The truth is that you can choose how you approach situations in your life-past, present, and future. I encourage you to begin imperfectly relaxing into the adventure of starting where you are starting, in the present, with "tests" in your life today. This is a perceptual skill or muscle, which requires a lot of practice to begin feeling natural. Jot down in your journal what you notice about your reactions to this filter. Do you need work changing your perceptions of life from a test into an adventure? Allow yourself to practice consciously looking at situations as opportunities to experience your adventure into change.

14. Shame, Guilt, and Regret are three different perspectives. **Shame** is a filter that kills your soul through suffocation and mal-nourishment at a spiritual level. Shame states that you are the main issue, who you are as a person is being attacked and rejected. You need to shift your attention to the action that is the real issue. **Shame** says that you are a mistake, a failure, unlovable, worthless, etc. **Shame is a rejection of self. It is a statement of identity. Shame is invariably involved with wounded inner kids.** It serves as a force field of rejection that tries to keep the lids on your Tupperware. Without loving connection with your wounded inner kids, you cannot help them become healthy. **Shame prevents healthy change!**

I work with my clients to recognize areas where shame is active, and help them learn to transform the shame perspective into healthy guilt and regret. **Guilt** can be a useful, healthy signal that you are going the wrong direction in the present, and need to change directions. This is a feeling of conviction. The focus of healthy guilt is on your action in the present, and not your personhood. God doesn't want you to feel badly, He wants you to change in healthy directions, for your own sake. That is why it is important to feel good about noticing unwanted things, as the first step in changing. God's Plan includes Grace, which is unearned love. Nothing you do can add to or subtract from His Love for you. His Love is unconditional and unchanging. Take your focus off hating yourself and begin to focus on changing in the present. **Guilt** about past things, that are no longer current, transforms into shame over time.

By comparison, **Regret** is a healthy, emotional reaction of grieving as you accurately accept past events and actions. **Regret** may be experienced in a variety of different ways, which need to be respected as part of the healing process. It is a fluid feeling of sadness at actions that have had a painful effect. **Regret** is not an intellectual notion; it is an emotional experience. Share your reactions to what you are reading in your journal. Notice what it is like to make the distinction between shame and healthy guilt/ regret in your life.

15. Who Defines My Reality is a filter that can create confusion in your personal interactions. It often leads to a reactive posture toward others. When you get feedback from someone, regarding your strengths and weaknesses, how things should be, or what you should or should not do in a given situation, do you notice a pressure to react in one of two ways? Do you feel that you either need to blindly accept their feedback, or you must convince the other person to change their feedback?

If you can't convince the other person to change their position, do you feel stuck with their perspective? Either way you react does not allow you to evaluate the feedback independently and define things for yourself. ***Reacting and responding are two very different experiences. Reacting focuses on the other person, responding comes from within you.*** Which perspective feels most natural to you in different situations? Jot down any examples of this filter being active in your life in the present.

Replay these interactions with the truth, that you can decide for yourself what is accurate. There is no need to convince others, only the need to believe the truth imperfectly yourself. ***There is a difference between sharing and defending, between being open and being gullible.*** You can be open to hearing what the other person wants to share, and you are free to decide ultimately what you believe, and what you choose. You can be open in sharing what is important to you in a situation, without trying to convince the other person. ***Remember that trying to convince prevents believing! The harder you try convincing, the more doubt and resistance you will generate.***

16. Mind Reading is the toxic assumption that either you can read other people's minds, or that others should be able to read your mind, or both. This assumption can focus on your ability to read body language, assuming that you know what the other person is thinking or feeling or intending because of what you read from their body language (this includes verbal modes). Mind reading helps create your Selective Movie, and distorts your access to truth. Common phrases that indicate mind reading include: "If you loved me you would…" "You meant to…" and "You know what you did!"

The truth is that no one can read minds! The best you can hope for is a working hypothesis of what someone else is experiencing. Allow your curiosity to be expressed through checking things out with others. Let others know what you want them to know, instead of assuming they should already know. Jot down examples of mind reading in your life. Do you see any patterns that are currently leading to toxic results? ***Begin practicing being unemployed as a mind reader and start using 20/20faith!***

When Sonia and I were first married 50 years ago, we moved into a house to begin our life together. I was the associate director of the Family Service Agency, and was living faster than the speed of feelings. We lived next door to an older couple with a retarded son, six months older than me, who worked at a sheltered workshop. His name was James. From time to time James would come over and want to "visit." When I would give him subtle signals that I needed him to go home, he would not get them. I would finally have to make a direct comment like "James, you need to go now."

As I was walking James out the front door one time after a short visit, it struck me that I had spent much of my life trying to read the subtle signals from others, to read their minds. My antenna were so well developed that I would sometimes pick up things that the other person wasn't even conscious of at the time. When I would respond to these perceptions, the other person would frequently deny what I perceived.

At that point, I decided to learn to become more like my neighbor James! I decided to "not get it" when others sent me negative or hurtful signals, so that they would have to become more direct for me to "get it." This was an important turning point in my life. I began to give myself the gift of allowing others to share what they wanted to share with me, without me trying to read their minds. What a relief!

17. Assuming That Feelings Are Fact is a filter that uses emotional reasoning to determine what is true. If you feel something, it must be true. You give your feelings some infallible authority in determining what is real and true. ***The truth is that feelings are neither true nor false; they are just real sensations of emotion.*** They are the result of your perceptual filters. If your perceptual filters are accurate, the feelings that come from them will be accurate too. If your perceptual filters are faulty, the feelings that come from your filters will be distorted too.

Do you have a tendency to react to your feelings as if they were true facts? Begin to explore the perceptual filters that are creating your feelings. Challenge those filters that are currently distorted, and replace them with healthy accurate ones. As you practice experiencing your new filters, they will become more natural. Remember practice, practice, and more practice!

You may be someone who has gone to the other extreme of believing that feelings have no place in making decisions, and that feelings should be blunted out as much as possible. From the time I was 14 until I began my recovery at 29, I lived my life as a Vulcan, like Mr. Spock on Star Trek. I gave up feelings and tried to live a life of logic and rational reasoning. The problem with this decision is that intimacy requires feelings to grow and flourish.

This Vulcan style was very hard on my marriage. When Sonia and I had only been married a few months, she was expressing some strong feelings about something important to her, and I responded that I would "talk to her when she was rational!" Some time later, when I was having a rare moment of emotional outburst, she turned to me and said "I'll talk to you when you are rational" and I suddenly experienced what she must have felt so many times. I looked deeply into her eyes, as tears were forming in mine, and told her how sorry I was for having said that to her all those times before. I have never said that to her in the many years of marriage since then.

If you have learned to survive by burying your feelings and worshiping logic, you can start by feeling good about noticing this toxic pattern, as the first step in change. Notice your resistance to the idea of shifting to a more balanced respect of feelings and logic as a dynamic duo to help you determine truth. Respectfully connecting with your resistance can help you make contact with the wounded part/parts of you. These parts are often afraid to open the feeling dimension for fear of being overwhelmed with blocked feelings from the past. You can learn to support these wounded parts as they respectfully learn to deal with their blocked feelings with your help and supervision. We will explore the Adult Child Character in the next chapter. Jot down in your journal what you notice.

I experienced a unique aspect of this filter on a drive up into the mountains recently. I have always had some anxiety driving around curves when the pull of centrifugal force "makes me feel like I'm losing control." There are a lot of curves in the mountains and I began to notice when my anxiety would spike. I was driving my Regal GS, which is a very stable car in the mountains. I would be following a big SUV or truck that was making the curves fine, and I would be touching my brake and feeling anxious about not staying on the road.

The feeling from centrifugal force is a real signal, but my conclusion was distorted. I flashed back to a serious car wreck I had had in my early twenties on Highway 17 between San Jose and Santa Cruz. In the middle of a curve my back tire blew and I rolled several times, ending up facing the opposite direction in the grassy meridian. I hadn't thought about that accident for years. It never ceases to amaze me how past experiences can filter our present moments.

I began to relax into the curves at the speed of the other cars and trucks, talking to myself as I began to experience the sensations differently. I reminded myself that the sensation was a natural principle of physics and did not mean that I was out of control. Each curve became a chance to practice interpreting the meaning of the sensations more accurately. I recognized the metaphor in this experience-the parallel at the process level between what you and my other clients are facing in your recovery and what I was experiencing on my drive up to the retreat. Past experiences may be causing sensations/feelings in current situations that affect your ability to function in the present. Reflect deeply on this aspect of Feeling Are Fact, and share what you notice with me in your journal.

18. Black And White Thinking causes you to experience life as a series of dilemmas, feeling that you must choose one or the other of two possibilities. ***It is all or nothing! This filter is closely associated with your wounded inner kids.*** It is normal development for children to look at the world in black or white terms. This filter creates tremendous stress as you try to choose between two extremes, neither one fitting as well as a point in between.

The truth is that your choices run the continuum from black to white. Notice what happens when you replace the word "or" with the word "and." I encourage my clients to never settle for less than three choices in any given situation. If you recognize this filter in your life, begin to practice generating at least three or four choices to situations where you would normally use your black or white filter. Make a game out of expanding your choices. It gets easier with practice. Jot down your reactions to the adventure of expanding your choices beyond the dilemma of either/or.

19. *Faulty Generalizations* filter your perceptions in a way that affects your ability to make accurate conclusions. You build a case for something being true, based on one or two examples. "I always screw up," "I don't need anyone," "Everyone has one," "You always hurt me," and "You never care about me," are examples of this filter. You can create a word picture through these generalizations, which can become more real than "reality." The truth is that words like "all" and "never" are usually not accurate statements.

Do you notice a tendency for using overgeneralizations and building a case to fit your expectations? Jot down any overgeneralizations you notice in your journal, and begin to challenge your faulty generalizations. Make a game out of spotting overgeneralizations in yourself and others. It is best not to be to quick to point out violations that others make, as this is usually given as a flashlight statement, and responded to with defensive-ness.

Notice the violations of others as useful information, to help understand possible areas that could use clarifying.

When you notice yourself using this overgeneralization filter, feel good about noticing and begin coming back to specifics like who, when, where, what, and how. It may feel strange, but you can begin stopping in mid sentence, and start becoming more specific in the present. It is amazing how many people do not realize they can affect how they process information.

You really can choose to become more specific, to practice consciously challenging your own generalizations when you notice them in your thinking. It is a wonderful gift to be free to notice and change. It strengthens your New Program and weakens your Old Program in the same action. It can be fun poking holes in your generalizations when you choose to also feel good about noticing the generalization in the first place. *Judging takes the fun out of recovery.*

20. Powerful Words create such strong emotional reactions that you end up reacting to the words rather than the actual situation, which affects your ability to choose. Words like "phony," "acting," "can't," "should," "stupid," and "but," are all examples of powerful words. The word "but" takes away the meaning of the phrase that goes before it. "I think you have a good point, but you make no sense." "I'd like to help, but…" One of the more toxic patterns is "yes but." Replace the word "but" with the word "and." Notice the kinds of words you use to describe difficult situations. Do you see a pattern of powerful words? Jot down any powerful words that feel familiar to you.

Do you notice different words having power, depending on whether they were coming from you or from someone else? *Take the time to notice the kinds of words that come from your inner "Commentator," that voice in your head.* Feel what it is like for you to tune in to the messages that are usually going on subliminally, and make them conscious. Notice the kinds of words you are using to describe yourself and others. Listen to the words used in describing the situation. Do you notice flashlight judgment statements or grace-filled lantern statements that shine with respect and valuing at the entire scene, including you. Keep coming back to this filter as you grow, to deepen your appreciation of the power of words.

A significant dimension in intimate communication is the tone that the words create during sharing. When there is an overall tone of valuing and respect, and the words convey that attitude, and the nonverbal channels congruently express the same valuing and respect, you have maximized your healthy power. Shining your lantern with a gentle, open light in all directions, allows healthy, intimate communication to come most naturally. ***When I shine my lantern in coaching sessions the first thing we usually see is that the client has been working with a judgmental flashlight.***

The language in this book is there for a reason. Notice what it's like to hear yourself reading the words sub-vocally, experiencing what you are reading. When you share honestly, with respect and valuing, the chances of a healthy outcome are much greater. Many people use judgmental words without even realizing or intending their impact on the communication. Some have the attitude that they need to "tell it like it is!" If a relationship is important to you, it deserves the gift of thought, particularly when sharing difficult things with your family and friends. Notice the impact your words have on those you care about-including you.

21. Time Machine takes you out of the present, which is the only place you can actually make changes in your life. Do you find yourself living in the past, hanging on to past negative experiences, allowing them to influence you in the present; or living in the future, anticipating and focusing on the unpleasant things that might happen, rather than living in the present? When you relive past scenes, experiencing that scene as if it were happening in the present, the original feelings and conclusions are reactivated.

When you come out of your Time Machine travel, you will bring back into the present these painful feelings as a hangover.

With traumatic events, the Time Machine allows you to experience the same painful scene over and over. When you project yourself into a future situation, experiencing that scene as if it were happening in the present, you bring your current resources into that future scene. This denies your ability to gain resources in the present to help deal with this future situation.

The truth is that you become the cause of your current pain by using your Time Machine. ***The truth is that you can learn to notice when you begin firing up your Time Machine, and choose to use New Program tools***

to change this destructive process. Gaining "frequent flyer miles" in your Time Machine allows you to feed your depression and anxiety. Travel into the past feeds your feelings of depression; travel into the future feeds your anxiety.

You can start to ask the key questions: "Who am I?" (Who's driving your bus in the present), "Where am I?" (What is the actual situation in the present), and "What time is it?" (Is it past, future or present time)? These questions help you orient out of the time machine and into the present.

The Time Machine is very different than allowing yourself to reflect on a past or future scene, while staying in the present. You are free to remember who you are becoming, and bring an attitude of nonjudgmental curiosity and caring into the scene. The difference has a lot to do with perspective.

When the camera angle is coming from your New Program Adult eyes in the present, looking at yourself in the scene, you can rally useful resources to help nurture yourself in the scene. When the camera angle is coming from your eyes in the scene, you tend to experience regression and a flood of painful feelings. Does this pattern feel familiar to you? Feel good about noticing this and shift your camera angle so you can begin seeing yourself in the scene. Jot down in your journal examples of time machine travel.

22. *It's Awful; It's Nothing* is a filter that works like a telescope. When you look through one end, everything looks far away and your feelings become dulled and blunted. When you look through the other end of the telescope, everything looks up close and huge, blowing your feelings out of proportion, making them much more intense and overwhelming. Either side of the telescope has a profound impact on your experience and feelings. Does either end of the telescope feel familiar to you?

Allow yourself to practice playing with both ends of the telescope, so you can recognize when it is happening and put your telescope down and deal with the situation without your trusty telescope. Gain familiarity with the end of the telescope that you don't normally use, so that you can expand your choices. Share your reactions to this exercise in your journal. What is it like to realize that you can change this filter?

23. *That's Just How I Am! That's Just How You Are!* This filter confuses action with identity. The fact that you (or someone you interact with) have been a certain way up until now, does not say anything about what is possible in the present. It only affirms that you will probably continue being that way as long as you remain functioning in automatic pilot in Old Program. The moment that you choose to shift to manual, becoming conscious, as chooser in your life, and begin to bring truth into that pattern, change becomes a natural outcome.

Remember that allowing and forcing have opposite effects on your ability to change. This filter, more than most, gets its power from believing the faulty perception. When you believe that "that's just how I am," it becomes true for you. Your believing gives it the power. If you expect me to behave in a certain way, you will tend to be affected by that expectation, and see what you expect, whether it is actually happening or not (see POM Filter #2: Self-fulfilling Prophecy). This filter actually helps create what you expect to see.

24. We Are Our Mistakes filters your experiences through a lens of shame or blame (or both). This filter assumes a negative overtone to your experience. If you are applying this filter to yourself, you will tend to maximize any failing, shortcoming, flaw, imperfection, looking through your telescope, using the close-up direction. You will believe "I am my mistakes." Your worth as a human being depends on hiding your imperfections from yourself and others. This assumption is a constant source of anxiety and depression. It acts like acid on your self-esteem, tainting your self-perception with shame, eroding your sense of worth.

When you apply this filter with others, you use the same telescope to see the other person. You will believe that "the other person is their mistakes, too." Again you will see all the negative elements in the other person, overlooking any positive elements that might balance the negative (you are blinded by your need to prove your case), or you deny any negative because you must see the other person as perfect. Either way distorts reality and makes choosing more difficult.

This filter may come from previous experiences in your life. If you were constantly being attacked for getting home late from work in a previous relationship, you will probably assume the same kind of response from your current partner. Your expectations will affect your nonverbal behavior toward your partner, increasing the chances of your partner becoming upset. When this happens, you see proof that they were really upset with you for being home late from work, no matter what they say. This increases their upset, feeding the vicious cycle. Does this feel familiar? Hold up your lantern, so you can see both of you at the same time. Notice what happens when you respond instead of react to your partner? **It may take several times before your partner notices the changes, but if you let yourself enjoy the adventure of learning how to break this painful pattern, positive change is likely.**

25. What If…? If Only… functions like a black hole in space. In astronomy, a black hole is created when a star collapses in on itself, creating such an intense gravitational pull that nothing can escape, not even light. When you fall for the trap of "what if.," you enter the Twilight Zone of endless possibilities. This filter feeds powerfully into feelings of anxiety and insecurity. It interacts with the Time Machine, causing you to experience these endless possibilities over and over, as if they were actually happening in the present. **When you shift from the Time Machine to looking at possibilities from the perspective of being in the present, it greatly reduces your anxiety.**

The truth is that you can not do more than apply the Prayer of Serenity in any given situation: ***"Lord, grant me the serenity to change what I can change, the freedom to release to You what I can't change, and a growing wisdom to know the difference."*** If the answer to the first part is that you have done what you can do up until now, then the second part guides you to release what is left that you can't change. This allows you to put your focus and energy on becoming in the present. We all have limitations; that is part of being human. Jot down in your journal any examples of "what if." in your life today. Notice what happens as you practice shifting time perspectives back to the present. Remember that it will get easier with practice.

"If Only." allows you to punish yourself (or others) for choices not taken. The truth is that you "can't go to the party I gave yesterday." It may have been a wonderful party, and you may be very sad about missing it, and feel a lot of regret. No matter how badly you feel, it is impossible to go back in time in order to attend my party. There is a dramatic difference between feeling healthy regret for missed opportunities, and torturing yourself (or others) for having missed that opportunity. If this filter feels familiar, take a few deep breaths, feeling good about noticing this pattern. Begin to experience shifting from shame to regret in these situations. Notice what happens as you learn to respect and feel healthy regret. Share what you notice in your journal.

A list of the 25 perceptual filters making up the **Power Of Mind Distortions** includes:

1. Expectations
2. Self-fulfilling Prophesies
3. Conditional Acceptance
4. Demanding Comfort
5. Learned Helplessness
6. Control vs. Influence
7. Fairness
8. Fault and Blame
9. Needs vs. Wants
10. The Comparison Trap
11. The Giant "Me"
12. Why, Why, Why?
13. The Test
14. Shame, Guilt and Regret
15. Who Defines My Reality?
16. Mind Reading
17. Assuming That Feelings Are Fact
18. Black and White Thinking
19. Faulty Generalizations
20. Powerful Words
21. Time Machine
22. It's Awful; It's Nothing
23. That's Just How I Am! That's Just How You Are!
24. We Are Our Mistakes
25. What If…? If Only…

3

A LOOK INSIDE YOUR PERCEPTUAL BUS

Now that we have looked at cleaning your windshield of distortions, we can begin to explore the inside of your perceptual bus. Are you willing to look deeply into where you are starting and how you want your life to change? Are you willing to explore the beliefs and patterns that have supported your current problems and made change so difficult up until now? Are you willing to be honest with yourself, noticing without judging your starting point? Are you willing to give yourself the gift of thought and time in order to gain healthy changes in your life today? Do you want to learn how to gain healthy personal power for growth?

It is important for you to consider what you want to gain as a result of our coaching relationship as you work through this book. It is the same question that I have encouraged thousands of clients to ask themselves, regarding how they wanted to use their time during our coaching sessions. I am guessing that you are interested in making changes in your life. Stop for a moment and jot down some of the areas you want to begin addressing in the present.

It is essential, at the start of our relationship that you understand what you are agreeing to bring to this adventure. It is your job to bring a willingness to gain and practice new perceptions that greatly increase your healthy powers of choice in your life. It is my job, as your coach, to help you recognize any distorted views of yourself or others, and supply useful tools and skills to help you see more accurately to reach your healthy goals.

I will make my 40+ years of experience as a full time therapist/coach available to you, as we approach your goals together. **You supply the "content"-the situations you want to change; I help you bring the needed resources to your "content." As your coach, it is my responsibility to help you see more accurately, in ways that allow you to "relax into your changes."** I believe God has some important "Nuggets" regarding *how* He wants us all to approach changes in our lives. In this book I will share these "Nuggets of Wisdom" about the change process, as I have shared them countless times with clients in **Therapeutic Life Coaching** *sessions*.

The Adult Child Concept

In 1987 I published my first article on treating the Adult Child Character using **Cognitive/Perceptual Reconstruction (CPR)** as a Therapeutic Life Coaching approach. I had developed this therapeutic process in the early 80's with the help of my wife Sonia and my partner at Psychological Associates, Don Strangio, Ed. D. My experiences with preschool children helped me recognize the Adult Child characteristics in so many of my adult clients during coaching sessions. I would see a competent, capable adult client suddenly regress into a scared, hurting little child.

Adult Children are like the Wizard of Oz. Their outer facade may seem powerful and competent, but inside it is as if a little child is pulling the strings and driving their emotional bus. Does this feel familiar to you? Do you often feel like a "fake" when relating to important people in your life? Do you often see yourself as a "phony" going through life in fear of being "discovered?" Does life feel like one unending drama of trying to survive to the next scene, trying to avoid the inevitable disappointments and rejections that you just know are coming? Do you often have significant difficulties in your personal relationships? Do you often ask, "Why Me?"

There are six qualities that seem to be present in most Adult Children prior to entering recovery. How many of these qualities do you recognize in yourself?

1. Reacting to life with a "survival" mentality.
2. Feeling that we are different from "normal" people and spending a lifetime trying to "pretend" that we are normal.

3. Looking at life through a "Black" or "White" filter.
4. Going through life judging very harshly. This judgment may be directed at ourselves, at others, or both.
5. Constantly looking for approval and validation from outside of ourselves.
6. Having great difficulty with intimate relationships.

The natural reaction of blocking painful feelings and experiences is what creates the Ault Child characteristics, dynamically like the frozen scenes that continue to break through for trauma survivors when certain triggers are activated.

Blocked Feelings

We have learned a great deal about Posttraumatic Stress Disorder from work with combat vets and survivors of traumatic events. Blocking an emotionally charged experience can cause the memory/experience mechanism in the brain to freeze that moment with the emotions fully charged. The memory leaves the limbic portion of the brain experiencing the fullness of the original emotions for the remembered scene, locked in the "on" position emotionally.

When the memory is activated, even subliminally, the emotions come flooding back into consciousness, so that you perceive yourself back in the original experience. I call this dynamic the Time Machine (see Power Of

Mind distortions in Chapter Two). Blocking unwanted feelings causes part of your "self-perception" to be stuck in a timeless state, as if in Tupperware and hidden away, frozen in the original scenes.

Adult Children were often forced to become "adults" as children, and often function as "little children" in aspects of their adult lives. Others never grew up because of the lack of safety and healthy models. They had a lack of support to risk becoming an adult with healthy self-esteem. They learned to survive by blocking out painful experiences and adapting to the demands of their environment.

Our wounds grow out of our decisions, perceptions of who we believe ourselves to be *at our core,* how we perceive the outside world, and how we choose to survive. This can vary greatly depending on whether regression is taking place at the moment. Do you notice any significant fluctuations in your perceptions of self and others?

It does not require "war stories" to create wounds in our character. Rejecting and hating yourself, trying to block painful feelings, and hating someone else can all create a frozen scene. This frozen scene can develop into a wounded part of self, forming its unique perceptions and sense of self. I am not talking about the pathological condition of Dissociative Identity Disorder, formerly Multiple Personality Disorder. I am talking about the sometimes subtle filtering of your perceptions without you realizing it is happening.

You need to be living consciously to recognize most of your regressions. What you may notice first is the old, survival feelings beginning to seep or flood into your current experience. A Second-Order feeling reacting to these feelings compounds the intensity and complexity of your feelings in the present. ***Feel good about noticing where you are starting at this moment. This cuts off the flood of Second-Order feelings that normally come with judging.***

Are you feeling guilty because you come from a normal family with no particular problems, feeling you have no right to be an Adult Child? The truth is that we all grew up in fallible families that came from fallible families, etc. We all learned who we are and what the world is going to be like in our childhood. This is not about blaming; it is about being accurate. Notice what you decided from these early experiences. Take several deep breaths and notice the reactions you have to this "Nugget." Share your reactions with me in your journal.

Normal life produces wounds! ***This concept of wounding is not about blame, it is about change!*** This book is an opportunity for you and me to discuss and reflect on your "Old Program" filters that support your current problems. You can learn to unblock your feelings in a healthy way that allows healing of your core self-esteem, using a "New Program" set of tools and resources to develop healthy esteem. I am a recovering Adult Child myself and will share glimpses into my own "inner kids" as the book unfolds.

Appreciating this Adult Child concept is central in the change process! The way I explain it to my clients is that I believe most people have some degree of Adult Child qualities. I believe that this is a normal part of being human. I coach them, and I will coach you to learn how to "parent" the wounded parts of yourself that are involved in the dysfunctional patterns in your life today. ***It is important to realize that the rejected parts of yourself retain their original perceptual filters, developmental resources, and the cognitive/thinking styles that were present at the time of disconnection.***

It is necessary to understand that you do not perceive the world directly, but rather through the filter of your beliefs, attitudes, and assumptions. ***When either internal or external factors cause you to regress to that dissociated "little child," you activate those filters and actually become that earlier age psychologically.*** The *ABC's Of Observation* in Chapter Four will give you a way of perceiving, that allows you to gain choice in situations where you had previously gone in circles. Jot down your reactions to this Adult Child concept.

Your unconscious mind is like at DVD with scratches on the surface, or a phonograph record with a skip that repeats over and over, or a 16 mm film with certain frames ajar. Specific scenes from your life keep repeating, in the form of perceptual filters that become triggered by situations in the present. These ruts are caused by experiences and decisions made at earlier times in your life. These scenes become frozen in timeless perceptions of yourself and others, usually experienced subliminally at a deeply emotional level.

I cannot tell you how many times, prior to beginning my own recovery, I would regress into one of my wounded inner kids and feel overwhelming anxiety in social situations, or dealing with conflict. I would go through long periods of feeling an empty depression, a sense of meaninglessness that would drive me to accomplish "enough," trying to fill the hole inside. I would go *"faster than the speed of feelings,"* to avoid the pain. When in my regressed states, I would feel a desperate need to gain acceptance and approval from others, just like I had experienced early in my life. At those times I could not give the needed validation to myself. **Logic and rational reasoning could not touch the overwhelming experiences of these regressions.**

As my personal recovery has developed over time, the way I know I am progressing is that these regressions happen less often. When I do regress, it's like my heart isn't really in it, because I know one of my inner kids is behind the wheel, and that I can take back the wheel whenever I want. This is not an intellectual knowing, but a spiritual relationship I have developed with each of my inner kids over time. I have a commitment to loving supervision and support for them, whether they want it or not. My core identity no longer changes because one of them is grabbing the wheel.

I no longer have to experience all the emotional pain associated with "their" living in those past scenes, instead I can provide the needed resources so my inner kids can feel more healthy today. I am free to be "becoming" in the present. ***The truth is that I am not them, and they are a part of me, and will always be a part of me, so the mission is how to deal with them in a healthy way.*** Have you ever felt the sudden flood of strong emotions, e.g., anxiety, anger, or insecurity, triggered by something happening in the present? Have you suddenly felt very young and overwhelmed by the familiar feelings of childhood? Do you notice a pattern of regressions in your life? Jot your reactions in your journal, noticing without judging any emotionally charged scenes in your life. As you learn more about healthy change, you can help these wounded parts of you heal in the present.

These emotionally charged scenes are stored in "Tupperware," where time has no meaning, yesterday, last month, or 40 years. When the lid pops off of the Tupperware, the original perceptions filter your current experience. The same shame and fear that caused you to block and reject the scene in the first place, make it difficult for you to reconcile and begin healing these wounded parts of yourself that are stuck in your Tupperware.

A key part of your recovery is learning to perceive the wounded parts of yourself with loving grace, giving them nurturing supervision and support, as you learn to deal with reality in the present, with your current resources.

Feel good about noticing any wounded parts of yourself as you jot down your experience, sharing what you are experiencing with your coach.

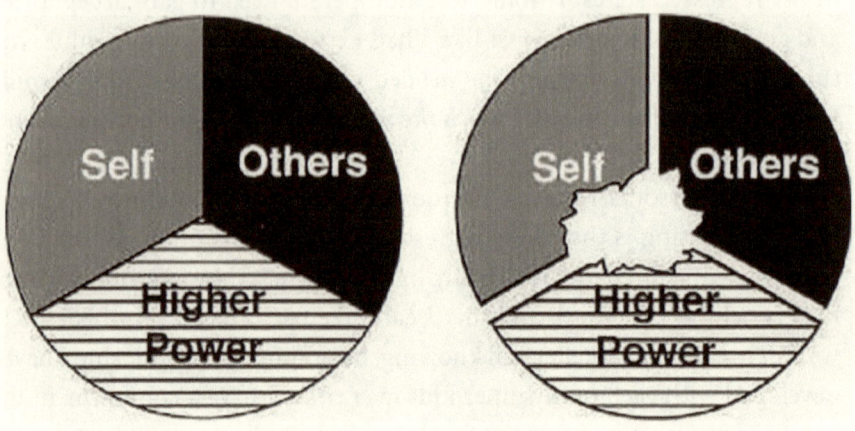

Healthy   Wounded

Many of my clients have tried to get rid of these unwanted, wounded parts of themselves, causing separations within themselves, between themselves and others, and between themselves and their Higher Power. I share with them that it is not possible to eliminate these perceptual parts of self. I explain that without these parts, they are left with vacuous, empty places where those parts of identity belong. Have you tried to ignore and reject parts of yourself? Take a few deep breaths and experience what comes up, as you are open to connecting with wounded parts of you.

Have you succeeded in creating a raw hole of nothingness in your core being through judging-creating shame and blame? ***Shame and healing cannot go together. Shame is an autoimmune disease, where the self attacks itself.*** The self is trying to protect itself from an unacceptable part of itself that is a perceived danger. It does this by trying to get rid of, or at least hide, what is unacceptable by rejecting that part of self. There is no distinction between "being" as identity and "doing" as behavior.

This confusing circle crushes your soul and destroys your self-esteem. It has not worked for the thousands of clients I have coached over the years, and it will not work for you! Embracing your wounded kids inside with loving supervision produces deep healing and growth. It is important for you to recognize who is driving your perceptual bus in the present moment.

Do you notice a pattern of who's been driving in recurrent problem areas? Share your reactions with me in your journal.

Notice the different feelings that come up as you begin to see who is driving your perceptual bus. ***Your resistance to seeing accurately is a normal reaction. Resistance to healthy change is a valuable source of useful information, and needs to be treated respectfully.*** Most clients have a hard time respecting their resistance, and acknowledging the impact their Adult Child characteristics have on their lives today. We will explore this in much more depth throughout the book. For now, jot down what you notice about your reactions to what you are reading, including your feelings about any resistance you experience. It is very helpful to keep a journal while going through this book, capturing your reflections on what you read. Writing helps you slow down enough to notice what is below the surface. ***Core change requires experiencing deeply!*** This is difficult in a superficial world where "30 second sound bites" and instant results contaminate your expectations.

Jill, a very competent woman I had the opportunity to work with had been struggling with a debilitating autoimmune disease for years. She also suffered from depression. She was an Adult Child, coming from a family characterized by unacknowledged alcoholism and high-powered, performance-oriented achievers. Never seeming to measure up to critical voices in her life, she felt shame and inadequacy. Jill began hating herself into perfectionism and placed rigid demands upon herself.

Later in adult life she continued the harsh demands, expanding them to those who were important to her. Eventually, she became driven by the "safety" of being in control and taking responsibility for everything in her life. The pressures placed a great strain on her physical and emotional health. Jill drew this picture of how she felt at her core as a teenager many years prior to recovery.

These problems were particularly frustrating for Jill because she deeply believed in God but felt her disabilities prevented her from living up to what she was supposed to be as a Christian, leading to even more guilt and shame. She rigidly held onto the truths of her faith intellectually, while emotionally holding herself at arm's length in her relationship with God. This is a familiar paradox that I see frequently: "I believe in God and love Him, and when I can finally earn His free gift, I will be able to actually experience His Love for me personally."

The paradox is trying to earn a free gift. The harder Jill would try to earn it, the less free it felt to her personally. Many people conclude that they will never be good enough to get His free gift and finally give up trying, resenting God for rejecting them. **Although their observation is accurate, their conclusion is faulty.** Since we can never be good enough to earn His free gift, we can give up and resent, or we can give up and accept His free gift. How have you chosen to react to this issue personally up until now?

This pattern of trying to earn Grace comes about when you begin to experience God through the perceptual filters associated with your parents or some key person in your childhood. At a relational level you feel you are relating to that person when connecting with God, projecting onto Him those personal qualities. Does this pattern feel familiar to you? Jill was trying to earn the acceptance and love of God, just as she had tried to earn it in her family, without getting too close to become hurt or disappointed. She had the Grace to see that she had been attributing the painful qualities of her family members to God. Having an inaccurate view of her loving Heavenly Father, resulted in an inability for her to have an intimate, trusting relationship with Him.

As Jill began viewing God on the basis of His own personal attributes, taking Him at His Word, she began to stretch, taking emotional steps toward Him in a growing, personal relationship. She began to experience believing her identity as a new creation in Him, as she learned to nurture wounded parts of herself through His Love. Tremendous freedom has also come as she has learned to forgive herself and others imperfectly. Her intimate relationship with God has blossomed. Feelings of shame are becoming less common as she learns to challenge and replace toxic shame with healthy regret and growth. Her depression has dissipated, and her overall levels of energy are gradually improving. We will have to see the ultimate effects of the recovery on her autoimmune disease over time, but the prognosis of physical improvement is as encouraging as that of the mental, spiritual, and emotional health she is experiencing.

A Personal Look Inside

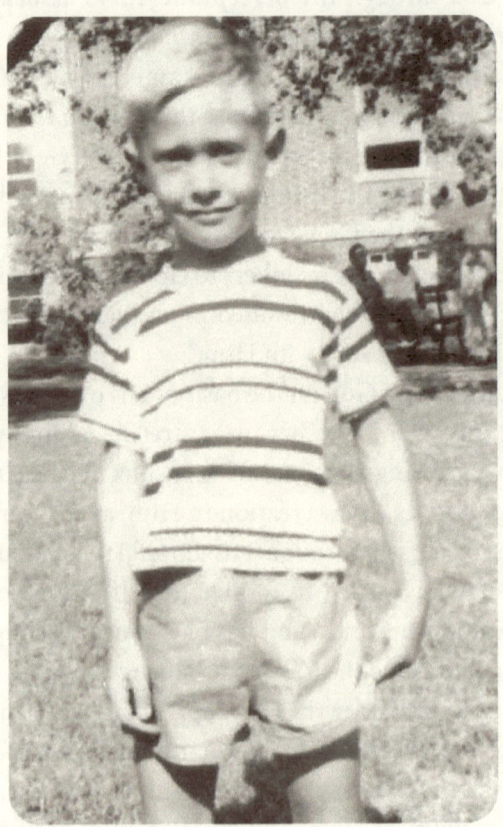

I met my first "inner kid" in 1977 while taking advanced training in Neuro-Linguistic Programming with Richard Bandler and John Grinder in the Santa Cruz hills of California. It was the last day of a week long, intense training. I picked someone I felt was safe, and asked him to be my support while I did some internal work that I couldn't put into words.

As I was sitting with him, relaxing into experiencing my feelings of anxiety and depression that had been such a part of my daily life as far back as I could remember, I suddenly saw an image of me as a six-year-old, with a striped t-shirt and short pants. The look on Jimmy's face was so sad and empty. I am not very good at visualization exercises generally, and it surprised me at how powerful the image of little Jimmy was at that moment.

As I was watching him in his sadness, I felt a strong, loving arm on my shoulder, and the insight that this little boy had been living much of my life for me, especially in the difficult times. I reached into the scene to him and began to hug him and tell him how sorry I was to have left him in such an impossible position. Both of us were in tears. I asked his forgiveness and told him I loved him.

I promised him that I would take care of him and help him feel better about himself. At the same time, I realized that who I am is becoming too, and it was my Big Brother Jesus who had put His strong, carpenter's hand on my shoulder and helped me see Jimmy through His loving eyes. **The Lord would help me grow as an adult, while I helped my inner kids to continue growing and healing.** This use of imagery allows the spiritual/relational dimension of the healing to be maximized.

When I was six years old I was in second grade at Lincoln Elementary School in Modesto, California. I later learned that I had mild ADD and dyslexia, along with serious anxiety and depression problems. Much of my emotional tensions would come out physically as gastrointestinal symptoms. I was sick frequently, and missed a lot of school. I remember looking around the room and feeling ashamed that I was in the lowest reading, spelling, math, and social studies groups. I was smart enough at six to realize what a dummy and loser I really was in the class. During physical education, I would stand with the other kids, hoping that they would not pick me last.

Most of the other kids wouldn't play with me, so I developed a plan to change that. I started stealing money from my dad's office (which was in the home), and would buy ice creams for the other kids so they would let me play. I hated myself for doing this, but I couldn't think of any other way to make up for being me. One evening my mom and dad were standing in line with me, attending the annual ham dinner at school. Along came Jeanie Campbell, and she stopped to talk to me in line. She was saying how cool it was that I bought ice creams for everyone, and my parents overheard everything. I could have died on the spot. After the dinner, I had to talk to my parents about where I had gotten the money and where the money had gone. Six-year-old Jimmy had absolute proof that he was inadequate and unlovable.

My personal relationship with Jimmy grew over the subsequent years since we first met. Jimmy began to see himself through my loving reflection of him and slowly became more confident, liking himself for the first time in his life. I no longer allowed him to handle adult situations, choosing to live consciously, dealing with life imperfectly as my adult self, becoming. As he blossomed, I felt less depression and anxiety in my daily life. I had had all six qualities of Adult Children. My entire life had been clouded with painful anxiety and depression. My ongoing relationship with Jimmy was like healing from the inside out.

It was over 10 years before I connected with another part of myself. While I was giving a talk on "Treatment For The Adult Child Character," in front of 250 people, I suddenly saw a scene from kindergarten when I was four years old. In the scene I watched as little four-year-old Jimmy waited as long as he could to ask permission to go to the bathroom. His teacher never said no, but his shy, self-consciousness made it so painful to ask. I watched as he ran from the classroom as fast as his little legs could carry him, across the yard to the boy's bathroom. There was a sandbox with a wood frame, about half way between the classroom and the bathroom. Just as he passed the sandbox he wet his pants and began to cry.

I watched him sit on the wood frame of the sandbox, waiting for his pants to dry. He was feeling total shame and self-hatred. I entered the scene from my adult perspective and sat down next to him on the wood frame. I put my arm around him and cried with him, letting him know how sorry I was that he had spent so much time in this condition. I told him I would be proud to sit with him, any time he needed me, and that someday he was going to grow up to be a psychologist, lecturing to hundreds of people about recovery. I had been so absorbed in my experience with Jimmy; I forgot that I was actually giving a talk. When I looked out on the audience, most of them were in tears, too.

A few years after meeting four-year-old Jimmy, I was suddenly introduced to an angry ten-year-old inside. I was taking a brake with Isie, a co-worker, when I was suddenly overwhelmed with powerful anger and resentment. I knew it was not coming from my sharing with Isie. I began to share what I was experiencing with her and the intense feelings came into focus as a very angry, scared ten-year-old.

I saw ten-year-old Jimmy standing in the bathroom with his father and his younger brother Bobby. Someone had left a dab of toothpaste in the sink and my dad was raging, demanding to know whose fault it was. He finally settled on me and decided that I should eat the toothpaste that was in the sink. I was very squeamish growing up, and there was no way I could eat that toothpaste. I remember standing there trying to figure out how I could make a living at age 10, how I could survive having to leave my home? It is no coincidence that I got my first job delivering newspapers a few months later after I turned 11, and I have worked ever since.

Twenty years later my younger brother Bobby and I were sharing in his back yard, enjoying his pool and the warm sun, when he looked at me deeply and said "Jim, you and I are very different. I work to live, while you seem to live to work." The year was 1977; I was up to my neck in my doctorate program and working in private practice. I stared back at Bobby, saying nothing for several moments. He was right! I have worked on my workaholic patterns from that time on. As I am writing this section, I realize that ten-year-old Jimmy, and his fearful determination to be able to support himself, was at the heart of my addictive pattern. I have made a lot of progress on this area over the years, but I need to be very conscious of my choices in this area of my life. Now that I understand Jimmy's role in the process, it will make it easier to address some of the underlying needs supporting this pattern.

I did not actually have to leave home at that time of the toothpaste showdown, but I believed I was faced with that choice. Because ten-year-old Jimmy became frozen in time, he didn't get the chance to see how things turned out. This is an important issue for you to consider as you begin your coaching. I have had countless clients try to figure out whether a particular memory was "true" or not, or they felt it didn't count unless the feared threat actually happened.

The truth is that when we believe something at the core depth of our being, it is real to us. In fact, it is more real to us than objective reality. We can filter out objective reality in many ways, but when we believe a painful event at that core depth, that event is powerfully real to us. Objective reality is not what is most important in the healing process, it is the spiritual relationship you have with the wounded parts of yourself that are stuck in a timeless Tupperware-the kids inside.

At school the other kids wouldn't tend to play with me during recess unless they had a personal problem that they needed help with. Although I wasn't good enough to play with, I was good enough to talk to about solving their personal problems. My caseload was nearly as big at age 10 as it is now. The difference today is that clients enter a healthy contract for help, while back then I was paid by the few moments of attention during the time I was helping them solve their problems. I accepted Jimmy with his anger, and assured him that I would no longer sell my soul to get others to like me. I assured him that I would help him grow and heal from his wounds. We have been in a growing relationship ever since. Over time his anger has generally subsided, replaced with healthy feelings of curiosity and adventure.

Ten-year-old Jimmy had a major role in my wrestling experience in high school (although I didn't consciously understand it until well into my recovery). Wrestling was one of the few sports that didn't require being able to catch a ball, so I decided to go out for the wrestling team at the 120-pound weight class. I was tall and wiry while most of the other guys were short and solid. I worked out and practiced in preparation for the first school meet, realizing that I might not be able to beat the others, but I could keep them all from pinning me. The team lost more points if one of our guys got pinned.

As the big day came up for the meet, the coach told us that the 120-pound kid was the section champion last year and pinned nearly everyone he wrestled. The coach asked who wanted to go against him, and suddenly ten-year-old Jimmy shot up his hand and said, "I'll bet he can't pin me coach!" I was shocked at what was coming out of my mouth. The coach said that if I could last the entire match without getting pinned I could have the starting position on the team.

I will never forget that match, he had me on my back in about 30 seconds of the first round and spent most of the two minutes bouncing on my chest while I bridged my back off the mat-using my head and feet. I felt all the rage and hurt of trying so hard to be accepted and at age 14 I channeled all that energy into sheer determination to keep from getting pinned. The second round I was on top-for about 15 seconds, and I was on my back again; he was bouncing, I was bridging. By the end of the match he was ahead about 100 to 2. I was so exhausted by the end that I could hardly walk. Two of my teammates came out to the mat to help me get back to the bench. My team gave me a standing ovation! The confused look on my opponent's face was priceless.

In my four years of high school wrestling I was never pinned! In four years I only won one match-pining my opponent. In my one victory the match was progressing like usual until he got careless and gave me the chance to bridge all the way over him and be on top, pinning him. He was so shocked that he didn't resist getting pinned. *I was shocked too, because my goal was "not to get pinned;" I really never thought about being able to actually win. I wonder what would have happened if my goal had been to win all along?* What does this example bring up in you right now? Share your reactions with me in your journal. Are you going through life, determined *not* to get pinned, or are you focused on winning your matches?

I have recently become aware of another pattern in my life that involves my ten-year-old Jimmy. Much of my life I have denied and suppressed my feelings. In my recovery my feelings are much more on the surface, including anger. Sonia and the boys asked me why I would occasionally "loose it" and react in a brief emotional tantrum? They see me as so much more capable than that, and wondered why I didn't change this pattern. I had always defended these occasional "meltdowns" as a sign of my fallibility and it felt good to allow my feelings out. I would not direct the feelings at anyone, but would express intense frustration and powerlessness. I didn't tie these tantrums with Jimmy. Even though it is obvious in hindsight, I never thought of it. I never made the connection.

At times when I am feeling a lot of pressures in my life, and I feel things are out of control for some reason, and I begin to feel very powerless, I am most vulnerable to one of these "tantrums." What I discovered was that at these times ten-year-old Jimmy would feel responsible to fix the problem, and would begin to feel a flood of inadequacy. He would "grab the wheel" and try to handle the current problem. Imagine how much more overwhelming a difficult situation would be to ten-year-old Jimmy compared to Dr. Henman.

As strange as this may sound to you as you read this, check your own times of feeling out of control. Be open to what you notice as you breathe into your intense feelings, with an attitude of openness for what comes. Most of my clients react with surprise when they finally allow themselves to experience the intense feelings respectfully, rather than trying to block the feelings, pushing them away. When they begin taking over the healthy driving of their perceptual bus, they experience living consciously in the present. They can allow themselves to notice **who** has been driving, beginning to nurture and remove the wounded parts from behind the wheel.

Now that I recognize the underlying dynamics in my "melt-downs", I can remind Jimmy that it is not his job to handle current situations. What I realize at a deeper level now is that I can respect my feelings without allowing Jimmy to "loose it" when he feels responsible and inadequate. Since learning this "Nugget", I have begun to connect with Jimmy whenever these feelings start to build.

By allowing myself to feel good about noticing, I can put my energy into comforting Jimmy and reminding myself of who I really am.

This is a great example of how healthy choices can blind us to needed healing inside. It has been wonderful growth to allow myself permission to own and express my feelings more openly over the past 25 years of my recovery. It has allowed growth in the intimacy of all my important relationships. As long as I was looking at the tantrums from this perspective, changing them seemed to work against my recovery. A Black or White filter was blinding me to see only two choices: either I could keep a lid on all my feelings, going back to being a Vulcan, or I could ask those who love me to accept the occasional meltdowns as part of me being a fallible human being. Given these two choices, I chose the latter. The truth is that I have many more choices than that!

It is also the truth that there is another important issue that was being totally overlooked-the supervision of ten-year-old Jimmy. It is never healthy to allow one of your inner kids to drive your perceptual bus without loving supervision. As long as I allowed Jimmy to shoulder the burden of dealing with my most difficult life situations, I was hurting him, and myself. He is a part of me, but I am not little Jimmy. Believing the truth of this allows me to relax into feeling OK about starting where I'm starting at this moment.

These are not just words! In the months since making this connection, it has become much easier for me to deal with stressful situations from my adult perspective and not toss the hot potato to ten-year-old Jimmy to handle. Sonia and I have tackled several home "fixing" projects in the past few weeks. This would be one of the times when Jimmy would be likely to "loose it." I am pleased to share that he hasn't even shown up, let alone felt responsible to do the handyman projects. I am continuing to update my Self-Image Thermostat to make room for these changes.

As a sophomore in high school I took Sophomore Goals, a class to explore different occupations and career paths after high school. I was in the non-college track, getting mostly C's, with a few B's and D's. During the course of the semester I discovered psychology and learned that Ph.D. Psychologists could earn up to $12,000 a year and help people too. I knew I could never get a doctorate but I thought I might be able to get a Masters Degree and earn around $9,000. That would allow a comfortable living and I had always been someone others would turn to for advice and guidance. Just think, getting paid a good salary to do what I had always done for free. I asked the teacher about becoming a psychologist, and I'll never forget what he said, "Get serious! Being a psychologist requires a lot of college, even advanced degrees, and you are barely getting C's in the "Y" track. You need to pick something you can actually achieve."

I went home and told my mom, and she went back to the school with me, demanding that I be raised to the "X" track of classes-college prep. The counselor resisted, but when my mom is determined, there is no stopping her. I was moved up to college prep classes my Junior Year, and my grades began to slowly improve. I graduated high school with a 2.64 grade average. I went to Junior College and my grades continued to improve, graduating from Modesto Junior College with a 3.26 average. I got an "A" in my first psychology class, without being able to spell psychology. By the time I was at San Jose State University, I was getting a 4.00 in my psychology major. I was developing an identity of being a successful student.

In 1978, as I was finishing my Doctoral Dissertation, six-year-old Jimmy grabbed the wheel of my perceptual bus. I was under tremendous pressures in academics and a clinical field placement 20 hours per week, working full time in my fledgling private practice, commuting 200 miles each week to school, and writing the final chapters of my dissertation. I was way out of my comfort zone-almost a doctor! Me, who almost failed elementary school, wasn't supposed to be going on to college, except in some trade; I was going to be a doctor, as soon as I completed writing my Discussion Chapter. Each time I would sit down to start writing this last chapter, I would regress into six-year-old Jimmy and begin to cry. I couldn't write.

A friend from school spent several hours with me, typing for me, as I would pull each sentence out of my soul. I would cry and pull, paragraph after paragraph, until it was finally complete. The closer to the completion, the more anxious and overwhelmed six-year-old Jimmy became. By the time of my orals, I was practically immobilized. The week before my final orals, I finally realized what was happening, and began to make contact with this wounded part of me that was being triggered by the prospect of becoming a doctor. By the time of the actual orals, I was able to reassure little Jimmy that I was going to do the orals, and that he could keep me company if he wanted, but he was not going to be allowed to respond during the exam. He was relieved and I was able to feel more normal stress during my orals exam.

Allow yourself to take a moment right now, put down the book after reading this paragraph. *Feel what it would be like to believe that it is your responsibility to take care of the wounded parts of yourself.* Feel good about noticing any resistance to giving yourself this gift. I believe these words with my whole heart because I believe this is how God wants us all to approach changes in our lives. My confidence is in Him and His Plan, which I apply imperfectly on a daily basis. Share with me your reactions to what you are reading in your journal. Noticing your resistances can help you contact wounded parts of yourself, and can bring into focus perceptual filters that are robbing you of choice.

Remember that when you cannot see your inner kids, the chances are that it is because you have let one of them drive your perceptual bus. Some people can see their wounded inner kids very clearly, while others can only experience a vague sense of these wounded parts. Sonia is able to see vivid pictures of her girls inside, while most of my contacts with Jimmy are more of a feeling experience with only vague images. What is important is the attitudes/feelings you bring to your relationship with your kids inside. It is your job to heal their wounds, it is my job to show you how, and support you as you do your ongoing healing. I hope that these personal glimpses into my inner kids can help you begin looking inside, listening respectfully to the real needs of your own inner kids. My kids inside are feeling overwhelming joy that their stories might help someone.

The Concept of Therapeutic Life Coaching

You can learn to "bring truth to the content" in your life, the situations you want to handle differently. You can bring more accurate perceptions and a deeper understanding of the Fundamental Principles of Healthy Change to difficult situations. This may seem like a strange and confusing notion for you as we are starting our coaching journey together. By the time you have experienced the entire book several times, this statement will make perfect sense. You can learn to freely bring healthy perceptions into difficult areas of your life; imperfectly applying the tools you are learning in New Program, and embracing a No-Fault attitude in the learning process. You can learn to recognize who has been driving your perceptual bus in any problem area.

Therapeutic Life Coaching actively brings the following resources into your change process:

(1) Brings judgmental, defensive, flashlight perspectives into consciousness and turns them into lantern perspectives that look nonjudgmentally from all directions,
(2) Encourages an attitude of curiosity, openness and accuracy,
(3) Provides New Program tools and resources from the Fundamental Principles of Healthy Change,
(4) Brings a desire to learn and grow into the situation, and
(5) Brings absolute faith in your ability to apply New Program in your life today.

I often tell my coaching clients that there is an automatic difference of 40 I.Q. points depending on which chair one sits in while in a coaching session. When sitting in the coach chair you automatically gain an additional 20 I.Q points from where you are starting, as you look at the client's blind spots; sitting in the client chair causes you an automatic 20 I.Q. point loss as you look at your own blind spots. A difference of 40 points is very significant. You can begin to gain these points as you learn to bring truth and accuracy into difficult situations in your life, without judging or defending, feeling good about noticing. **You gain healthy power as you learn to listen to your own inner coach.**

The goal of Therapeutic Life Coaching is to help you experience your life as an adventure of recognizing these Fundamental Principles of Healthy Change in daily life, and taking action on what you notice. The difference between "experiencing believing-in-ac-tion" and "intellectually holding on" to concepts has a direct impact on the possibility of successful change! Holding on to beliefs, whether true or not cannot produce healthy change. Only the process of putting your believing into action produces meaningful change in your life. This is what I call recovery.

Recovery is putting your healthy believing into action, one day at a time, imperfectly. Really reflect on this distinction in your own life. Share with me in your journal what comes up as you make this important distinction. List the areas in your life where there is intellectual knowing of important facts, but you have not been able to put your knowing into action. Also list areas where you know something is untrue and unhealthy, and yet your actions are as if you believed it to be true. Remember to feel good about noticing the things on your list as a beginning of the change process.

My clients usually describe me as very intense, passionate in the belief that change is possible. Don't be surprised that some of that intensity comes across in this book. It is not easy sitting across from me in a coaching session, and it won't be easy to sit across from me as you experience this book. My clients are ready for a nap after a 45-minute coaching session. We often make an audiotape recording of our sessions so the clients can listen back several times to what has been shared in our session.

Clients often come to coaching wanting an A, B, C, set of rules to fix things, what they leave with is an appreciation of a different way of approaching life. Perception has a profound effect on us all. *The truth is that you actually do have the ability to achieve transforming personal changes. The secret is how to approach your abilities in a way that makes them come alive.* When you embrace the "Nuggets" in this book as healthy perception, you can practice believing them consciously as you go through difficult situations. The truth is that there are Fundamental Principles of Healthy Change that can affect the chances of success in your recovery.

Please don't expect yourself to pick up these resources immediately, like a set of rules to follow, with white-knuckled demands of perfection. Let yourself have fun with me as we approach your life differently. You can use this book as a resource that can bring a healthy perspective and New Program tools to whatever situation you may need added help. The more you use it, the more helpful it will become as you build your own personal coach inside. Are you willing to invest in your recovery? Share your reactions to having a coach at your disposal in your journal.

There are two motivational strategies for approaching healthy change in your life that have very different affects on the resulting process. In one motivational approach you are motivated by the desire to avoid negative/painful consequences; in the other strategy you are drawn toward a desired goal. Which one feels most familiar in your life up until now? Fear and pain can motivate a person to abstain from drinking or using drugs; it cannot draw a person into sobriety. Trying to avoid a negative tends to create the dynamic I call "Don't Think Of Purple!" The harder you try to not think about the color purple, the more the color floods your mind.

New Program and Therapeutic Life Coaching focus on learning to motivate yourself by the positive desires to continue becoming and growing. *It is not fear-generated; it is motivated by grateful humility. You are drawn toward a positive goal. This key "Nugget" makes all the difference in your recovery process. Take several deep breaths and look deeply into how you have approached motivating yourself up until now. What do you notice? Share what comes up in your journal, sharing with me how you are feeling about what you are noticing.*

As you begin to experience this reflection on your life, how are you feeling about what you are noticing? Remember that you have feelings about what you are feeling? These *"Second-Order feelings"* are often much more powerful than your original feelings. You may feel angry about feeling hurt, anxious about feeling anger, or afraid of feeling anxious. Most people are not aware of this Second-Order process in their feelings. They tend to lump all their feelings together under a single label. They then assume their "feelings" are the direct result of the situation they are struggling with at the moment. This can easily lead to misunderstandings and confusing reactions within Adult Children. What kind of patterns do you notice as you reflect on your "Second-Order feelings?" Jot these patterns down in your journal, feeling good about noticing more accurately where you are starting.

I was recently working with a bright, capable woman named Sara who wanted help dealing with an intense fear of driving on the freeway because of trucks. She reported it had been a problem for years. Even thinking about being near a truck would produce strong anxiety feelings. She had learned to avoid driving on the freeway most of the time, but recent changes required her to drive on the freeway regularly. She would be nearly sick after a short, 20-mile drive on the freeway.

When I had her imagine being in her car on the freeway right now, seeing the trucks around her, the anxiety went off the charts. She had very good visualization skills and when I had her breathe into the fears and move toward the signal of the anxiety as a way of finding the core of the reaction, she was able to see a scene from seven years ago, when she was traveling with her father, and mother and her young son. Her father was driving recklessly on the freeway and there were trucks everywhere. She knew that her father would not listen to her and would just put her down for being so stupid. She hated herself for being afraid of him, and for letting that fear put her son in danger.

The freeway, the trucks, and the feels of shameful powerless-ness all came together at that moment. She had not consciously thought of that painful experience for years, and had not tied it with her fears of trucks and freeway driving. The freeway/truck association would trigger off these painful feelings, and as the feelings would flood over her, Second-Order feelings would make the anxiety even more unbearable.

Sara learned to comfort the 30-year-old part of herself that was feeling the overwhelming shame and fears, and remind herself that she would never let something like that happen in the future. She was able to learn how to release the tremendous pressures of emotion, that had been frozen in Tupperware, in healthy ways, and forgive herself for not being able to take action at the original time. Remember that Tupperware can hold scenes from any age, childhood or adult.

We walked though her experience of driving on the freeway a frame at a time, noticing what she was saying to herself, and what she was picturing in her mind while driving. It was apparent that Sara was very upset with herself, and was giving herself a hard time for feeling so anxious. These Second-Order feelings were increasing the overall intensity of what she was experiencing. She practiced seeing herself driving on the freeway, following trucks, passing trucks, and having trucks follow her. When she had the scene in focus, she would step into the scene, experiencing it as if it were happening in the present. As she experienced driving next to trucks, she practiced hearing her relaxation tape in her mind while driving.

She practiced talking to herself in a gentle, comforting voice, respecting the truth that trucks can be dangerous, and appreciating that it is natural for her to feel some nervousness. By accepting these feelings and respecting her need to keep as far away from trucks as possible, she began to respond to the anxiety differently, with slow, deep breathing, releasing the tension with each exhalation, and giving herself credit for learning to cope with this difficult situation. She learned to stay in the present. With practice, Sara has become more comfortable driving on the freeway, although she still doesn't like trucks. She only needed a few coaching sessions to gain freedom in this area of her life. She may need an oil-and-lube at some time in the future, time will tell.

Therapeutic Life Coaching helps you appreciate the difference between shame, guilt, and regret in the recovery process. **Shame,** is a destructive, condemning judgment of self. It is a feeling and perception of self-rejection and self-hatred. Shame says: "I am bad and wrong," "I am a mistake," "I am a failure," rather than being a statement about specific actions.

Guilt can be a healthy, useful signal (conviction) when I am going the "wrong direction" in the present. It is a feeling signal to an action, rather than a statement about self. We need to feel good about noticing guilt in the present, turn toward a healthy direction, and release the feelings of guilt. God only wants us to feel guilty as a motivation for change; guilt is not a goal in itself. Guilt about past events or actions, no longer present, tends to transform into shame over time.

Regret is a healthy grieving reaction. It can be experienced as a variety of different feelings that come with the accurate acceptance of past events. Regret says: "I feel bad that this happened and wish things had been different." "What can I learn from this to help me move forward in my recovery in the present."

Change comes about when you accept that you are "starting where you are starting in the present," and begin parenting these wounded parts of yourself differently. As you experience the material in this book, you will learn a different way to approach the change process. You need to learn which perceptual frames you are working with at any given moment. It is for this reason that what appears to be an overreaction for you as an adult, may be developmentally normal for your "little child" within. This is not an excuse, but rather an accurate description of what is actually happening inside.

The key is introducing loving supervision for your child within. Therapeutic Life Coaching is the process of learning to apply "the Fundamental Principles of Healthy Change" in your daily life, gaining the ability to become your own Therapeutic Coach in your personal recovery.

The Twelve-Step Concept Of Healing

In 1990 I took a big step toward writing this present book. I began working with a steering committee of people with a wide range of different problem backgrounds to develop a free support group, whose focus was creating a safe place to share and practice building healthy self-esteem. Out of that sharing process came Changing Attitudes In Recovery-A Handbook On Esteem (Henman, 1990).

Working with the CAIR Steering Committee, the CAIR Handbook became the foundation for CAIR Self-Help Groups that met for the first time in 1990 and have been going strong to this day. The CAIR Handbook gave a format and structure for a group process, and provided helpful tools and concepts about building healthy esteem.

These free support groups were formed in the Twelve-Step tradition of people helping people, but the organizing principle for the meetings was different. Whereas the traditional Twelve-Step meetings are organized around a common problem, the common bond that draws members together in these free CAIR Groups is a shared commitment to growth and development of healthy esteem.

We have created two paths to help you with your adventure/journey into a recovery process of building healthy self-esteem: CAIR Self-Help Groups share the Twelve-Step tradition of a loving Higher Power, while the CAIRing Grace Groups share a Christ-centered perspective. Both are free and open to anyone desiring healthy changes in their lives. There is free material on developing these groups on our Web site www.CAIRforYou.com. It only takes two to have a group. Alan, who has facilitated many CAIR and CAIRing Grace Groups since their beginning, has shared that even at times when he was the only one to show up for a meeting, he would go ahead and spend time with himself and God. Sharing with yourself and me in your journal is a start.

In the traditional view of Twelve-Step recovery, **Step One** states "We admitted we were powerless over alcohol-that our lives had become unmanageable." Since these words were first written in 1939, the "First Step" has been applied to many different problem areas. CAIR welcomes you, regardless of what motivates your desire for change. The foundation of CAIR is Steps Two and Three in the Twelve-Step tradition: **Step Two** states "We come to believe that a Power greater than ourselves could restore us to sanity," and **Step Three** states "We have made a decision to turn our will and our lives over to the care of God, as we understand Him."

Are there areas of your life that feel unmanageable, where you feel powerless to choose differently? Are there patterns in your life that keep you from being all you want to be? Are there past memories that torture you, creating depression or anxiety? Give yourself the gift of noticing, without judging. Share your reactions with me in your journal.

The Concept Of Spirituality

Dear Lord,
Allow me to see myself and others
Through Your loving eyes,
And to respond to what I see
Through Your Nature.

Many of us assume that good things should happen to good people and bad things should happen to bad people, and that life should be fair. What is your reaction when things aren't fair and just? Do you blame God and demand to know why He let it happen, or do you share your sadness with Him, as He also feels your pain deeply? These different perceptions dramatically change your experience of spirituality.

The concept of spirituality applies to the personal experience of relationships-within yourself, between yourself and others, and with your Higher Power. Is spirituality a familiar issue for you to reflect on? Have you always lumped spirituality and religion together, and put it all under "going to church?" Spirituality is one of those "Powerful Words" filters (Power Of Mind Distortions) that require respectful, nonjudgmental reflection, noticing the Second-Order Feelings generated by subliminal reactions. The truth is that trauma often brings your spirituality closer to the surface, making more conscious choices possible.

The specific name we give our Higher Power has to do with the question of salvation and religion, while the personal qualities we see in our Higher Power have a direct impact on our recovery. ***We have found that as human beings, we do have a basic need to feel a sense of meaning and purpose in our lives. This need to feel a relationship (within ourselves, between ourselves and others, and with a force greater than self) is what we call spirituality.***

The CAIR Handbook describes the kind of relationship with your Higher Power that is helpful in your recovery: "We can practice the experience of relating to our personified Higher Power. We can feel what it is like to look into the eyes of our Higher Power and see the unconditional love that is felt for us. We can begin to feel the absolute faith and confidence our Higher Power has in our ability to grow, and move forward on our journey into recovery. We can safely be open to the honest, accurate feedback our Higher Power gives us as an expression of caring respect. We can feel a powerfully supportive arm around us as we walk through difficult times, remembering that we never again have to go through it alone. (Stop and discuss)"

It is important for you to have your own personal relationship with whatever Higher Power you choose. What is key is that your Higher Power reflects this affirming, nurturing faith in your healthy becoming. How does your Higher Power fit with this description? What I tell my clients is that if their Higher Power does not help their recovery, fire Him/Her and hire another one! Jot down your reactions to this issue of spirituality in your journal. What do you notice as you reflect on the difference between religion and spirituality for you personally? Describe your personal sense of spirituality as you begin your recovery journey. What is it like to look through the eyes of your Higher Power? Share your reactions with me in your journal.

There are four key qualities necessary in your relationship with your own personal Higher Power to make healthy growth the path of least resistance. How you experience your personal Higher Power is often at a subliminal level of consciousness. I am speaking of a relational experience, not an intellectual construct. *I am referring to spirituality in your recovery, not religious questions about your salvation!*

These four Higher Power qualities capture the core elements of the Fundamental Principles of Healthy Change:

(1) Giving unearned grace and love,
(2) Giving unchanging consistency about Truth,
(3) Giving honest, accurate feedback nonjudgmentally,
(4) Having absolute faith in your ability to continue moving forward in your recovery.

Notice your reactions to these key elements of spirituality in your recovery. Share with me in your journal the different feelings you have as you explore these qualities in your own personal relationship with your Higher Power. Take the time to reflect deeply into this issue.

The Concept Of Self-Esteem

The definition of self-esteem used in my coaching and in all of the CAIR material, has been adopted from the California Task Force to Promote Self-esteem and Personal and Social Responsibility: "Appreciating my own worth and importance and having the character to be accountable for myself and to act responsibly toward others" (Toward A State Of Esteem, 1990, p. 1).

We formed the core elements of the Task Force definition of esteem into the eight Fundamental Principles of Healthy Change used in this book.

These Fundamental Principles are the foundation of a "New Program" designed to help you develop healthy self-esteem. The process of healing wounded self-esteem is termed recovery. What is your reaction to this definition of self-esteem? How healthy is your self-esteem when examined from the Task Force's perspective?

The Task Force definition of self-esteem has four components that you need to consider as we begin your coaching process. I believe that each component adds healthy strength to your core esteem:

1. ***Appreciating your worth and importance*** involves accepting yourself where you are starting today, setting realistic expectations for yourself, forgiving yourself for your fallibility-past and present, taking risks, trusting, and expressing your feelings respectfully to those who are important to you. It also includes appreciating your creativity, your mind, your body, and your growth as a spiritual being.
2. ***Appreciating the worth and importance of others*** involves affirming each person's unique worth. It includes demonstrating respect, acceptance, and support toward others in an open, honest way, being sensitive as others express their feelings to you. This component includes setting realistic expectations of others, forgiving others for their fallibility-past and present, and appreciating the benefits of a multicultural society.
3. ***Affirming accountability for yourself*** involves taking responsibility for your decisions, choices and actions, being a person of integrity and honor. It includes understanding and affirming your values, attending to your physical health, and taking responsibility for yourself in the important personal relationships in your life.
4. ***Affirming your responsibility toward others*** involves respecting the dignity and value of being human. It includes you encouraging independence and growth in others, creating a sense of belonging, fostering a democratic environment, recognizing the balance between freedom and responsibility, balancing cooperation and competition, and serving humanity.

The Task Force concluded that self-esteem could be a "social vaccine" that allows you to live a more healthy, meaningful life. Self-esteem helps you deal more constructively with emotional, addictive, and relational problems. Reflect on the four components of self-esteem. Do you have difficulty in one or more component areas of healthy esteem. Are you currently experiencing problems related to low self-esteem?

Depression, anxiety, and panic are common symptoms for people suffering from low self-esteem. ***They experience the gamut of addictive problems including chemical dependency, eating disorders, co-dependency, and sexual addictions. Their emotional/ spiritual turmoil and the*** *resulting internal stress are associated with physical symptoms such as headaches, gastrointestinal problems, and sleep difficulties. Intimacy and the capacity for healthy relationships are elusive for those with low self-esteem. Are any of these toxic patterns familiar in your life today? Do you have a past history of struggling with any of these symptoms of low esteem? We will be addressing your changes at this core level of self-esteem.*

As a relational Christian, I believe my esteem is based on my true identity in Christ, as a new creation. "Such confidence as this is ours through Christ before God. Not that we are competent in ourselves to claim anything for ourselves, but our competence comes from God. He has made us competent as ministers of a new covenant-not of the letter but of the Spirit; for the letter kills, but the Spirit gives life." (2 Corinthians 3:4-6)

My esteem comes from seeing myself through His eyes. My identity draws its core value from Him. "May the God of hope fill you with all joy and peace as you trust in him, so that you may overflow with hope by the power of the Holy Spirit." (Romans 15:13)

Jesus described His feelings about me in John 15:15: "I no longer call you servants, because the servant does not know his master's business. Instead, I have called you friends, for everything that I learned from my Father I have made known to you." **What greater esteem could I have than to be called friend by my Big Brother Jesus?**

As Paul counseled Timothy, "This being so, I want to remind you to stir into flame the strength and boldness that is in you, that entered into you when I laid my hand upon your head and blessed you. For God hath not given us the spirit of fear; but of power, and of love, and of a sound mind." (2 Timothy 1:7). **What impact does your relationship with your personal Higher Power have on your self-esteem? Reflect deeply on what determines your sense of esteem and share these reflections with me in** your journal.

I will help you learn how to make changes in your life, and will supply helpful tools to aid in your change process. I will help you apply the Fundamental Principles of Healthy Change in your life through an esteeming New Program-a nurturing map for your recovery. If you are willing to invest the thought and energy into your growth, and are willing to be clumsy and awkward in the process, you can make whatever changes you want to make in your life today. You can learn to have abundance in your life by living each day as if it might be your last, and living each day as if you were going to live for a very long time.

This book is to be experienced, not just read. Journaling your reactions with me, as you go through the book, is like sharing with me in a coaching session. Begin to dialogue with me in your journal, as you relax into believing the truth at an experiential level, rather than just holding on to the truth at an intellectual level. Write about what you notice on your adventure of becoming. You do not have to take the journey alone—I am proud to be your coach!

DRIVER'S TRAINING-LEARNING TO READ THE SIGNS

The 25 *Power Of Mind Distortions* summarized in Chapter Two, interact with other perceptual filters to create your *Selective Movies.* One of the most important skills I work on with clients early in coaching is to help improve their ability to recognize their perceptual filters, feel good about noticing and replace the faulty filters with more accurate perceptions. I help them experience bringing openness and curiosity into difficult situations. They learn to respond through these healthy filters, with lots of practice, practice, and more practice. The *ABC's Of Observation* was developed for the CAIR Handbook in 1988. It allows you to organize a complex amount of information into an approachable form, starting where you are starting in the present.

An important aspect of God's plan for healthy change is our freedom to "feel good about noticing" things we don't like, as the first step in the process of changing what we see. I believe the "Knowledge Of Good And Evil," without God's loving reflection, results in feelings of shame when you begin to see accurately. The overwhelming feelings of shame trigger a normal reaction of judging and defending. God's Plan neutralizes this toxic dynamic through His lantern of Grace so that we can feel good about noticing, and begin relaxing into a healthy direction as His Spirit draws us into health.

When you begin to see past scenes more accurately, you can learn to parent the wounded parts of yourself that are stuck in the painful scenes, bringing healing in the present. When you begin to see present situations more accurately, you can relax into the Prayer of Serenity-giving yourself the freedom to approach the present situation with the serenity to change what you can change, to release what you can't change, and continue growing in the wisdom to know the difference. What is most important in both past and present situations is to approach it with an attitude of nonjudgmental, openness, and accuracy. You can't do more than that! When you try, you will actually make change more difficult.

ABC's Of Observation

"A" reflects the Activating Trigger, which includes the time and date that the situation happened, person or people involved in the situation and where the situation took place. Is it happening in the present, or is the trigger coming from your Time Machine? Briefly describe the situation that triggered your unwanted feelings and behaviors.

"B" reflects your Belief Filters that are active during the situation. Write down briefly the assumptions that must be true for your feeling/behavior consequences to make sense. Look deeply into your underlying presuppositions that are filtering your experience of the situation. Next write down the Power Of Mind Distortions that are active in your assumptions.

"C" reflects the Consequences, the feelings and behaviors, that are resulting from your current Belief Filter. Allow yourself to feel good about noticing your ABC's as accurately as possible in the present, without judging. Let yourself have some fun bringing your tools to this situation as you begin to challenge faulty perceptions and replace the toxic perceptual filters with healthy truths about life and the process of change. Remember that you can approach this process as an adventure or as a test. The choice Fred reported the following situation in a coaching session. "I had a horrible fight with my wife, Mary, the other morning; I got so angry that I began yelling at her, and walked out of the room when my feelings felt like they were going to explode into a million pieces." When I asked him what the fight was

about, he reported: "She was feeling hurt that I needed to work late for a few evenings to catch up on needed work. She got upset and said I didn't care about her or want to spend time with her. She should know me better than that." As Fred was describing what had happened, the original feelings would keep flooding over him as he went into his Time Machine. I asked Fred to fill out an ABC's Of Observation sheet to organize his experience more clearly and accurately.

A B C's of Observation

A	B	C
ACTIVATING TRIGGER	BELIEF FILTERS	CONSEQUENCES
TIME:	ASSUMPTIONS:	FEELINGS:
DATE:		
PERSON:		
PLACE:		INTERNAL PHYSICAL:
SITUATION:		
POWER OF MIND (P.O.Wl) DISTORTIONS: BEHAVIORS: (EXTERNAL)		

We went through the situation, looking for Power Of Mind Distortions and noticing the assumptions that grow out of these distortions. Whenever Fred would start to get back into his Time Machine and feel the original feelings again, I would remind him that we are looking at a past situation. It is not happening in the present. I would remind him to feel good about noticing the faultyperceptual filters and faulty assumptions, and to put his energy into learning and growing in the present. When he would start to judge I would remind him that judging prevents changing, and he was going to have to choose whether he would rather spend his time judging (and feeling the results of judging), or spend time growing and changing? I would remind him that change can only take place in the present, and that he can't change other people directly. He can learn to gain healthy influence as he learns to apply New Program in his life. The following is Fred's ABC's

A B C's of Observation

A ACTIVATING TRIGGER	B BELIEF FILTERS	C CONSEQUENCES
TIME: 10:00 AM DATE: 1/20/91 PERSON: Wife PLACE: Family room SITUATION: Fight with Mary about me needing to work late.	ASSUMPTIONS: 1. If she really knew me she would know I love her and would rather be home with her tonight 2. She never thinks about my feelings 3. I must be a lousy husband & father 4. I should be able to make Mary happy all the time	FEELINGS: Angry, guilty, resentful, pressure, scared and sad INTERNAL PHYSICAL: tight stomach and headache
	POWER OF MIND (P.O.M.) DISTORTIONS: Mind Reading Faulty Generalizations Black & White Thinking Powerful Words Who Defines My Reality	BEHAVIORS: (EXTERNAL) Yelling, defending her 'attacks', walking out of the room, hiding my feelings

Make copies of the blank ***ABC's Of Observation*** form so you can fill them out to help organize and bring into focus the filters that are robbing you of your healthy power of choice. You can use the ABC's for any situation, whether from an internal source, or from dealing with others. When dealing with an internal experience, write out the situation in your mind, noticing filters and consequences coming from your internal experience.

Once you are aware of your assumptions and Power Of Mind Distortions, you can begin to challenge and replace the toxic filters with truths (imperfectly), and experience believing the truths about the situation. This skill comes gradually for most clients, and requires a lot of thought and practice. The more you use the ABC's, the more natural it will feel to recognize and replace toxic filters. You need to be living consciously, living manually to begin practicing these new perceptions. ***They will not feel natural at first!***

Additional Observation Tools
Constructive Problem Solving

This eight-step approach to interpersonal conflict allows you to practice using New Program tools in difficult relationship situations. Pick a situation you are currently facing. Really focus on it and begin using a lantern of nonjudgmental curiosity to illuminate 360 degrees in all directions, shining on everyone involved in the situation. If you notice your lantern turning into a flashlight, shining a judgmental light in only one direction, feel good about noticing this and switch back to the lantern. The flashlight can shine on you or the other person, but not both at the same time. The light of noticing is different than the light of judging, causing two different emotional reactions. If you notice your Time Machine becoming active, take the time to get solidly grounded in the present before proceeding with the exercise.

1. Clarify the situation and begin to focus on the issues as you see them. Use your lantern to see if others have the same issues or if they have different issues. What is your goal in this situation? What specifically do you want to accomplish in this exchange? Does this situation feel familiar? Is it a repetitive pattern?
2. How do you want to be in this situation? What proactive attitudes and behaviors can help you be the way you want to be in this situation? What resources do you want to bring with you into this situation? Is it more important for you to learn and grow, or is it more important for you to be right?
3. What would your Old Program (automatic pilot) look like in this situation? How would you normally approach this situation? As you play out your Old Program way of handling this situation in your mind, do you like the results that predictably come from this approach? What assumptions are you bringing into this situation?
4. What Power Of Mind Distortions and truths regarding the Fundamental Principles of Healthy Change are involved in your perceptions? What is it like for you to experience believing the truths you bring consciously to this current situation? Challenging,

replacing, and experiencing believing more accurate perceptions is a skill that improves with practice.

5. What have you taught the others in this situation to expect from you up until now? What impact will past history have on this current situation? What expectations are likely to be present in this situation, both your own and others?

6. What can you say to give a clear message to the others involved in this situation regarding what you want and how you feel in this situation? Do you appreciate what the others want and how they feel in this situation? What is it like for you to actively bring mutual respect and valuing into this situation? It is an active bringing rather than a passive finding.

7. Have you let the others involved in this situation know that you have heard their positions? Have you been open to explore their perspective as well as share your own?

8. Have you embraced the fundamental principles of New Program throughout this situation? This is an imperfect process and becomes more natural with practice, practice, and more practice. Have you been as nonjudgmental, open, and accurate as possible in this situation? Do you accept that you are all fallible human beings reacting through perceptual filters? Are you accepting that you are starting where you are starting at this moment? Have you experienced an attitude of mutual respect and valuing in this situation?

Does this situation activate your inner kids in any way? Do you notice one or more of them affecting your perceptions in this situation? Have you shared this situation with your Higher Power, gaining His/Her guidance and perspective on the situation? Can you experience this situation as another opportunity to practice applying the wisdom and tools of New Program in your life?

What was it like for you to apply these eight steps/questions that help you develop and build healthy power in your interpersonal areas of conflict? Are some of the steps easier than others? Do any of the steps seem too difficult for where you are starting right now? If so, what resources can we bring to make the step more possible for you? What seems to be most difficult about taking this particular step right now? What assumptions are you making about taking this step? Share with me in your journal the process of going through these problem-solving steps.

Movie Check

The Movie Check is an observation tool that helps you develop more ability to gain healthy perspective in your interpersonal relationships. Start by noticing what you see when you look through the camera lens from your own perspective. Notice what assumptions you are making, what the key issues and players in this scene are from your camera angle. Now allow yourself to shift to a different camera angle, looking through the eyes of the others in this situation. Notice what assumptions the others are making and what the key issues and players are from these other camera angles. When you remember that we all have **Selective Movies,** it is much easier to have curiosity and a desire for clarification as the scene unfolds. Finally, allow yourself to look through your camera using the eyes of your Higher Power, seeing from that perspective what seems most significant and important.

Role Reversal Check

The Role Reversal Check is an observation tool that helps you spot double standards in your relationships. Double standards are toxic situations where the two sides are unevenly balanced. An example would be having the right to spend as much money as you want, without asking or consulting your partner, but getting very angry if your partner spends any money without getting your permission. When you let yourself experience the other person's position, seeing through their eyes how you are coming across, and what seems fair, you can begin to spot and change your double standards.

Five-Step Deep Sharing Exercise

When you find yourself in a repetitive pattern of "getting nowhere" in communicating about something with someone you care about, you can use this exercise to help break out of the destructive circles:

1. Allow the other person to go first-have them express the core of their position on the issue that has produced the ongoing circles, without interruption, for up to two minutes. *If it goes any longer than two minutes it will take the power out of the exercise.* Your job is to listen deeply to both the content they are sharing with you and the underlying feelings in their message. Release any urges to disagree or correct the other's message, accepting that this is their perception up until now. *It is important not to interrupt during their sharing time (interruption will take the power out of the exercise).* Allow yourself to experience their movie as fully and deeply as possible. This does not mean that you agree with their perceptions, only that you care enough to experience it openly.
2. When the other person has shared the core of their position on the problem area, it is now your job to accurately reflect back to them their sharing. You are to feed back both the key areas of content and the underlying feelings from their movie. You are not to add or interpret their message, only letting them know you have received it accurately without judging it. When you have succeeded it reflecting back to them all the key elements of their sharing, they are to acknowledge that you have received their perceptions accurately. If you have missed or distorted some element of their sharing, they are to repeat that element again, and you are to reflect back until all the key elements have been received and reflected. *They are the final authority on when you have successfully fed back their movie accurately.* There can be no debate on this issue! Any debate will take the power out of the exercise.
3. When you have successfully reflected back all of their perceptions about the original problem area, you can take up to two minutes to share your feelings and reactions to their shared perceptions. It is now their job to reflect back your sharing until they have

reflected back all the key elements in your shared reactions, both the content and the underlying feelings you were sharing. They are not to add or interpret your sharing, only letting you know that they have received it accurately without judging your movie. ***You are the final authority on when they have successfully fed back your shared reactions to what they originally shared.*** There can be no debate during this step. Any debate will take the power out of the exercise.

4. When the other person has successfully reflected all the key elements of your shared reactions to their original sharing, then reverse positions. It is now your turn to share the core of your position on the original issue with them for up to two minutes. They are to listen deeply to both the content you are sharing with them and the underlying feelings in your message. They are to release any urges to disagree or correct your messages, accepting that this is your movie up until now. It is important that they not interrupt during your sharing time. They are to allow themselves to experience your sharing as fully and deeply as possible. This does not mean that they agree with your movie, only that they care enough to experience it openly. When you have finished sharing your core position for up to two minutes, they are to repeat *Steps 2* and *3.*

5. The first four steps can be repeated as many times as necessary to explore all the core issues in the problem area. When you both agree that you both have given and received as clear and accurate a representation of your core positions as possible, and have given your reactions to each other's sharing, you are almost done with the exercise. The final step is for both of you to experience updating your old perceptions to reflect what you have learned during the exercise. This is a very important step. ***Over the years I have found that unless you consciously update your old perceptions to reflect new learning, it will not happen automatically.*** Share with each other how you are feeling as the exercise comes to an end. Feel what it is like to see both yourself and the other person more accurately with a lantern of grace. Notice any resistance to updating your perceptions of this issue to reflect what was learned during the Deep Sharing Exercise.

5

INSIDE A DRIVERS TRAINING SESSION

This chapter will allow you to sit in on two different Therapeutic Life Coaching sessions from the past, to get a feeling of the process. I will call the first client Emma. She describes herself briefly before her transcript. I will call the second client Bill, who describes himself before his transcript. While I've respected their anonymity, both Bill and Emma wanted to share these insights into the healing process because they are both committed to recovery and health. These examples are very typical of Therapeutic Life Coaching sessions.

Notice that the focus of the session is truth/accuracy experienced at a deep level, in a spirit of "No-Fault" learning. Identity is a key issue in both sessions. Shame is a powerful force in both of them, as are inflaming defensiveness and self-rejection, creating circles that exhaust, leading to feelings of hopelessness. Notice what you identify with in these examples. Notice any familiar patterns as you read the transcripts out loud so you can experience them more fully.

Introduction from Emma

Fifty years later it is hard to determine what is real and what is a figment of the imagination of a four-year-old little girl. What I do know is that I was left at my grandmother's house and my mother never came back to get me. I have always felt like the child with her face pressed against the window looking into the lives of others. Always wanting a mother who went on to have six more children. Never understanding why she didn't want me.

I was raised by my grandparents and I believe with all my heart that they loved me, but I don't remember my grandmother ever holding me. What I do remember is her constant referral to me as "a poor little orphan," along with her referring to what she gave up to raise me. It was never done maliciously to make me feel bad. It was all about making herself feel better.

I know now through what I've learned in CAIR that she did the best she could with the tools she had to work with, it just wasn't enough.

I went throughout my adolescent years wanting her so much that at night as I would lie in bed, I would smell my armpits because the musty smell reminded me of my mother. At the birth of my daughter I remember the first thing that went through my mind was "how could any mother give up her child?" I went through a love-hate period after that where I wouldn't drive two miles across town to see my mother if she was in town visiting my grandmother.

When my mother died at age 65, I don't know what happened to me. I literally could not say the word "mother" and I couldn't stop crying. That was when I first met Jim, eight years ago. I remember telling Jim it was like my eyes were leaking. I knew if I didn't get help I was going into a deep dark hole and never coming out again. The first time I ever met my inner little girl was in Jim's office. It was so clear, even the way I was slouching in the chair was that of a four-year-old. Four-year-old Emma Ann was scared to death, and I didn't have the tools to take care of her.

I became active in the CAIR Groups and would see Jim when I was ready to take another step in my healing. Years would pass between sessions and I would stop going to CAIR Groups because I had "more important things to do with my time than keep going to group when I know all the tools anyway, and I'm feeling good." Sometimes I could coast for years before beginning to crash back into depression and self-hate. By the time I would begin to notice the growing problem, I would feel too ashamed to go back to the CAIR Group (I had been doing so well when I was last there) and would wait to call Jim until I was in the middle of crashing.

This pattern happened over and over, each time I would get a little healthier, before slipping back into autopilot, ignoring Emma Ann, and slowly I would regress back into being four-year-old Emma Ann again.

There would usually be some crisis or other that triggered the free-fall. I was always a little surprised and thankful at the loving reaction of the CAIR Group members and Jim when I would finally reach out.

Emma's Therapeutic Life Coaching Session
(Read out loud-Experiencing the dialogue)

Jim: It's been a long time. Give me a thumbnail sketch of where you are starting right now, so we will have a context, and we can work from there. How does that sound?

Emma: I don't even know where to start because there are about five things. I'll start with the other day when I called you and said, "I need you!" What had happened the night before was that three of my friends were in town and they wanted to get together with me. They had started calling several days prior to their arrival, and I never even returned their calls. Twenty years ago the four of us went on a trip to Mexico. It was the greatest trip I have ever been on. We started laughing from the time we left going to the airport till we came home. We talked about doing it again, but knew we could never repeat a trip like that. I hadn't seen one of them for 15 or so years, and the other one for about 10.

The night of the get-together, even though they had not heard from me, they started calling and the later it got the more determined they were for me to come over. About 10:30 P.M. they called and said they were coming over to get me. Of course they were leaving these messages on the recorder, as I was not answering the phone. At about 11:00 P.M. the doorbell started ringing and it was them, laughing and giggling, telling me to come out. I pretended that I wasn't home.

The next day, when I realized what I had done and the reason why I did it, the fact that I didn't want them to see me because I am so fat, it just broke my heart. To do that to people I love…I couldn't believe I did it.

Jim: Good, because that is a healthy response. Feeling that kind of honest, heartbreaking regret is healthy, regret that can lead to action. Feel the difference between these healthy feelings and the shame you feel so often.

Emma: (Taking a slow, deep breath) Yeah, they do feel different.

Jim: Remember that Second-Order feelings can stack shame on shame on shame, so the feelings grow to tremendous intensity. **Shame prevents change! You need to choose what you want; you can't have both self-hate and change!** Take several slow, deep breaths and experience choosing to respect your regret at this moment, releasing the shame with each breath.

Emma: Well, I am ashamed of myself for sure!

Jim: Ashamed of yourself for.?

Emma: I am ashamed of myself for getting so fat that I would do something like that to people I love.

Jim: Your weight had nothing to do with what you did, in truth. Now, it is true that being incredibly judgmental and arrogant about your weight did cost you that whole wonderful time with your friends.

Emma: What do you mean? I couldn't help feeling what I was feeling.

Jim: You need to realize and acknowledge your decision that your weight is who you are, and therefore you are ashamed of yourself as you are, and therefore you do not want these people you care about to see you.

Emma: Yeah.

Jim: You really need to begin looking at the assumptions that must be true for your reaction to make sense to you. **Remember that reactions always make sense, finding the right camera angle to see it is the trick.**

Emma: I've been so busy crashing on the rocks I haven't really been looking at my filters. I guess I need to dig out the CAIR Handbook and dust it off again. I haven't thought about the Tool Box either.

Jim: Sounds to me like you have a Black or White filter working overtime-fearing that if they saw you at your current weight, they would either reject you outright or pity you by pretending they are willing to take time to be with you.

Emma: It's more about how I feel about me! I know they wouldn't pity me or reject me!

Jim: ***I am not talking about reality.*** It's all about what you truly believe in your heart that drives these perceptions. What you know intellectually doesn't change the deep believing in your heart. ***You keep it nice and tidy by saying "its just how I feel about myself." Do you see where I am coming from?***

Emma: I know these friends of mine could care less about what I look like, when I'm honest.

Jim: You know that, but the part of you driving your emotional bus at that time didn't know that, and still doesn't!

Emma: I hate the way I look, and I don't want them to see me like this.

Jim: I see…so instead of caring enough to take proactive steps…

Emma: (interrupts) I don't care enough! I just don't care!

Jim: Well, isn't that a problem?

Emma: Yes, that is why I am here. I'm disgusting!!!

Jim: No, the problem is you think…believe that your weight is disgusting and you believe that you are your weight, whereas in truth that attitude is disgusting if anything is disgusting. In truth this attitude is sad and painful, and this is the place you have not been willing to go over our years together.

Emma: It's hard to get past the attitude when you are married to someone who doesn't touch you because you are fat, and tells you your weight repels him.

Jim: No question. But that is like saying as a painter you are going to decide the value, the quality of your painting based on my opinion, and I am color blind and have absolutely zero appreciation of perspective, contrast, or anything else artistic.

Emma: I can understand that!

Jim: But you aren't letting yourself believe it as it relates to you personally, intellectual knowing plus a dollar can get you a cup of coffee, believing needs to be experienced at the core level of your being.

Emma: I understand your metaphors.

Jim: But you don't believe it.

Emma: I believe that I should not look through my husband's eyes based on his vanity and his hang-ups. I weigh 250 pounds; that is reality!

Jim: I am not questioning the weight. These friends of yours, are they all thin?

Emma: Yes.

Jim: And among all the people that are dear to you, are they all thin?

Emma: **No.**

Jim: Do you see any as "grossly, disgustingly overweight" as you see yourself?

Emma: No, not really.

Jim: So you have them in a special category?

Emma: Yes, they are the ones I like to be seen with so I look thinner. I'm really kind of teasing about that.

Jim: I know. But the point is you do have the capacity, because you are very bright, to see things on many different levels of motivation, and you do have the capacity to turn around and judge the heck out of yourself for any of those levels of motivation that you don't like seeing.

Emma: Well, I guess so; I guess I do that a lot (deep sigh).

Jim: That's my point! So, then what you are saying is that there are people you care about whose weight is comparable to yours?

Emma: I am beginning to think not. I believe I have gone over the edge.

Jim: Okay, lets say that that is true. In point of fact I have seen quite a few people…

Emma: Yeah, me too, on Jerry Springer!

Jim: There are in truth many women that are 250-350 pounds or more, that I have seen right here in this office. They do exist and they have value!

Emma: But.

Jim: Look what you are doing right now. I am being truthful, notice what you are experiencing inside as you consider the truth. Feel your resistance to believing the truth about your double standard, and feel good about noticing your resistance.

Emma: I know you are being honest with me. I guess I just don't care about them.

Jim: I understand. Do you care about you or do you care about your weight? The truth, as you know intellectually, is that they are two very different things.

Emma: You know I care about my weight.

Jim: Right, and therefore…

Emma: I do nothing!

Jim: No, you do a lot! You are very active in hating yourself, and shaming yourself, and demanding of yourself proof that you are going to drop to a weight that makes you acceptable before you begin accepting and nurturing yourself.

Emma: I can't help feeling that way.

Jim: If I recall from the Tool Box this would be called a "Conditional Acceptance" filter. This pattern prevents healthy change, no matter who uses it. It didn't work for me when I used it in my Old Program, and it can't work for you either.

Emma: Yeah, I can see that.

Jim: I'm also hearing "Powerful Words," "That's Just How I Am," "Shame, Guilt and Regret," "Feeling Are Facts," and many others.

Emma: Is there any filter I'm not violating?

Jim: Honestly, there are a lot of them. The Camera Check and Role Reversal Check can help change the double standards. Get back to the Tool Box to freshen up your access to your tools. It's really important right now. Recognize the filters as you listen back to the tape.

Emma: I'm going to have to listen back tonight; it is a relief to be here with my coach.

Jim: ***I'm proud that you felt safe after all this time to call when you needed honest feedback and guidance.*** The problem is that your self-hate and shame are generating an equal and opposite resistance to everything you try to do, that leaves you stuck in a black hole, obsessed about your weight, which in turn causes you, if anything, to gain weight.

Emma: You know that I actually followed that! No wonder I keep feeling like I'm going in circles, I am! (Both laugh)

Jim: When a person tries to DIET invariably that person will have a net gain of weight from the starting point of the diet. It may drop briefly, but ultimately it will end up with a net gain. It is because the healthy part of you resists as long as you insist upon changing before accepting yourself. Take a deep breath and feel the healthy resistance.

Emma: That is strange and confusing.

Jim: Accepting where you are starting is the beginning of change for you. As long as your weight is more important than you, you are not going to reach your goal of being a healthy weight. That is a fact. That is the truth.

Emma: I have never been important to myself (pain and sadness in her voice).

Jim: Well, now would be a wonderful time to start, wouldn't it? So you could show your granddaughter what it is like to be with someone who is learning to value herself because that is what you want for Heidi.

Emma: I am at my best when I am with Heidi.

Jim: I believe you, and that is the problem.

Emma: Why is that?

Jim: Just imagine here you are with these wounded little girls inside who are starving for acceptance, approval, and that they have their noses pressed against the window watching from outside while this wonderful filet mignon dinner of love and grace and affirmation of blessing is being poured out towards Heidi, while they are digging rancid tube-steak out of the garbage can. Take a deep breath and notice what it must be like for Emma Ann, not good enough to partake of the blessing. It would keep her wounds fresh.

Emma: I understand, but don't totally agree with you. I try to do things with Heidi that I think my inner children would like to do. We have fun. I like to think I am taking care of myself.

Jim: So you, as an adult, are having some time to enjoy some child's play with Heidi? Enjoying her having the experiences you didn't have growing up?

Emma: I believe that to be true. Not all the time, of course.

Jim: Of course! Sometimes you have to be an adult setting the limits, etc.

Emma: I believe my job here is to teach Heidi how to be a responsible adult. I want her to be capable of taking care of herself when we are gone.

Jim: I understand, and therefore when you hate yourself for your weight, is that what you want Heidi to feel about her body? Do you want her to be burdened with hating herself for not being good enough in some area?

Emma: I don't discuss it with her. I suppose it comes out in ways. (Heavy sigh)

Jim: Do you remember the story in the CAIR Handbook "Seen Through The Eyes Of Jean?" Jean was very much the way you are describing yourself being with Heidi. Jean was very loving to her kids. She was able to give amazing grace, affirming blessing to her kids. She couldn't give it to herself. So one of her kids, who was very bright and perceptive realized that the real point is to give selflessly of yourself, while withholding good things from yourself. He became Dr. Henman.

Emma: Jean is your Mom?

Jim: Yes, and she is still active in a CAIR Group at her church. It was so cool to share this with her. Once I was able to appreciate that part of my Old Program, I was able to tap into that grace, that unconditional love she had given me so freely, as part of the fuel for my journey into recovery. I am consciously choosing to approach myself with the same love and grace that I share with others. No more double standards!

Emma: I can't just choose to feel differently about my weight. I agree I have a double standard, but so what!

Jim: The truth is that you can begin to challenge any double standard, including this one, and do the work necessary to make healthy shifts. You can choose to begin applying the Prayer of Serenity in all areas of your life:

"God grant me the serenity to change what I can change, release what I can't change, and continue growing in the wisdom to know the difference."

Emma: I guess I really know that when I honestly look back over the years. There have been many times over the years when I have applied New Program and my life would begin to go better. I just feel so stupid right now!

Jim: Feel good about noticing that reaction, and release the judging.

Emma: That's so hard right now.

Jim: Change can come with a lot less pain when I'm not judging and hating myself. I'm constantly learning more about myself, growing, loving the adventure. What's next? Looking forward to learning more. I know it may sound dumb, but it's thetruth.

Emma: You have always been that way as long as I've known you. I want Heidi to feel that way about her life! I hope I haven't ruined her already.

Jim: Now, I have no doubt that in terms of you and Heidi at this point, at the age she is now, that the of inoculation of your unconditional love has been her key experience. Even though she is very bright, she still is her age. But as she gets into 11 or 12 and begins secondary sex characteristics and adolescence, that's when your filters will be most likely to activate, and that's when if you don't decide to accept this assignment of change, the odds are that without intending to, you will contribute to her having the same conditional attitudes towards herself that you have towards yourself.

Emma: I can't let that happen! If I do, I have failed the one person who depends on me totally for everything. Please help me so I don't let that happen!

Jim: Now if anything would motivate you to get off the dime, and use the tools you already know how to use, that would be it! I know that! ***I believe your love for her is stronger than your hate of your weight.*** What do you believe? Take several deep breaths and experience deeply what you notice, without judging. Feeling good about noticing what's coming up inside.

Emma: I hadn't thought of it like that. You would think that should work (hesitance in her voice).

Jim: Take another deep breath and let yourself experience the truth-you have never thought about it that way. This is new territory, out of your Comfort Zone!

Emma: Well, the truth is that in time she will see me as a martyr rather that someone who takes care of myself.

Jim: And to find someone who is as bright and competent as you are, and has the kind of positive qualities you share with her; to relegate yourself to that position of self-hate, where isthe hope for us mortals?

Emma: Well I guess there can't be much. (Both laugh)

Jim: Right. Without judging, allow yourself a feeling of openness; let yourself share what you are noticing.

Emma: Well, I guess what I am feeling is that I have become my grandmother, something I swore I would never do. I do everything for everybody else and I don't do anything for myself.

Jim: Well, except hate yourself.

Emma: Yes!

Jim: You do that for you.

Emma: Yes, I do that.

Jim: And ironically, and as weird as it may sound, that is something that you do for yourself.

Emma: You know what I was thinking on the way over here. This is so sad. I actually would enjoy being in the hospital, and the reason is because it takes away the pressure. But what happened to me that day was that I was so upset with myself because of the realization of how much I hated myself and how much of life I am giving up because of that.

Jim: And you felt good about noticing that?

Emma: I knew I had to come talk to you about it.

Jim: You felt good about noticing that?

Emma: I never thought about feeling good, no!

Jim: Now feel good about noticing that you didn't think to feel good about noticing that profound awareness.

Emma: Feel good about not noticing?

Jim: **No! Really hear.** Feel good about noticing that you didn't feel good about noticing when that awareness first hit you and you made the call.

Emma: Why?

Jim: Because I said so (both laugh), and it is the best way to give your granddaughter a healthy grandmother. Okay?

Emma: Okay.

Jim: This is your coach speaking.

Emma: Well, if I had noticed right away what would have been the significance of that?

Jim: You noticed. You did notice! What you didn't do was allow yourself to follow New Program in that noticing. Remember that the first principle in New Program is "Non-judgmental openness and accuracy." Judging what you noticed took you in a different direction. Noticing was a very positive thing. What you noticed was a very painful thing.

Emma: Yes, the pain was overwhelming.

Jim: Feeling good about noticing that pain allows you to approach the whole process differently. *So* right now is the only place and time you can start feeling good about noticing. So let's start by feeling good about noticing that you didn't feel good about noticing at that moment.

Emma: Yes…(reflects deeply)

Jim: So you may as well do it right now. Actively choosing life gives you more motivation to live consciously and invest in becoming healthy in the present. The start is feeling good about noticing!

Emma: I was feeling good about myself until all the crap kept crashing in, and I'd eat to numb the anger and pain, and the weight poured on, and my self-hate went through the ceiling. When I liked myself, I thought that I was a good person, a person I would want to be a friend with, then I went over here…

Jim: Over here?

Emma: I went all the way…I am referring to my marriage…I went from being a bitch to trying to be good enough to get him to love me, ultimately losing myself. That's what happened to me. And now I have come back to this. You told me years ago that I could change, but not if I waited for my husband to change first. And he did change, in that he let me work my tail off trying to please him. And the farther I went the more he liked it, and then one night he tells me he is not interested in me physically because I am fat. So on that day I went all the way down the pit, to the bottom of the self-hate pit.

Jim: Yep.

Emma: I know I should have handled it differently, but that was such a crushing blow. Looking back now, I can see how my tools could have allowed my very different choices. I had worked so hard to change. And now I am probably fifty pounds heavier than I was when he told me that.

Jim: Yes, it is sort of like "Up yours".

Emma: Exactly! That was so devastating to me and there is nothing that he can ever say to erase that. I know he is human, but I would never say anything like that to anyone, ever.

Jim: Okay, except you are lying.

Emma: I am?

Jim: Yeah!

Emma: In what way?

Jim: When you say I can't imagine saying that to anyone.

Emma: You mean because I say it to myself?

Jim: Yes.

Emma: I know but.

Jim: Stop! Stop! Stop! You know just enough to be dangerous.

Emma: Why do you say that?

Jim: ***You know things.some.*** You know things intellectually…some. But you don't have the permission to believe them at a feeling level. Those things you know intellectually, and you have not yet had permission to let them become part of your believing-they trip you up.

Emma: Yeah.

Jim: They make you feel doubts about your program because you are trying to apply New Program, but you are trying to do it from the left side of the Split Screen-judging and shaming while trying to use New Program. You cannot hate yourself into change. It's not possible.

Emma: Well you have to admit I gave it the old college try! (Both laugh)

Jim: But you can honestly choose for Heidi's sake. Okay? We're not purists here. We will take any motivation. Okay? I know how pure your love is for Heidi, how precious she is to you. It is for that reason that it is a gift to her for you to decide that you are committed to learning how to be as loving to you and the kids inside as you have been to her. Take a deep breath and notice the resistance.

Emma: Sometimes I feel like food is all I have. I don't even **Inside A Drivers TrainingSession** care. It's the only pleasure I am getting, that I can count on.

Jim: To take away food, the only source of pleasure besides Heidi would be a punishment.

Emma: Yes!

Jim: Yes, a punishment for not being good enough, and therefore there is a healthy resistance to doing that. There is a healthy resistance to depriving yourself of food. Feel the difference of being free to eat in a healthy way. Where you, the Adult, are responsible for eating, rather than letting the wounded girls inside control eating. Now take a deep breath and let yourself feel all the way to your core, listen, and see all the different reactions to this commitment to learning a different way.

Emma: Long silence

Jim: Out loud.

Emma: There are all these pressures coming at me right now, and my husband won't touch me for being so fat, and I'm supposed to be thinking about how I am going to eat healthy? On the grand scheme of things, it just doesn't seem to matter. Its like, who really cares?

Jim: Oh, I see.

Emma: Well, that is what was going through my mind.

Jim: And as you look at that, can you see that through the eyes of your Higher Power?

Emma: I can't even comprehend that.

Jim: Okay then, let's go for second best. As you look at it through my eyes what do you see? Honestly.

Emma: There are two things. The number one thing is how do you expect to get through all those things if you are not healthier? The second thing would be you thinking, "After all these years she is still a nut".

Jim: That's good. Well, at least one of those things needs Windex to clean your dirty filters.

Emma: Seriously, do you have any other patients whose lives always seem to suck? Year after year something new just seems to happen. There doesn't seem to ever be a light at the end of the tunnel. Its like one thing after another and it never quits!

Jim: Yes, because Life is a chance to continue practicing and choosing differently.

Emma: I don't ever feel happy any more unless I am with Heidi. Other than that, I would like to be taking a nap, hiding out.

Jim: Okay, so for now, what say you start claiming back your life-both for Heidi and for yourself?

Emma: I guess I would just hate you to think of me as a nut (crying).

Jim: Then take a deep breath and feel the truth. Feel the truth and notice the resistance to feeling the truth.

Emma: I would just like you to think I have come a long way, when in fact I haven't.

Jim: ***You really need not to quit your day job to become a mind reader. Is this the best mind reading you can do?*** Now for myself, I'm always in New Program. I'm always in New Program, except when I'm not. Isn't it interesting that you expect more of yourself than your coach expects of himself?

Emma: No, I have quite an imagination, actually. (Both laugh)

Jim: I would appreciate it if you wouldn't put my name to your mind readings. At least make it more accurate if you are going to do that. I have total faith in your ability to grow and change. I have seen you blossom and become alive! I have seen you do well for long periods of time. I have also seen you abandon yourself and Emma Ann when you felt overwhelmed with rejections from others. You are not a nut; you are a very competent, capable woman who hates herself for her weight and shames herself into periods of depression.

Emma: I'm just being honest, Jim.

Jim: So am I. I appreciate your being honest; I want you to hear that. I do. Can you hear that? And I am being honest too. I respect your honesty and I am being honest back. Take a deep breath and feel both of those honesties. Can you respect mine?

Emma: I guess I am feeling relief that you feel that way. I don't even know why I brought it up.

Jim: Because it was a question from the perspective you were coming from. That's how the filters work. The filters stack on top of each other so that things that are truths become inaccessible or become accessible only intellectually…feel that…feel the filters preventing you from actually believing…breath deeply. This is a very important point.

Emma: **My filters are really out of control lately!**

Jim: You end up either not thinking about what you believe, not even thinking about what is true, not even thinking about what you truly believe to be true; or you don't think about it at all because you are drowning in the condemnation and shame. Take a deep breath and feel good about noticing the trap that has kept you stuck over and over during times of crashing-The Embarrassment Cycle.

Emma: Yeah.

Jim: Notice how busy you have been, hating yourself, feeling ashamed of yourself, feeling disgusted by yourself, hiding away. Notice how exhausted this effort makes you feel. Notice how often you tap in at an intellectual level to things that you believe to be true intellectually, and wonder why that awareness doesn't help you change.

Emma: It feels so different when I'm not judging. I know I have looked at things that way before in my life, it's just that when I'm on the rocks I forget that.

Jim: There have been times in your life when you would believe the truth of New Program at that level of action. At that level of experience, and during those times you would blossom. You would blossom! Your work productivity would go up, your experience of day to day living would be very positive. Things would be going so well that you weren't "needing" to consciously bring your New Program tools into daily life. New Program was coming more naturally…then something would happen that would hit you sideways and you would begin to forget what you believed.

Emma: Yeah.

Jim: You would begin to slip back into old familiar ways you felt about yourself, old ways of treating yourself, and old ways of experiencing yourself with the rest of the world. Take a deep breath and feel that. That is called normal. Addiction To The Familiar! Take a deep breath and really feel the truth of that. That is normal for Adult Children.

Emma: It feels like my life is just a black hole. I look around, and obviously I don't know what goes on behind closed doors, but I see people who seem to be happy and have what appears to me as normal lives. I see people with children, people with friends and successful careers. I have friends who have daughters that are their best friends. I lost my daughter!

Jim: And that's where you are starting, isn't it?

Emma: It doesn't seem right.

Jim: It doesn't seem fair?

Emma: *No!*

Jim: *Its not.* And the truth is, life isn't fair.

Emma: I know that! I do know that.

Jim: And the truth is, the more difficult the circumstances that you are facing, the more important it is to be aware of the filters you are using. In a life that is going real smooth and real easy you can get by with pretty smudgy filters. But in a life that is very difficult, the need for truth, the need for healthy New Program, as a vest to protect yourself from very real toxins, is even more important.

Emma: But that's not the point! I believe I can be adult enough.

Jim: Right! I agree absolutely that you can be that healthy adult; I have see her before, but until you are willing to take care of Emma Ann and believe the truth of your identity as a New Program Adult becoming, the chances are that she will grab the wheel and try to handle the most difficult situations that come up in your life.

Emma: Well…I guess we have both seen that happen over the years, haven't we? (Both laugh)

Jim: Give yourself the chance to turn around and begin building some healthy new identity muscles, cleaning your faulty filters, and accepting yourself in the present. Feel what it's like to really accept yourself where you are starting, and learn to nurture yourself, as you are becoming healthy in the present. That is how you would treat Heidi, isn't it?

Emma: I don't have a lot of time.

Jim: Then you might as well start right now!

Emma: Well I will, but you are saying that I need to get stronger before I try to tackle the important and difficult situations in my life now?

Jim: You at least need to get clear about "who" you really believe yourself to be, before confronting the key people in your life…for it to have the best chance of success. Allow yourself to feel the truth of that deeply inside, breathe slowly into the truth that coming from your healthy New Program Adult would have the best chance for a healthy outcome… to convey healthy changes to the important people in your life. **The truth is that you really are the New Program Adult becoming, and the wounded girls inside are a part of you.**

Emma: I know that's true; I believe that!

Jim: It seems there are more and more reasons to chose to believe yourself becoming.

Emma: To really see myself as "becoming" feels strange, but it takes a huge weight off my back. I'm so tired of hating myself! I love when I've been in New Program for long periods. After a while New Program feels more natural.

Jim: You need to get back to CAIR Groups and use the CAIR Handbook to focus on what you truly believe and who you really are. Replace faulty filters and experience believing the truth at the level of action. It means walking your walk!

Emma: You know, I really can do this; I've done it before. This is the first time for a long time that I feel some hope and can see some light.

Jim: Small steps forward, learning from the steps backwards. Listen back to this tape over and over, so you can gain more each time you listen. Remember No-Fault learning.

Emma: I have several old tapes that I can listen to also. I remember that was very helpful before. I'm feeling some excitement, but I'm afraid to get my hopes up.

Jim: The truth is that you have nothing to loose. Heidi needs a healthy grandmother, your husband needs you to be healthy-whether he knows it or not, and most important from my point, you and Emma Ann need you to be healthy in the present.

Emma: Boy is that true! I never looked at it that way before. (Long pause)

Jim: Today is a great day to start! Take several deep breaths and experience leaving the session on an amazing adventure, for all those you love. See yourself becoming as the New Program Adult you really are, and feel a growing commitment to taking care of the girls inside.

Notice the patterns that unfolded during the Therapeutic Life Coaching session. Can you recognize the assumptions Emma was making to fuel her circles? Do any feel familiar to you as you reflect on your own life up until now? Although your issues may be different than Emma, are the underlying patterns in your life similar? Feel what it is like to be in Emma's seat and allow yourself to experience the session with the issues you are facing today. Take the time to experience deeply what you notice in your session.

Introduction From Bill

I have had what I always thought was a normal male existence. I was a product of a family that never thought to talk about feelings or share what was going on inside with each other. I learned about sex the same way thousands, if not millions of other teenage boys did-from my friends and from trial and error. Unfortunately, I found some pornographic material my father had in the house and I began to think that was what being sexual was all about. Having pornography as a barometer, I began to view women from that perspective. I thought that sex and love were the same thing, which caused my relationships to by very dysfunctional, and they never lasted very long. I was a user and abuser of anything that would bring me immediate gratification-including women.

Then I met the woman, who is now my wife, and things began to change, but I withheld parts of myself that I felt ashamed of and would try as hard as I could to get rid of these "terrible" parts of myself. I tried to hate myself into health! I received Christ while involved with porn, praying for deliverance after each time I would fall into my sin pattern. I figured I would be delivered from it if I prayed about it enough. God had other plans. My wife discovered what I had been doing on the inter-net, and to make a long, painful story short, laid down the ultimatum that saved me from myself-get help or get out. I got help.

I also began, through the help of loving and caring Christian counseling, to see that each day I was living according to what I thought was reality. I failed to see that I was living in the past and letting the person I used to be before becoming a Christian be in control of the person I truly am. I am a new creation. I am learning to allow my new self to be a loving and gentle shepherd to my old self (what a contrast to beating the crap out of myself for each failure). It is freeing and wonderful to be able to recognize that I am a wonderful and capable person because of, and in spite of, who I was before! I hope this sharing will be of help to others.

Bill's Therapeutic Life Coaching Session
(Read out loud-Experiencing the dialogue)

Jim: First of all I've got to tell you something.

Bill: What's that?

Jim: I would encourage you to give yourself some real credit for giving yourself permission to be sitting in this chair at this moment, instead of finding a million reasons not to. Take a deep breath and just appreciate how you got here from the time you made the call and we talked briefly on the phone. How did you make the decision? Really feel that.

Bill: It's like everything else; nothing's real clear. There's no clarity at all. In every.

Jim: Compared to what?

Bill: I guess when I've been more aligned spiritually with Christ and who I am in Christ. It's never been super apparent to me. I've always been kind of a cynic and a skeptic.

Jim: Skeptical of.?

Bill: Where I am in the whole scheme of things, in His plan for me.

Jim: The scheme of things in terms of God's Plan?

Bill: Yeah.

Jim: Tell me about that skepticism.

Bill: Well, I've only been a Christian for about 3 or 4 years, and before that I was a devout atheist, no God, and we're all dust and that's pretty much it. And I would have gone to the mat with that. I surrounded myself with people who believed the same thing I did. Ya' know, those who didn't, were fools. And that creeps in, just questioning everything. Never settling down and just taking a deep breath. Doubting that I have enough faith. So I.

Jim: Bill, Bill, I'm hearing an assumption…you don't mind if I be myself? (Both laugh) I understand; I wouldn't want to sit in that chair unless I really wanted to change! It takes courage to sit in the chair you're sitting in. It really does.

Bill: Yeah, but that and 2 bits gets you what?

Jim: Accuracy. And accuracy is essential to the process of healthy change. Accuracy allows you to choose, and the more difficult the situation, the more important that you be able to choose consciously. That is the 2 bits!

Bill: Okay.

Jim: Because you knew when you sat in that chair today that you'd have a very deep, deep, honest conversation about things that you've danced around, things you've been fogging over, things that you've been closing your eyes to, things that you've been ignoring, things that you've been judging yourself about, old patterns that have sneaked in. You knew that we would look at them in a very bright, loving light of grace. This isn't a surprise, because we've danced before.

Bill: Right, right, right.

Jim: That's the reason that I want you to acknowledge you being here, instead of using a million excuses to avoid being here today. (Long pause) Take a deep breath and notice what comes up as you do that.

Bill: I don't know. I'm fighting it. I'm just not there. I'm not in the "giving myself benefits of being here" mood.

Jim: Okay. What is the resistance saying?

Bill: With all our financial pressures, the money for the session today is hard to come by.

Jim: Bill, the fact is that you have already paid for this hour, you may as well get the most out of the session. Practically speaking, being as healthy as possible during difficult times gives you the best choices possible. What doesn't make sense is spending this hour feeling bad about being here, instead of gaining all you can from our time together.

Bill: There ya' go.

Jim: See Bill, the biggest problem you have is that you've never learned to respectfully listen to Bill without judging what you notice. **God wants you to be His ambassador to the wounded parts of yourself.** Take a deep breath and notice how you are treating yourself during this difficult time in your life.

Bill: But I think it goes even further than that though, because I don't have a clear sense of even who I am. And I go in circles with my wife about that, ya' know, I don't have my own identity.

Jim: What does that mean?

Bill: That means I don't...uh...interests, hobbies, things that make up a person. It just seems it's all about the labors of life.

Jim: You mean, working 2 jobs and going to school?

Bill: And a new family, and struggling with my wife. There's not a lot of joy there. And that's who I am right now. No-joy-Bill.

Jim: That's who you are? So you do have an identity!

Bill: (Laughter) Not the one I want, you see. I'm lacking contentedness.

Jim: How do you expect to have contentedness when you see yourself as the "Bill" you were just talking about a second ago?

Bill: I don't know...(heavy sigh)

Jim: Well, it's not possible!

Bill: I'm finding that out. (Both laugh)

Jim: It's as if I put a board with nails sticking out where you're sitting and then say, "You're not comfortable?" You'd look at me like I was weird. But you're sitting on all kinds of nails and thinking you're weird for not being comfortable. Take a deep breath and look at that; let yourself see accurately without judging. (Long pause) The fact is that your true identity comes from becoming as a new creation in Him.

Bill: I know that intellectually. I just can't seem to feel it. The "without judging" part, I think I'm so wrapped up in doing it

Who's Really Driving Your Bus? so much I don't even know when I'm doing it and when I'm not.

Jim: Right, so it's kind of helpful to give yourself permission to feel good about noticing when you're judging. Feel good about noticing when you're judging. And as you feel good about noticing when you're judging, you can add, "Never mind" like Gilda Radnor from the old Saturday Night Live. You can release the judging and defending like Gilda. Do you remember her?

Bill: Long time ago, yeah.

Jim: Remember when she would make a huge mistake on the Saturday Night Live News segment and everyone else wanted to lynch her, she would look at the camera and say "Never Mind" in a way that showed no shame or defensiveness. You can see Gilda and laugh as you release your judging to the Lord, going back to using His plan again. God's plan is for nonjudgmental noticing with a perspective of grateful humility…take a deep breath and feel your resistance respectfully.

Bill: I feel nothing but resistance. Respectfully? What does that mean?

Jim: It means taking an attitude of respect, a desire to learn from, and a desire to know more about the signals that are coming from your resistance. Imagine if it was more important to learn and grow, than defend and judge.

We call this attitude Powerful Vulnerability. That's what it means. And notice the resistance to that. Take a deep breath and really notice that resistance. What does it say?

Bill: Like you said earlier, it's like I need a chiropractor. I'm just completely out of alignment.

Jim: Great! Feel good about noticing that you're out of alignment. Notice that the pain that you're feeling makes perfect sense; given the fact that you're out of alignment. That's not who you are, it's what you're feeling-out of alignment. Now that's true!

Bill: Yeah!

Jim: Take a deep breath and feel what it's like to experience that truth at the core of your being.

Bill: It's a little sense of relief.

Jim: Then take another slow breath and notice what it's like to experience believing this truth about your identity even more deeply.

Bill: It's like…when I actually stop and experience this truth, everything seems to change, to be more possible…I just can't seem to keep this clear (deep sigh).

Jim: I don't understand. What can't you keep clear?

Bill: It's clear right now and I'll be able to leave for a while and say, "That's right I'm not my circumstances." And then my circumstances just come back up again and again.

Jim: **Remember part of the Introduction to the CAIRing Grace Groups that they read at each meeting,** "I am not my story and my story affects where I am starting today. How I'm feeling and how I'm doing does not define who I am." **You are starting today!**

Bill: Yeah, I guess?

Jim: What?

Bill: Well I don't know, I have the good feeling of being connected right now, it's there, and then it's not. It's taken over by other things.

Jim: Okay, other things crowd in and you lose that good feeling. Right now you are living consciously, as life becomes more demanding you slip into automatic pilot. I call that normal! So how did you create that good feeling here now?

Bill: By having an objective party saying, "Take a deep breath, think about it, and experience it."

Jim: Trust me Bill, having sat across from you more than once, having an objective party suggesting something to you, plus a buck gets you a cup of coffee unless you choose to do something. So if you chose to do something right now and you got the result-feeling that good feeling-it's because you chose to do it. Not because I said it. Now that's the truth.

Bill: (Laughs) I see your point.

Jim: I'm reminding you of things that you know to be true from previous experiences, that you have forgotten.at the moment. **Forgetting your true identity is what causes you to become out of alignment. I call it "Identity Alzheimer's Disorder."** Take several slow, deep breaths and check it out… does that feel accurate?

Bill: Yeah. And that's probably the sum total of what's going on, and putting it into practice. And there are reminders to me but…you know. we don't seem to do the homework you want us to do…we don't do anything.

Jim: It is true that doing the homework would make having the good feeling a lot easier. I'll give you credit for approaching your recovery the hard way, a way I don't think I could do. I hate pain and love pleasure. That's why I consciously approach things in New Program, actively choosing to do it. **I often say "I'm always in New Program, except when I'm not."** How do you and your wife decide when to practice New Program, and what is that practice process like for each of you?

Bill: Yeah. (Laughter) And I think it's true that I'm doing it the hard way. She wants to read the CAIR Handbook together and discuss the material, like you have suggested in each session so far. I'm so tired by the time I get home that the last thing I want to do is study and work on my problems. I feel she thinks I'm not committed to my recovery when I tell her I'm too tired.

Jim: Bill, homework is not about focusing on your problems, it is about learning and growing in the present. The more difficult the situations you are in, the more you need your New Program tools. Feel what it is like to see your homework as a gift, a drink of cool water, when you are in need.

Take a deep breath, experience this at your core, noticing any resistance.

Bill: It feels very different that way. I always approach the homework as one more thing on my list-a list that has no end.

Jim: Up until now! I wonder what it'd be like for you to have permission to believe-in-action the truth that your homework is a loving gift to both you and your wife?

Bill: It's just that I've got a lot to do. And there's the burden of being the sole provider for my family, without enough income. So there's a sense of failure.

Jim: Or at least a sense of pressure. Now, how you go from pressure to failure is an interesting point too.

Bill: That doesn't seem interesting to me. It's just a pain in the ass.

Jim: It's painful.

Bill: Yeah

Jim: But let's keep with accuracy for a moment. Having the baby and your wife being off work taking care of the new baby, you're down to one income. Now my guess is that both you and she know that one income is less than two.

Bill: Yeah, we got that much figured out. (Both laugh)

Jim: Okay, and the importance that how both of you feel about her being with the baby is keeping her at home at this point. And the two of you chose that up to this point? So, circumstances are that suddenly the whole financial load has fallen on you, and now you're working two jobs. Why aren't you working three?

Bill: I don't have time. The third job is school. (Both laugh)

Jim: That's right. and you're going to school in order to.?

Bill: To get my bachelors, to go into teaching is my current plan. We may be reviewing that. I'm just not sure what I'm cut out to do?

Jim: So it all comes back to the question of identity, doesn'tit?

Bill: That seems to be the big struggle at the moment.

Jim: Isn't it interesting that that's also God's focus? It's God's position that you are a new creation in Him, and He calls you to be His ambassador of reconciliation to the wounded parts of yourself that are stuck in your old nature. Allow yourself to see your identity through His eyes. Take several deep breaths as you experience deeply the truth of God's view of Bill.

Bill: What I believe? You mean how I use the knowledge of God in my daily life? What do you mean?

Jim: When you see yourself through the Lord's eyes what do you see?

Bill: I see. I'm going. I just don't get it. What else do I have to do? C'mon! The Lord says: "Let Me help you," and I'm not letting Him help me! (Anger and frustration in his voice)

Jim: Okay, feel the resistance to allowing Him to help you. What does that resistance say? Take a few deep breaths to help feel what the resistance is saying.

Bill: I can't be sure He's going to come through. I'm scared to trust Him! (Deep sigh)

Jim: Now feel good about noticing that. Isn't that normally what you use to bash yourself in the head, not knowing if you can trust Him?

Bill: Bash yourself in the head? Tell me if this is what you mean: I don't know if I can trust Him, I go with my own plan, my struggles get harder, but I still don't trust Him. Is that bashing myself in the head?

Jim: **No, that's just being human.** The bashing yourself in the head is judging yourself harshly for not having enough faith to trust him.

Bill: Oh yeah. I do that all the time!

Jim: And that's where we started, talking about how you keep questioning.. and I was going to ask you something and I got distracted, but at my age I have senior moments. We're going to be gentle with me, aren't we? (Laughter)

Bill: Oh, of course! Your age, my age, what's the difference?

Jim: Exactly, we're all human! Are you assuming that if you're questioning issues in your faith that it means you don't have enough faith?

Bill: That's a sticky area. Faith is a sticky area for me. Is there actually a quantifiable issue surrounding faith? Faith of a mustard seed, or faith of a mountain? I don't know.

Jim: Let's bring it down to "Bill." Take it away from the world and bring it down to "Bill" personally. How much faith is enough for you? So you can feel good about the amount of faith you have in your walk with the Lord? Take a deep breath and experience deeply, at your core, this essential question.

Bill: Uhhh…I don't know that I can answer that.

Jim: Take a deep breath and feel what it's like not to know the answer to one of the key questions in your life.

Bill: (Laughter) You have a way of putting that, don't you. Ya' know, it's either some-some is enough, or unquestioning, undying faith. If some gets it done then I can live my life with some faith, and that's enough to.

Jim: Get by? I also hear a Black or White filter.

Bill: Well, not even get by…it does sound kind of Black or White.

Jim: Hear the tone in your voice and feel what it's like to just "get by."

Bill: Enough to get it done. Yeah, I guess so.

Jim: A little faith is enough to get it done, in terms of surviving. But God, because He loves you perfectly, is not willing to settle for you surviving. He wishes for you to have abundant living. And for that, getting by is not the same as living life more and more abundantly in Him. But notice that you put yourself above Him as judge and jury about whether or not you have enough faith to count.

Bill: I'm a little thick. I'm not sure I'm getting that.

Jim: What is it that you're not getting?

Bill: I'm judge and jury above God?

Jim: About whether or not you have enough faith to ante up to the table in the poker game of life-yes!

Bill: Isn't that the whole "Catch 22" thing? How do I release that? How do I release the fact that I'm judge and jury and that I demand more faith than I have?

Jim: Well, you start by noticing it...realizing the role of choice in the believing process. Then you really ask yourself, "Is that truly how I choose to believe?" and, "Is that truly how God wants me to believe?" The fact is that believing deeply, at the level of action, is very different than intellectually believing that same truth.

Bill: (Heavy sigh) I can't seem to make myself believe God's view of me.

Jim: Believing-in-action comes out of a growing personal relationship with Him, starting where you are starting at the moment...feeling what it's like to deeply experience His free gift of Grace...feeling any resistance to believing His Truth...feeling yourself as a new creation in Him.

Bill: Well, I'd like to think I believe that.

Jim: What do you truly believe about that? Do you truly believe that God does not want you to be judge and jury, but instead wants you to put your focus on the process of "becoming" as a new creation in Him?

Bill: Yeah.

Jim: How much of you truly believes that He wants you to be His ambassador of reconciliation to the wounded parts of you that have been disconnected and put in Tupperware. At times of great stress, the lids often pop off from time to time? This is particularly important when things get hairy and difficult, and the pressure and the time and the tiredness all start to feel overwhelming.

Bill: I don't know.

Jim: What don't you know?

Bill: Oh, I don't know how much of that I believe.

Jim: Then feel free to pay attention right now to that question. It's important enough; it deserves your attention. And notice what you experience inside as you really look at that question. The fact is that God does want you to be His ambassador, to take on His Nature when dealing with wounded parts of yourself…He states that in His Owner's Manual.

Bill: It's a core issue. And I'm getting a lot of resistance to that right now.

Jim: Cool! And, of course, you're feeling good about noticing that resistance, right? (Both laugh) God's Plan calls for you to continually remember your true identity in Him, no matter what is going on in your life. He wants to share the load with you, drawing you into His Nature through His Spirit so you can have the best chance of a healthy life.

Bill: (Laughter) No, I don't naturally go right to that. I don't go, "Oh, I feel good about that!"

Jim: I'm not saying to feel good about that. I'm saying to feel good about noticing accurately about where you're starting, without any condemnation. That is, if you want to use God's plan, as His ambassador. Of course, if Bill's plan is better than God's plan. then feel free to use Bill's.

Bill: Ya' know, He needs my help sometimes (laughing).

Jim: Which really brings up the other issue, doesn't it?

Bill: Which?

Jim: Have you ever had the experience in your life of the kind of unconditional love represented in Scripture? As scripture describes Jesus as your big brother, Jesus as your fellow traveler, Jesus who sends you His Holy Spirit so that you can be transformed through His Spirit into His likeness?

Bill: No (deep sigh). There has always seemed to be a catch, a hook that clobbers me when my guard is down.

Jim: Right. Feel good about noticing that you've never had that kind of experience before. That is why it's such a foreign feeling for you, even though you understand the words intellectually, you do not experience them at the core level of relationship. It's like, if I said to you, "Bill, Let's go have lunch on Mars." You're not going to go home and pack a lunch. You're going to think I'm nuts. People don't have lunch on Mars. So you understand the words, but you don't believe at the core that it's true.

Bill: Right…I always feel a pressure to be good enough tohave Him proud of me. I just can't let Him in completely…I feel so guilty (heavy sigh).

Jim: You will never be good enough to earn His Love or bad enough to lose His Love. He wants you to come to Him as you are and begin an honest relationship with Him, a personal relationship where you can really be yourself, a new creation in Him…resistance and all. It is His Nature that makes it all possible, not how good you can make yourself. Allow yourself to experience believing this truth, at the level of action.

Bill: Okay, so it has to be a "come as you are party," like we talk about in the CAIRing Grace Groups. I need to remember that there are parts of me that are very afraid to let their guard down…and that He loves all of me, flaws and all.

Jim: Yes, you need to get into the habit of connecting with these wounded parts of you, and being His ambassador, with His Nature flowing through you to these kids inside. The more you practice, the more natural it will feel.

Bill: Well, I do believe it but I haven't had personal experience with it. My wife is the closest, and she will not continue with me if I slip back into my addictions. She has her limits too.

Jim: What I'm saying is, "Yes, you've never had the experience of unconditional love." So intellectually you try to hold onto the truth of Scripture. But it becomes like a bad feeling at your core, a sick joke, a torturous lie that is just waiting for you to believe it, hook line and sinker, and then it will be ripped out from under you and you'll be left devastated… Take a deep breath. Check it out for yourself. Don't take my word for it. Very gently, very respectfully, notice what's going on inside.

Bill: Uh-huh, I can feel the fears inside.

Jim: Which is an honest fear, it's an honest part of where you're starting.

Bill: Right, it's just all that confusion, that's how we get back to that.

Jim: Confusion? It's not confusion. In truth, there is an honest fear that you have, not all of you, but much of you has. Most of you inside believe that if you really, truly believe, at that moment you're most vulnerable, it's going to be ripped out from under you and you're going to be devastated.

Bill: That may be, I really haven't thought about it that way. That may also be the same thing as, "Let's go have lunch on Mars." I do know that I get anxious when I get too close to Him for very long. I begin to feel like I'm losing myself.

Jim: I know that feeling! The truth is that when you are feeling that loss of self, you are more fully your true self in Him. Notice that feeling and begin to relax into the tension, realizing that the resistance is an important signal that part of you needs His loving care.

Bill: I never thought of it as a signal. I just feel guilty that I could even question His commitment.

Jim: Not so, Bill. You have lots of proof. If you were Pinocchio right now, you'd poke me in the eye with your nose! Shame on you!

Bill: (Laughter) What? Clarify that. What do you mean by that?

Jim: As you look back over your life you have many examples of proof of getting your hopes up, only to have it snatched out from under you.

Bill: Well sure. But.

Jim: Stop, stop, stop! So when it comes to the fear that believing leads to pain, and hurt, and abandonment, and devastation, you have lots of proof. True?

Bill: Yes (heavy sigh).

Jim: Then feel what it's like to feel that truth. Respect that truth. That's part of where you're starting.

Bill: It goes back to, "Come on, let Me help you, let Me help you. You're not letting Me do any work in you."

Jim: Right. You mean this person is asking you, "Why won't you let me help you," when you have ample proof that being vulnerable and allowing yourself to trust someone has so often led to devastation, and He's going to judge you for being hesitant about that? That's the Jesus you know? Take a deep breath and experience sharing your fears openly with Him, sharing with your Big Brother in whatever way it comes out. **Look into His eyes and see His amazing love for you personally.**

Bill: (Tears flowing) I can actually feel Him…this is too cool…He really does love me as I am…He just gave me a big hug and has a warm smile as He tells me how He wants to help me live life abundantly.

Jim: Take a deep breath; respectfully, gently notice what you're feeling inside.

Bill: I'm noticing-how did I go from salvation and all high on the Lord to.

Jim: To how it is today?

Bill: Yeah, to "What's it all about, Alfie?"

Jim: You mean, the messy part of relationship building?

Bill: I guess I always thought it should be nice and tidy.

Jim: It has not been tidy in my experience. Life is an ongoing process of "Got It's" and "Ain't Got It's." "Got It," is allowing Him to be living through you, for you, with you. "Got It," is you're becoming as a new creation in Him. That includes becoming His loving ambassador to the parts that resist His Love. The key is that He loves you the same whether you "Got it," or "Ain't Gotit."

Bill: That just goes back to the resistance. Not letting Him in to walk with me.

Jim: Because...He'll let you down?

Bill: Yeah. I want to take that step of faith off a cliff. And land on a cloud or something.

Jim: Isn't it neat how we always want something dramatic? He isn't asking for that. Do you want me to tell you something? You sitting here right now, at this moment, is an example of allowing the Spirit to work. The urge for you to call in the first place is an example of the Spirit through you...and your wife's loving nagging. (Laughter)

Bill: Yeah, she doesn't put it in so many words. She just wants me to do something. And I'm not doing anything.

Jim: Yes, you are. That's not true.

Bill: Well, maybe today.

Jim: No, no, no! I'm not talking about right now. You have been very busy! Hating yourself, shaming yourself for not having enough faith, feeling guilty that somehow you would see Jesus as someone who would do something as hurtful as promise to be with you only to let you down.

Bill: Yeah?

Jim: Yeah, you've been busy hating yourself. You've been busy wanting to counteract that by doing something as dramatic as stepping off a cliff in faith to prove that you have enough faith to warrant His love. You've been busy, just not anything productive! (Both laugh) It's not a lack of business… what do you notice?

Bill: You're right! No wonder I get so tired. It just seems like taking the easy way out. if I don't judge myself. keep myself accountable.

Jim: God's Plan allows you to take the struggle out of the change process by feeling good about noticing the things you want to change, giving yourself permission to start in the present, and relaxing into the adventure of practicing the changes.

Bill: I never really looked at it that way.

Jim: Accountability is accountability, judging is judging. The truth is that judging makes accountability more difficult and painful. Feel this process, feel what it's like to approach your recovery in this new way. Listen to the audiotape of today's session-over and over.

Bill: I'm going to share it with my wife. This can be a new start in my marriage too. I'm actually feeling hopeful. I really can start with the faith I have and bring that faith to Him so more can grow out of our relationship together. This feels possible!

Jim: Share it with your wife and discuss how to change the whole homework experience in a way you two can enjoy and have fun with it. Give yourself the gift of thought by reading the CAIR Handbook. Call when you are ready for another session. Keep going to CAIRing Grace Group meetings when time allows. Build the habit of seeing yourself as His ambassador to your kids inside. Remember that resistance is only a signal to bring His Light to where it is needed. Good work!

Notice your reactions to Bill's session. The focus on his judging and demanding unrealistic faith is common in coaching sessions. Do any of his responses feel familiar to you in your own spirituality? Although Bill's issues may be very different than yours, what do you notice as you experience sitting in his seat during the coaching session. Share your reactions with me in your journal.

Prayer Of Trust And Confidence

*My Lord God,
I have no idea where I am going.
I do not see the road ahead of me.
I cannot know for certain where it will end.
Nor do I really know myself,
And the fact that I think that I am following your will,
Does not mean that I am actually doing so.
But I believe that the desire to please you
Does in fact please you.
And I hope that I never do anything
Apart from that desire.
And I know that if I do this, you will lead me
By the right road though I may know nothing about it.
Therefore will I trust you always,
Though I may seem to be lost
And in the shadow of death.
I will not fear, for you are ever with me, and Will
never leave me to face my perils alone.*

Thomas Merton

6

CORE ELEMENTS OF DRIVERS TRAINING

In this chapter we will be exploring five "Nuggets of Wisdom" reflecting "Fundamental Principles of Healthy Change" in learning to drive your perceptual bus. These "Nuggets" impact your ability to make healthy changes in your recovery: "Truth Transcends Our Perceptions Of Reality," "We Become Addicted To The Familiar," "Change Is Possible In The Present," "Personal Change Is An Active Participation Process," and "Freedom Is The Willingness To Accept The Consequences Of Your Choices."

Each of these "Nuggets of Wisdom" helps you approach the process of making changes in your life with the least effort and pain. Allow yourself to approach these "Nuggets of Wisdom" at an experiential level of action rather than intellectually holding on to them. Learning to apply these "Nuggets" experientially makes change the path of least resistance. We will explore other "Nuggets" in future chapters.

Nugget: Truth Transcends Our Perceptions Of Reality!

I often find myself sharing with clients that they need to learn "to not be so confused by the 'facts' as they perceive them." They would be so busy drowning in the situations with which they were struggling, that they could not recognize the beliefs and assumptions that filtered their perceptions. I use a lot of metaphors in my coaching to convey complex clinical issues in ways that clients can understand and apply in their recovery. I use examples from TV, movies, etc. I will often share a scene from the movie "Robin Hood" with Kevin Costner, where Robin Hood meets Little John for the first time, as an illustration of truth transcending our perception of reality.

Coming from opposite directions, Robin Hood and Little John were each wanting to cross a stream. They met in the middle of the tree bridge and after verbal sparring, began to battle. In the process of the fight Little John and Robin Hood both fell into the stream. Although Little John had been winning the battle before entering the water, once they were in the water he began to panic. Little John believed he was drowning, and surrendered to Robin Hood. After the surrender, Robin Hood helped Little John to his feet. It was then that Little John experienced the truth. The stream only came to his waist! Are there areas of your life where your beliefs and fears have caused you to give up unnecessarily? How often do you believe in your "limitations" so strongly that, like Little John, you surrender needlessly?

There is amazing power available to you in understanding your perceptual filters more accurately. I will show you how to recognize, challenge, and replace dysfunctional perceptual filters that are currently robbing you of your ability to grow and make the changes you want in your life. We will look deeply into your filters, and *I will coach you, as you learn to shift from surviving to living.* You'll learn to apply a New Program set of beliefs and assumptions as listed in the Introduction. It is important to practice throughout your day, thinking about how the "Eight Fundamental Principals Of Healthy Change" can help you perceive more accurately. You can experience the comfort of applying the Prayer of Serenity throughout your day.

My younger brother, Bobby, shared an experience he'd had driving up to our mom's cabin in the mountains on a busy holiday weekend, feeling in a hurry to get up there so he could relax. The two-lane road was packed, and after passing a few cars, he realized that he couldn't go faster than the flow of traffic. He was feeling more and more uptight by the moment. Suddenly he heard himself say, "I've got to hurry up and get to mom's so I can finally relax."

He began to laugh at himself, settled into his captain's seat, turned up the Eagles on the stereo, and took several slow, deep breaths. He realized he could start relaxing right there, on the road to mom's cabin. He didn't have to wait until he got to the cabin to start relaxing. When he told me about his experience, I realized immediately how profound a "Nugget" he had experienced. I have shared that story many times in coaching sessions. It is a great example of how truth transcends our normal perceptions of reality.

There is a profound difference between the perceptions coming out of "living" compared to the perceptions coming out of "surviving." Do you approach your life as something you have to endure and survive, or something unfolding that you get to experience and live? In the 40+ years that I have spent as a therapist/coach in people's lives, a number of patterns emerged over and over in sessions that came from a survival mentality. The same patterns would appear with different "content"-the situation the client was dealing with at that time-through the course of therapy. I began to notice that the same identifiable patterns would show up with different clients, even though their diagnoses were not the same. These patterns would rob the person of the joy of living.

The common denominator across the dysfunctional patterns was that the people were struggling to find the truth, to "make sense" of the situations in their lives, while being blind to the unconscious filters they were using in their situations. They wanted to understand why things were happening the way they were. They would feel trapped and stuck in their painful situations. They would be totally unaware of the assumptions that would filter their perceptions of events, and that others might have a very different set of assumptions filtering their perceptions also.

They were stuck on the surface, drowning in the content, reacting without any awareness of the underlying presuppositions they were bringing to their experiences. In many cases the truth was that the water only came to their waist when they could finally perceive accurately. Share with me in your journal the different reactions you notice regarding your desire to understand.

People operate within the "truth" as they perceived it on au*tomatic pilot* (like Little John). The situation/story would provide the content that the client usually focused on in their struggle. **The real power for change is not in the content; it is in the accurate awareness of the assumptions and attitudes you bring to the situation.** Most people have little or no awareness of all the presuppositions they are reacting to, and whether they truly believe the things they are assuming automatically. Addiction patterns can help illustrate this dynamic.

Bob came for coaching when his wife became very upset with his Internet use of pornography, and tensions were getting to a crisis point in the marriage. Bob was in his early 40's and was a very successful professional. He had been married for 15 years to Helen, and was an active participant in the life of his ten-year-old daughter. He worked very hard at whatever he did-work or play. Bob felt driven most of his waking day. He admitted that he had tried to quit going to the pornographic web sites many times, but the tension would build and he would "find himself on one of the sites." Sometimes he would masturbate while watching the site, and at other times he would feel intense sexual arousal, but would release the sexual tension with Helen later.

They both reported an enjoyable, active sex life together. Helen felt that Bob was cheating on her when he went to the web sites. She would feel hurt, that there must be something wrong with her, something lacking, for Bob to want to go to the sites. Bob swore it had nothing to do with Helen, and he felt she was beautiful and desirable. All he could say was that he couldn't stop going to the sites on his own, and needed help with this problem.

I had Bob use the Time Machine to activate the feelings in the pattern by going back to a recent time he "found himself on a site." As Bob began to experience the entire process again in the present, step by step, starting before he actually made the decision to go to a site, feeling good about noticing consciously what was going on inside and out as he went into his "addiction trance." We would notice how different parts of Bob seemed to be in conflict, without Bob being consciously aware of this battle going on inside.

Respecting the feelings, applying the principles of New Program in the process, and allowing himself to start where he was starting, made it possible for Bob to connect with a very driven seven-year-old Bobby who desperately needed relief. It was difficult at first. Bob would judge and feel shame about what he was noticing, and then a Second-Order feeling would kick in-defen-siveness. The more accurately Bob began to see the pattern, the more choices he began to have in the present. What we discovered in Bob is a common pattern in the addiction to pornography.

A strong drive of conditional acceptance (see **Power Of Mind** "Conditional Acceptance" filter) leads to a lot of "self-sacrifice," which in turn leads to feelings of entitlement/resentment and finally acting out the addiction. Bob worked long hours. When he really began to experience the feelings surrounding the addiction he realized that the pornography was one of the few things he really did just for himself. It also acted like a drug on his anxiety and depression. The truth is that pornography does tend to create a physiological reaction that does help reduce feelings of anxiety and depression. I believe that in Bob's case he would begin to need the "fix" of physiological reactions to the pornography when he began to feel resentful about the many things he was doing in his life.

When he began imagining life without his addiction, he began to feel empty and resentful. These feelings would scare him and increase his anxiety, which would cause him to push the entire thing out of his mind, making it impossible to proactively work on change. All of this leads to even more urgency to act out with the pornography to relieve the growing anxiety caused by judging what was being noticed. Although he intellectually knew that it wasn't true that his sexual addiction was the only thing he did for himself, the feeling perception was very strong in the addictive trance.

He learned over time to comfort his little Bobby inside, and remove him from behind the wheel of his perceptual bus. He began to live more consciously, becoming aware of choosing to experience his life as an adventure and a gift to himself as well as others. From this perspective of grateful humility, Bob became able to supervise his wounded parts, and use the urges to go to the porno site as a signal that he needs to respectfully notice and respond to them in healthy ways.

The urge became an early warning signal for Bob to hold up his lantern of grace and see himself and others with humility. He was bringing truth into his life as a new perspective, a New Program that generates healthy choices in the present. Bob was pleased that the urge could take on a different meaning and activate very different choices.

The insight God gave me was that **"Truth Transcends Content,"** which is the antidote to the toxic patterns so many people struggle with for their entire lives! **It is very different for you to bring truth into a given situation, rather than try to find the truth in your situation.** Are there situations where you continually end up losing your healthy power of choice, no matter how much resolve you make prior to entering the situation? Begin to examine the assumptions you are making about yourself and the others in the situation. What beliefs and assumptions are you currently treating as truths? Use your ABC's Of Observation to help bring things into focus. Do your current assumptions prevent you from having healthy choices? Do you often end up feeling overwhelmed by the content of the situation, ignoring the filters you bring with you? Feel good about noticing this and share it with me in your journal.

Jenny came for Therapeutic Life Coaching when her depression and anxiety became unmanageable. At 35, she had achieved a solid reputation in her profession and was making a respectable income. Her friends and co-workers looked up to her as a strong, competent person. She had been married at 17, and was very frustrated with her marriage. Her husband, Larry, had active sexual addictions and alcoholism, with no interest in making any changes. In addition, there were long periods when he was not working at all.

He was verbally abusive and had threatened her physically, but had not actually been physical with her. He demanded her to keep the house perfect, and constantly put her down. He was pathologically jealous of her, and very controlling. Her friends couldn't understand why she felt she couldn't make it without him. The turning point of crisis for Jenny was when a man at work began showing interest in her, and seemed to enjoy hearing what she had to say. She had never been with anyone besides Larry, and was shocked that a man might actually find her interesting.

Jenny's father left her family when she was very young, and her mother blamed Jenny for her father leaving. Her mother was very angry and resentful toward Jenny, and put her down constantly. Her mother went through a series of men, several showing unwanted attention to Jenny. She met Larry when she was a freshman in high school and he was a senior. They married when Larry got a job out of town and told her that if she didn't drop out of school and come with him, he would drop her. Over the years she got an education and started working her way up in her profession. He was always putting her down with statements like, "Just because you have an education doesn't mean you know sh—" "No one would ever want you;" "I can't hardly stand you myself" and other hurtful messages.

In her coaching sessions Jenny discovered a little four-year-old inside who felt absolutely dependant on Larry to "take care of her," and a nine-year-old inside who tried as hard as she could to please him by doing everything he wanted. At first, she hated these parts of herself. We worked on building a healthy, supervising relationship with these wounded girls inside, and helping Jenny notice when she was regressing. She began to recognize her "addiction to the familiar" in the marriage. She started attending free CAIR Self-help Groups and working with the tools in the CAIR Handbook between sessions. As she got healthier, she began to relate with Larry differently. Instead of coming from her scared little girls inside, she began to use assertive skills and set healthy limits in the marriage.

Larry blew up and threatened to leave if she didn't stop "this craziness." We had practiced this moment several times in our coaching sessions, and she was able to look him right in the eye and say, "If that's what you want, that's up to you. I will not accept how things have been, and if you aren't interested in working with me to build something healthy, then it is best that you go ahead and leave." He left, expecting her to collapse into a heap, and was shocked that she seemed to be fine.

He increased his threats and finally crossed the line and was physical with her. She called the police-which we had also practiced in coaching sessions-and filed for divorce the next day. She continued attending the CAIR groups after finishing our coaching sessions, in order to support the healing relationships with her kids inside. Her depression and anxiety were no longer an issue. She learned to bring truth into the content of her relationships.

Intellectually, Jenny knew she made a good living and was carrying the load in the marriage. At the core level of believing, she perceived herself as needing Larry to survive. The CAIR Handbook makes this distinction: "There is an important difference between knowing something at an intellectual level, and knowing it at a feeling level. A.A. makes the distinction between "talking your talk and walking your walk." When we think we know something about our Old Program, we tend to move on to other things, and turn our backs on what we think we know. The fact is, until we can apply our knowing in our daily lives, we don't know it! It takes time and practice to allow things to go from intellectual knowing, to KNOWING. It's what we think we know that often gets us into the worst trouble. (Stop and discuss.)"

Over the years I have noticed a pervasive problem that is shared by most of the clients I have seen. This problem is **Identity Alzheimer's Disorder,** the fact that we keep forgetting who we truly are in the present. We keep slipping back to our rear view mirror view of ourselves as we have been in the past, and forget that we are really becoming, as we look through our windshield, in the present, toward the future. ***The present is the only place change can take place!***

James 1:22-25 says: "And remember, it is a message to obey, not just to listen to. So don't fool yourselves. For if a person just listens and doesn't obey, he is like a man looking at his face in a mirror; as soon as he walks away, he can't see himself anymore or remember what he looks like. But if anyone keeps looking steadily into God's law for free men, he will not only remember it but he will do what it says, and God will greatly bless him in everything he does." *To obey is to put into action. Intellectually knowing is not the same as believing at the level of action. Healthy change is possible when you put our coaching into action.*

Share with me times you have suffered from Identity Alzheimer's Disorder (IAD). Do you see a pattern of when this disorder affects you? Your Self-Image Thermostat setting will tend to remain fairly constant, even though your behavior and emotions may fluctuate greatly. A fundamental principle of healthy change is that you are drawn toward your comfort zone. To make change the path of least resistance, you need to learn to adjust your setting on your Self-Image Thermostat (explored in the next "Nugget"). Truth does transcend our perceptions of reality-if we allow ourselves to believe that truth (imperfectly) and put our belief into action. This is particularly true in the area of identity. Are you willing to begin living consciously, remembering the truths of your identity?

Write what you notice as you explore the "Nugget" that "truth transcends our perceptions of reality." Keep an ongoing journal where you can share thoughts and feelings about your coaching experience, while working through this book. Share your reactions and what it is like for you as you learn to believe this truth at a feeling-level-of-action.

Nugget: We Become Addicted To The Familiar!

We are naturally drawn to relationships that are similar to the ones in which we learned to survive. The more you are stuck in a survival mode, the more powerful the subliminal attraction you will feel when you enter a relationship with someone that allows you to move into your familiar roles and patterns. This is an important principle of change. **The fact that you hate these roles, and hate the feelings that come from these patterns does not diminish the attraction. The subliminal nature of the draw makes it harder to see the dynamics in action.**

I can't tell you how many times I've sat with a client who reports such a pattern. In A.A. they have a saying: "Insanity is doing the same thing over and over, expecting a different outcome." By this definition, are you insane in areas of your life today? The truth is that the "addiction to the familiar" is a powerful filter that plays a subliminal role in your emotional and addictive problems.

George, who grew up in an unpredictable, explosive, alcoholic environment, and learned to survive by reading the signals from his alcoholic parents, reported a history of failed relationships. His first relationship was with an abusive alcoholic, who made him feel just like his parents had growing up. When he left that partner, he was determined not to get into that trap again, and so put his focus on making sure perspective partners did not drink.

He entered a relationship with a very religious woman who did not drink at all. As time went on, he began to experience the same abuse when he did not do or feel what his partner felt he "should." Her rigid, insecure, demanding style created the same emotional climate that alcohol had produced. **The specific content of each relationship was different, but the underlying patterns and resulting roles were the same.** George was unconsciously drawn to these roles where he knew he could survive. His self-image included these relationship patterns. He desperately wanted to be in a healthy relationship but was afraid to try again.

He came to coaching when he met a woman at church who seemed very different than anyone he had ever been with before. George really liked her, and all his friends thought she was perfect for him. His concern was that "something was missing" in the relationship with Sandra. There was a spark that was not there. He felt he should want her, and was getting very upset with himself. As our coaching unfolded, it was clear that George had several wounded parts of him that were activated when a woman came into his life. He learned to recognize and connect with these wounded kids inside, beginning a loving, supervising relationship with them. He became God's ambassador to his wounded kids inside.

George started attending free CAIRing Grace Groups at his church and began slowly to believe the truth of his identity as a new creation. He began to apply what he was learning in all areas of his life, including his relationship with Sandra. It became clear that Sandra had several significant issues that needed to be addressed before George could go further into a healthy relationship with her. Sandra agreed to work with him using the CAIR Handbook, and began attending a different CAIRing Grace Group herself. They both grew individually and the relationship blossomed. George's healthy adult could fall in love with Sandra's healthy adult, and both learned to take care of the wounded kids inside.

This leads to another important truth in the process: At some time in the past, the dysfunctional patterns that you are now wanting to change were the "best choices you had available to you at the time." It is illogical and unjust to judge past patterns without first appreciating the original context for the decisions you made. When you appreciate this truth, it changes your attitude and approach to these patterns. **Respecting the positive intentions in your dysfunctional patterns makes the change process much easier, reducing the resistance.** By respecting the underlying intentions in a pattern, you can begin to explore other ways to meet the intention without the cost of the current dysfunctional pattern. This greatly reduces the internal experience of resistance in the change process.

As a child in an explosive family, learning to avoid conflict at any cost may have helped you survive safely. In your adult life, this same avoidance pattern may cost you your marriage and feed into a serious problem with depression. The trauma of being abandoned in childhood may lead to a pattern of not letting anyone very close to you in adult life, or a pattern of clinging and being anxious in your adult relationships. **What you may not notice is that you are often the one to abandon yourself. Really feel good about noticing that fact and begin to apply your tools to strengthen your unconditional commitment to "never, never ever** abandon your inner kids for any reason, or fall for the lie that you are defined by your rear view mirror perceptions from the past."

It is very different for an adult to be abandoned than it is for a vulnerable, young child to be left alone. The problem most people have is that when they feel abandoned by someone, they tend to abandon themselves too. They leave their wounded kids inside with no one to take care of them, thus feeding an appropriate feeling of anxiety and despair from the inner kids.

The patterns that may have worked OK for surviving are often dysfunctional for healthy living. As you look at some of the dysfunctional patterns in your life today, can you begin to see how these patterns formed?

This is not an attempt to justify, blame or defend the dysfunctional patterns, but rather helps you approach your change process more respectfully and successfully. Share in your journal reactions to this concept of addiction to the familiar. Do you notice patterns in your life that fit this dynamic? What is it like for you to respect your dysfunctional patterns for helping you survive at a time in your past? What is it like to feel good about noticing painful patterns as the first step in the process of healthy change? Notice any resistance that comes as you look at these patterns differently.

Self-Image Thermostat

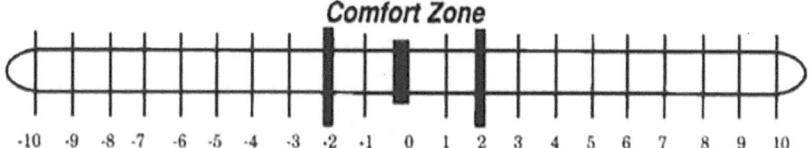

The CAIR Handbook states that "We make predictions about who we are and how we will respond based on our self-image. *As* long as we don't change, there is no problem. But when we begin to make changes in our recovery, the tension that develops between our old self-image, and our new behaviors, is like pulling on a rubber band. Even slight change in our behavior from the usual patterns creates tension if it is beyond a narrow range. This degree of change is called our 'comfort zone.' (Stop and discuss)"

Our comfort zone is often anything but comfortable! It simply means it is familiar and reflects our self-image. The tensions that come from moving out of your comfort zone are the same whether the changes are positive or negative. I will help you learn to change the setting on your self-image thermostat in a way that does not create tension.

Consider something you would like to be able to do more comfortably, or maybe an addictive pattern you would like to reduce. See a movie screen with a vertical line in the middle, separating it into two sides. This tool is called the ***Split-Screen Technique. Make the size and distance of the screen*** *comfortable for you to see accurately, without judging.* Pick a scene you would like to change. Put this picture on the left side of the Split-Screen- your Old Program view. On the right side, let yourself picture how you would like it to be becoming in the present. What would you like to see on the right side of the screen? *Since you can't really change others directly, how do you want to be feeling/behaving differently in this situation?*

Many clients get stuck demanding that the others in the situation be different. Do you fall into this trap? When you have to really think about how you want to be different, are you often blank? Are you able to picture your goals clearly? If not, feel good about noticing that you can't picture it, and begin considering the question now. Jot down elements of how you want to be different in your journal. Keep building on, and fine tuning the right side of your Split-Screen. I will often work directly on building the right side picture, teaching clients how to do this in future situations. Most people don't realize they can learn to do this, once they stop judging and feeling ashamed, and allow themselves to do it imperfectly.

Once you can see the Split-Screen clearly, both the left (Old Program) side and the right (New Program) side of the screen, go into the left side and experience noticing what assumptions and beliefs you are bringing into the situation. In what ways are you being like Little John, scaring yourself into feeling defeated? Feel good about noticing the thoughts and images that are associated with the unwanted feelings as the first step in the change process.

What are you saying to yourself, what are you picturing in your mind on the left side? Come out of the left side, and go into the right side of the Split-Screen.

Begin to notice the perceptions/assumptions/beliefs that are associated with the desired experience on the right side of the screen. Is there more truth/accuracy on the left side or the right? Remember that change is an imperfect process of steps forward and backward. *Believing that your identity is "becoming" is a key to quality living.*

An example of using the Split-Screen in Therapeutic Life Coaching came out of a conversation I had with Les. She had been suffering from a growing number of migraines requiring visits to the E.R. and pain shots. She had suffered from a painful migraine all day, with nausea and vomiting, struggling not to go to the E.R. because of her addiction to pain medications:

Jim: So you say that after barfing your guts up and trying to arrange for someone to get you to the hospital to get a shot, you noticed that you had been in Old Program all day?

Les: Not all day.

Jim: When did you start?

Les: When I was at the NA meeting this morning.

Jim: And how did you shift into Old Program at the NA meeting?

Les: I was thinking about seeing a Neurologist-it's been a long time since I saw one-but I know he's going to say I have Classical Migraines... that's what they say every time. But I, I don't know if that's what was bothering me but.I can't get into the pain management program unless he clears me for it.

Jim: You don't know if it was bothering you?

Les: I feel on hold again. I'm really ready to work hard in the

Core Elements Of Drivers Training pain program and now I have to wait; it's out of my hands.

Jim: What is out of your hands?

Les: Getting into the program. I need the program to deal with my addiction problems. I wanted to do something now, and I felt like if I didn't do it now, I wasn't going to do anything.

Jim: OK, now take a deep breath and really experience what it feels like to believe exactly what you're saying.

Les: (breathing slowly with her eyes closed)

Jim: And really share honestly what you are noticing…without judging what you're seeing, from the right side of your Split-Screen, coming from New Program. Remember to use your tools.

Les: Yeah, feels better. That I can be doing something now, it doesn't have to be at the program or so.?

Jim: You sound like there's a question in your voice.

Les: No.

Jim: No?

Les: I mean I know I can be doing something now as far as staying on the right side of my Split-Screen, staying in New Program but.

Jim: But that's not going to make any real difference because you are not in the pain program. Right? Be honest with yourself about what you are really believing inside, not what you think the right answer would be or what you "should" feel, but rather what you believe at the level of action. Experience the right side of your Split-Screen; breathe into this perspective.

Les: I think it's going to make it easier for me in the pain program. Otherwise I'll be stuck piddling along with little changes

Who's Really Driving Your Bus? now and then, up and down on a roller coaster.

Jim: And how do you feel about the changes you do make?

Les: I felt good about the changes, but I want more and I want it all NOW. I'm so sick and tired of being disappointed. The changes just don't last.

Jim: So you had little itty, bitty embers of change and you expect to put a big oak log on those tinny embers of change and demand a roaring fire. You feel you shouldn't have to use twigs and paper to get the embers started, like the rest of us? Because of all of your past suffering, you feel you should be able to put a log on and forget about it?

Les: I've tried so hard, for so many years…I'm so tired…(tears flowing)

Jim: So the program is going to do it for you? What do you imagine when you think about going to the pain program? What will make this experience different than the many stays in the hospitals up until now? What do you notice?

Les: (sigh) I guess that's what I'm hoping…(deep sigh)

Jim: So really feel that hope…really feel how much of you is hoping that the program can finally give you the peace that you so desperately want… really notice who's believing what inside, from the right side of the screen.

Les: It's my Adult that's feeling it.

Jim: It's your Adult that's feeling what?

Les: Believing that I need the program in order to change this cycle of headaches and need for pain meds.

Jim: I see…so what is it that your Adult is basing that on?

Les: That I haven't been able to do it on my own up untilnow.

Jim: Right…take a deep breath and really feel what you're saying. Feel what it's like to look at it that way: 'Because I haven't done it up until now, it means I can't do it without something different!' Feel how true that statement is… and how you are using this truth to stop your recovery process.

Les: I'm not saying I can't make some changes and be more on the right side. I'm just saying as far as the pain management goes…I need something more… because I, it's not working…(tears flow down her face).

Jim: What's not working?

Les: Staying on the right side of my Split-Screen...even if I'm on the right side.

Jim: Les, can I ask you a question?

Les: What?

Jim: I'm confused...I'm confused because what you told me earlier was that you had spent much of the day in Old Program, on the left side of your Split-Screen...So what does the right side of the Split-Screen have to do with what you have gone through today?

Les: Huh?

Jim: The fact is that you bailed into the left side of the screen and began to feel your worst fears in the Time Machine...the horrible loss of becoming a bag lady because you never would get the help you needed... Close but no prize! THAT'S JUST THE WAY IT IS!

Les: (breathing slowly, focused inside)

Jim: Or did I miss something?

Les: No...(deep sigh)...Well, I know I must be choosing the left side because I'm embarrassed, because that's what happened.

Jim: Hear the tone of your voice... notice what you are feeling as you blame yourself for "choosing" the left side.

Les: Angry with myself, and frustrated because I didn't want to choose Old Program. I hate the left side, why do I keep choosing this way?

Jim: Take a slow, deep breath and notice any other feelings going on...I sense something else, but I'm not sure what it is.

Les: I'm feeling a little defensive because I swear that I'm not choosing the left side, but I keep ending up on that side, up to my eyeballs in Old Program.

Jim: Feel the truth in what you are saying…you are not really choosing Old Program…in fact you are not making any conscious choices in these key areas of your life, if I understand correctly…Not choosing is a choice too… **Not actively choosing New Program has the same impact as choosing Old Program.** When in default mode, on automatic pilot, you will naturally end up on the left side of the Split-Screen. Notice what you are feeling.

Les: I never looked at it that way…it's true that I'm not choosing New Program very much (whine in her voice); I forget, and before I know it I'm in the middle of it.

Jim: Feel good about noticing the difference between blaming yourself for being in Old Program and taking responsibility as chooser in your life today. Take a deep breath as you feel the difference. **You can spend your time hating yourself for where you are starting, or you can begin relaxing into the right side of the Split-Screen and begin noticing what happens as you apply New Program in the present.** It's good to have a choice!

Les: I was starting to do that…and I slipped back on the left side… feeling embarrassed that after all these years.

Jim: So, what let you know you were on the left side was the fact that you were feeling embarrassed?

Les: Yeah.

Jim: Good for you! You are so right! Notice what it's like to see that and feel good about seeing it accurately. Feel what you notice on the right side.

Les: Yeah.?

Jim: You sound real hesitant.

Les: No, I feel good about seeing it.

Jim: It doesn't sound that way in your voice, so I'm confused…take a deep breath and notice deeply.

Les: (sigh). I guess I'm afraid to hope for this "right side" and "left side" business.

Jim: Tell me more.

Les: Because I'm afraid it won't work…that it will turn out to just be something else that didn't work…for me anyway.

Jim: Something else that didn't work?

Les: That I couldn't use, that I couldn't do.

Jim: Like what other things?

Les: I mean something else that I…couldn't sustain for very long.

Jim: What are other examples?

Les: Other New Program stuff…anything.

Jim: So somehow you were afraid that this "left/right sided Split-Screen" tool would disappoint you like everything else in New Program has?

Les: No! I don't feel New Program has disappointed me; I just haven't been able to get it or something.

Jim: Get it? I don't understand being able to get it. What does that mean?

Les: Well…like we've talked about, that I have a learning disability around that or something. And I'm not just attributing it to that, I'm just saying that's what I was afraid to hope.

Jim: You were afraid to hope because of your learning disability, and your learning disability is that you would have to work a lot harder than some people would to remember to relax into the right side of your Split-Screen?

Les: Yeah, I keep trying so hard and it doesn't work.

Jim: When you try so hard, White Knuckle Sobriety doesn't work for you?

Les: I can't seem to do it. It works for a little while, but it just goes back to the same.

Jim: That it's harder for you than it is for many people to pay attention in a loving, caring way to what's going on inside you. as you go through your day-day in and day out, 24/7? Noticing what your girls inside are feeling and what support they need from you at any given moment?

Les: Yeah.

Jim: That whenever you look on the right side of your Split-Screen all you see is blank…because you can't picture yourself perfectly in New Program?

Les: (deep sigh)

Jim: What was that sigh saying?

Les: That I was feeling that I couldn't picture myself perfectly, I can't do it perfectly…And I'm not saying that you are saying that…It's my expectation, I can't blame anyone else.

Jim: So you have expected something of yourself that makes it impossible to succeed. It's your expectation, but because that expectation is at the level of your core beliefs, you appropriately feel defeat and a sense of hopelessness… that there is no chance for anything good to happen, and therefore why hope? The Black and White Filter demands all or nothing!

Les: No, I don't mean there is no chance for anything good to happen… (heavy sigh)

Jim: But nothing significant that would be transforming, allowing you to really be OK?

Les: Yeah. I can make little bits of changes from time to time, but there's no use getting my hopes up that I could really be a happy, healthy person who feels really good about herself and is excited about growth like you experience so much of the time, and the adventure of day-to-day application of New Program into whatever is going on in your life at that time…(deep sigh)… I really want to feel that.

Jim: You want to feel what? Notice which side of your Split-Screen you are on right now.

Les: O.K., I'm back on the right side (deep sigh). I want the day-to-day life of living New Program.

Jim: And what stops you Les?

Les: I don't think that it's just that I don't practice it enough; I think there is more to it than that.

Jim: That's probably true…so take a gentle look inside, from the right side of the screen…to see and hear and feel what that might be.

Les: I'm thinking… I don't, I don't see anything else…I went inside and didn't see anything.(heavy sigh) It's the belief that somehow I don't deserve to have good things happen to me.

Jim: Great! Feel good about noticing this ticking time bomb, and how it was that you were not aware of it ticking until just now? Noticing without judging on the right side…good work, Les.

Les: I don't understand how I could have been carrying that belief without noticing it. When I stop and experience the belief that, "I don't deserve to be happy and have good things happen to me," I begin to feel hurt and resentful. I wonder why I don't deserve these good things? My 12-year-old has the proof of not being good enough to be adopted…It seems that every time something good happens, there is something bad that takes away the good feelings.

Jim: You are so familiar with this pattern that you give up like Little John fighting Robin Hood. Take a moment to connect with your 12-year-old and comfort her as you share her pain of not being adopted, and let her know that you have adopted her-that she is your little girl and you are proud that she is part of your family. Feel what it's like to really mean this commitment to her. Notice her reactions to what you are sharing with her from the right side.

Les: She so badly wants to believe me, but she is afraid to trust me.

Jim: Shows that she is a smart little thing! You have not shown her much to build trust with you up until now. Feel what it's like to appreciate her honesty, and let her know that she can watch your actions and decide for herself when she is ready to let down her wall. Your adoption of her is solid whether or not she needs to keep her wall up at any given moment. Breathe slowly and deeply as you share this with her deeply.

Les: (tears flowing down her face) She is so scared, but so desperate that she is allowing me to hold and comfort her. I feel so good right now…I can feel myself on the right side.

Jim: Share the truth with her that you aren't very good at parenting her yet (both laugh), but you are committed to practicing. Let her know that any time you forget to be there for her, she is free to get your attention. Share with her from the right side of your Split-Screen.

Les: I just seem to get on the left side whenever I see things that I feel bad about. It gets so frustrating, over and over.

Jim: Everything you notice is a chance to celebrate on the right side, to learn from it and grow. Feel the hunger to learn, feel the hunger to make contact with those little girls inside who are so badly bruised and abused. Connect with them from the right side.

What did you notice as you went through my conversation with Les? Did it help you understand better how to apply the Split-Screen Technique in problem areas? Does this help you appreciate the "Addiction To The Familiar Nugget"? What feelings came up as you read the dialogue? How would you like to be able to use this technique in your recovery?

Take the time to experience believing in your ability to see more accurately while in difficult life situations. I usually have the client picture on the right side what they have been able to do at least once, at least a little, and own the truth of that experience. It can be something they have seen someone else do, and feel they can do too. I also help them build new images of themselves for the right side of the screen. You may find that helpful.

Experience being in the situation on the right side of your Split-Screen, as if it were happening right now (positive use of the Time Machine). Notice what it is like to believe your right side experience. As you begin owning it, you can move the setting of your Self-Image Thermostat. You can start to clean your perceptual filters toward 20/20 vision, noticing "Nuggets" in the situation. You can learn to apply New Program imperfectly. Focus deeply so your changes can be experienced at the level of your core self-image.

Continue to respectfully notice your resistances to believing yourself on the right side of the screen. Experiencing your resistances helps you stay in healthy relationship with your kids inside, and with your Higher Power, because most of your resistance will come from one or the other. Practice this Split-Screen exercise to help move your comfort zone in a healthy direction with your **Self-Image Thermostat.** There will be more about the **Self-Image Thermostat** later in the book.

The "Success Trap" is a common pattern of sabotage feeding your Addiction To The Familiar. When you begin to make positive changes in your life, there is a natural tension between your new experiences and your "normal" Old Program self-image. If you do not consciously and deliberately change your self-image setting to accommodate these new changes, the tension will grow increasingly uncomfortable. Since you do not expect positive changes to create tension, you will tend to look around for some other explanation for your growing discomfort. You will probably find an explanation that will allow you to slip back into your familiar "comfort zone" of Old Program. The feeling of relief that comes from the reduced tension of moving back into your comfort zone reinforces the move.

Many clients develop a "Not" model for their life. If they hated their life growing up, they will try very hard not to be like their parent, not be with someone like their parent. They would try not to be in the kind of relationship they hated while growing up. The problem with this "Not" model is that the unconscious mind does not register negatives. Imagine playing golf on a difficult course. As you look down the fairway you see a sand trap to your left. You keep reminding yourself not to hit it into the trap. Where do you think your ball will end up? In the sand!

Each time you come to that hole, you try even harder not to hit it into the sand. As long as you remain blind to underlying truth, your insanity will continue and the ball is even more likely to end up in the sand. Together we can learn to do things differently by bringing truth into your situations. You can learn to see in your mind the ball going straight and long down the fairway, rather than trying hard not to hit it into the trap.

I often ask my clients to try the following exercise: "For the next five minutes I want you to try as hard as you can not to think of the color purple." Your recovery depends on you not thinking of purple! Try with everything you have not to think of purple. Don't think of the color purple! What do you notice? When I have tried this exercise in groups of 250-300 people, there would usually be a few who were able to succeed by not following the instructions. If you follow the instructions exactly, you cannot succeed, and the harder you try, the more intensely the color purple floods your mind.

The only way to succeed is to cheat by thinking of another color instead, such as green or blue. The moment you try not to think of something, your mind has to bring up that thing to make sure you aren't thinking of it. It is one of the Fundamental Principles of Healthy Change. As you think of the things you want to change in your life, I want you to put these things in a positive form. Being calm and relaxed is not the same goal as trying not to be so anxious. Learning to feel calmer in tense situations is not the same goal as trying not to get so mad. Take a few slow, deep breaths and really experience this truth at your core level of feeling. Notice any resistance, feeling good about noticing your resistance, as you begin relaxing into focusing on positive perceptions rather than the "not." This will be an ongoing process of noticing. Practice, practice, practice!

It is important to remember that there was a time when the addictive behavior created a desired effect. ***The addicted person came to believe that the addictive behavior was the only way to achieve the desired result, and that belief often becomes unconscious. The addictive pattern becomes part of identity, of self-image. The*** Alcoholics Anonymous Big Book ***has a great example with the addicted jay-walker:*** "Our behavior is as absurd and incomprehensible, with respect to the first drink, as that of an individual with a passion, say, for jay-walking. He gets a thrill out of skipping in front of fast-moving vehicles. He enjoys himself for a few years in spite of friendly warnings. Up to this point you would label him as a foolish chap having queer ideas of fun. Luck then deserts him, and he is slightly injured several times in succession. You would expect him, if he were normal, to cut it out. Presently he is hit again, and this time has a fractured skull. Within a week after leaving the hospital a fast-moving trolley car breaks his arm. He tells you he has decided to stop jaywalking for good, but in a few weeks he breaks both legs."

"On through the years this conduct continues, accompanied by his continual promises to be careful or to keep off the streets altogether. Finally, he can no longer work, his wife gets a divorce and he is held up to ridicule. He tries every known means to get the jaywalking idea out of his head. He shuts himself up in an asylum, hoping to mend his ways. But the day he comes out he races in front of a fire engine, which breaks his back. Such a man would be crazy, wouldn't he? (p. 37-38)"

As strange as our jaywalker may sound to you, there may be areas of your life that make the same kind of sense. How has your "addiction to the familiar" affected your life up until now? Jot down in your journal your reactions to believing that you are drawn toward familiar dynamics, whether you want them or not.

Realize that these dysfunctional patterns were once the best choices you had available for survival; and you are free today to learn more healthy choices to replace the familiar. What is it like to recognize how your self-image defines your reactions, and that you can begin to change your self-image using the Split-Screen technique? What is it like to begin changing your "not" model into positive goals?

Notice the initial positive goals in your addictive patterns that you now want to change. Respecting these positive goals, and exploring other ways to meet them, can help in making changes in your addictive and emotional patterns. You are not trapped by the Addiction To The Familiar pattern. Choosing to live consciously, applying the tools and principles of New Program in your daily life, allows you to make profound, deep changes in your life today. Share your reactions with me in your journal as you reflect deeply on the Addiction To The Familiar.

Nugget: Change Is Possible In The Present!

In this book I am taking you through the same process that I have successfully shared with countless clients over the past 40+ years. I am sharing "Nuggets" from my understanding of God's Plan for change, and how these "Nuggets" can help you make meaningful changes in your own life today. We will continue to examine many commonly held beliefs and assumptions that may be affecting your life, and your ability to really exercise choice in your life, up until now.

One of the most important truths that you need to face is: **Change is possible for you!** Notice what reactions come up inside as you allow yourself to experience this truth at a feeling level. Does it feel familiar and normal to be noticing your emotional reactions? If this is not familiar for you, begin practicing now.

Start by taking several slow, deep breaths as you experience believing the truth that change is possible for you in the present. Notice what thoughts and images come with the feelings. Notice without judging. *If you try to continue in the book without building this perceptual muscle of noticing, you will severely limit what you are able to gain!*

One of the common mistakes you can make is ignoring the feeling reactions you can have as you experience believing truth. Thinking something is true, is not the same as experiencing believing it at the level of identity. Your resistance to experiencing truth at a feeling level is an important source of helpful information for change. *You may have tried very hard to make changes in your life, with little or no real success. What you may not be aware of is that how you approach your change process determines your chances of success.*

For example, when you try to hide all the unacceptable aspects of yourself from the outside world, you create a natural source of anxiety, and make it impossible for you to really believe what you receive from others. Since they are responding to your mask, you cannot know how they would feel about you if they really saw you accurately. *Your choice to hide the rejected parts of yourself actually feeds anxiety, depression, and a growing sense of insecurity and self-doubt. Is that your goal?* The Fundamental Principles of Healthy Change will work against you, and the chances are high that, in frustration, you will finally give up trying to change.

The truth is that no matter who or how you are, some people will like you, some people won't like you, and most will be too self-absorbed to really notice one way or the other. What struck me, and made a profound impact on my own recovery, was realizing that when I was wearing masks, the people who seemed to like me were often people I didn't particularly care for, and I couldn't believe the reactions of the people whom I liked, because I didn't know how they would react to me without my masks. This vicious circle is a common trap for Adult Children.

Since I've chosen to live without masks, there are some people who really don't like me, and to be honest, I don't care for most of them either. Now, the people who seem to like me are seeing the real me, and I can believe their caring. *I can choose how much of me I want to share at a given moment, which is so different from wearing a mask.*

The quality of my personal relationships has grown as I have learned to tolerate being myself with others. It required me being in ongoing contact with my kids inside, particularly at first-it gets easier over time, with practice. It is the unconditional love and faith that I receive from my loving Big Brother Jesus that allows my unconditional love for my kids inside.

Grace is not about following rules; it is about our free, unearned relationship with God. I see Jesus as being a liberal fundamentalist. He didn't try to be perfect, He was in perfect relationship with His Father, and everything came from that relationship. He is the model for my "becoming." No matter what happens to anyone in my world, including me, I believe in His unconditional love.

Somehow knowing that I can always count on these foundational relationships makes it possible for me to live without masks. Share with me in your journal what you are feeling as you read about this concept of Grace and transparency. Do you recognize this cycle of wearing masks and having difficulty trusting how others feel about you in your life? Really take the time to deeply experience your reactions to this pattern.

Another common trap is generating isometric tension from demanding changes in your life. *When you try to force positive changes in your life, you create an equal and opposite resistance to making these changes. There is a healthy resistance to conditional demands.* In this case, the harder you try, the greater the resistance, until you finally collapse in despair, with proof that change is impossible. Throughout the book, we will be exploring many Perceptual Filters from the perspective of the Fundamental Principles of Healthy Change. *Filters have a direct impact on how much change is possible in your life.*

As you look back over your life, notice different times when you were trying to make changes. Were you successful in making the desired changes? How would you approach the change process in those different examples? Really take the time to notice each example. In coaching, I spend a lot of time walking through examples with my clients, not the content but the underlying presuppositions affecting the example. Together, we would begin looking at the different assumptions that were being made in each example. You and I need to do the same thing, for you to learn to live more consciously, aware of the assumptions you bring into situations.

Do you notice yourself expecting others to read your mind? If something is bothering you, do you try to ignore it until the pressure builds to such an extent that you finally explode at the other person? Do you use a judgmental flashlight, shining brightly at the other person without seeing yourself too, or do you shine your flashlight in your own face, blinding yourself to the other person's part in the situation?

New Program illuminates with a nonjudgmental lantern rather than a flashlight. A lantern gives light 360 degrees, allowing you to see yourself and others at the same time, making it possible to see how the interaction between the two of you helps create the current situation. The question you may be having right now is, "How can I be sure that I am doing the best possible for healthy changes?" *Take a moment to reflect deeply into the Prayer of Serenity, noticing your different reactions to it.*

The Prayer of Serenity
Lord, Grant me the Serenity to change what I can change,
The freedom to release to You what I can't change,
And give me a growing wisdom to know the difference.

I encourage you to apply the Prayer of Serenity to those patterns you would like to change in your life today. The truth is that you cannot do more than apply this prayer in the present, but you can do less by trying to do more. Really reflect on these words of truth. This is a key focus in coaching sessions. Share with me your experiences of applying this prayer in your recovery. Write about any resistances that you notice. Use these feelings of resistance to connect with wounded parts of yourself.

Write what you notice as you explore the truth that "change is possible in the present." Share with me your thoughts and feelings about your reactions, assumptions, and what it is like for you as you learn to believe this truth personally. Explore any resistance to believing this truth experientially.

What is not possible is to change perfectly. *Small steps forward, with steps backward along the way, is the natural process of change; accepting that it will feel awkward and unnatural at first, and that it will become more natural with practice, practice, and more practice.* The key is taking the steps and actions you can make at any given moment in the journey. *Be honest with yourself, without judging what you notice.* Allow your Higher Power to nurture you along the path, as you nurture your wounded kids inside, and imperfectly walk your walk in the present with your coach walking along with you.

You can pray to your Higher Power to want to change an area of your life that you know is not healthy, even though you currently don't want to change it. *In many areas of my life that have changed over the years of my recovery, I started with an attitude of resisting the change, and praying to want to want to want to change. What was important was that I accepted where I was starting, and believed that He would help me make the changes I was currently resisting.*

He is with me when I'm resisting healthy change just like when I am allowing Him to lead. His loving me doesn't change; it is constant and unchanging. He continues to shine a gentle lantern in my life so I can see more accurately where I am becoming, and learn more deeply from what has been. His loving Spirit helps draw me into healthy change, as I relax into becoming as a new creation in Him. His Grace can transform a painful, anxiety-producing ordeal of survival into an exciting, meaningful adventure of living. You can have fun on your adventure of shifting from survival to living!

Nugget: Personal Change Is An Active Participation Process!

You need to consider how active you are willing to be in the process of your growth and change. Most people do not even consider this question, and do not see this as a choice. Allow yourself to stop for a moment and really reflect on the question of how active you truly believe yourself to be in making changes in areas of your life that you choose. ***Without judging what you notice, accept that this is where you are starting, and not "how you are." Remember that healthy change is only possible in the present, and only when you are an active participant in the process.*** The first printed words in the CAIR Handbook are: ***"Recovery is a Participation Sport"*** and those words are there for a reason. I have spent many hours (at significant cost to the client!) sharing the same "Nuggets" I am sharing with you in this book.

The truth is that the only way change is going to take place in your life is for you to believe that you are an active participant in the change process and to take action congruent with that belief. No amount of money spent in therapy or coaching will change this truth. This means you need to be "Walking your talk," imperfectly, as you grow. I can promise that you will often feel clumsy and awkward practicing what you learn in this book. So what? It is normal and healthy to feel clumsy and awkward as you are learning to perceive differently, consciously choosing to notice the filters in your perceptions with an attitude of "No-Fault Learning."

The "Nuggets" in this book are truths that have a profound impact on your ability to make changes in your life. I will share more in the book later about the importance of identity-your Self-Image Thermostat. You can learn how to begin making changes in the setting of your Self-Image Thermostat, to help in your growing process. Take a moment now to consider your perceptions of how active you are willing to be in order to succeed in making healthy changes in your life. ***Your sense of identity, the person you believe yourself to be, needs to accept that you are the ultimate chooser in your life. This is true whether you believe it or not.***

The question is how much influence would you like to have on your life? If you don't care about having significant impact on your life, I would suggest you put this book down now, because you are wasting your time. If you want to have as much impact on your life as you can, choose to believe that you are an active part of your recovery. ***This truth is believed as all truths are believed-a layer at a time.*** Notice the resistance you feel to this truth. Allow yourself to take the time to listen respectfully to the messages coming from your resistance. Allow your resistance to help you connect with wounded parts of yourself that need your loving supervision.

You live in a very fractured, compartmentalized world with more demands on your time and energy than you could possible give. Many of my clients get so caught up in the business of their lives that they have difficulty "finding" time to do their homework. Does this sound familiar to you? The truth is that there is no extra time to "find." ***I'm telling you what I tell all my clients, if you want to make healthy changes in your life you need to make the difficult decisions regarding making time to reflect and focus on learning New Program and applying it imperfectly in your daily life.***

Experiencing this book takes time and thought. Practicing what you are learning does not have to take more time, and can actually help you gain more time. What it does require is living consciously, intentionally looking for opportunities to practice experiencing yourself as "becoming" in difficult situations. ***Instead of looking for time to practice your homework, allow whatever you are doing at the moment to be practice. Those who approach change in this way have a very high success rate at reaching their goals because they choose to live their learning in the present.*** What do you choose?

Write what you notice as you explore the "Nugget" that "personal change is an active participation process." Share in your journal thoughts and feelings about your reactions, assumptions, and resistances to believing yourself to be an active participant in your recovery. What it is like for you as you learn to believe and apply this truth?

Nugget: Freedom Is The Willingness To Accept The Consequences Of Your Choices!

We live in a society that prizes freedom. At the same time we live in a society that is obsessed with finding out whose "fault" things are, who should be blamed for any given event. This emphasis on blame has lead to a defensive reflex of needing to justify why you couldn't help what you did, or that what you did was really the fault of someone or something else. ***This fear of being blamed, and needing to avoid and defend has created a significant paradox that leads to anxiety and prevents learning and growth.***

The paradox is that as long as you are defending against the consequences of your choices, you are not free to learn from them and make healthy changes in the present. ***The moment you accept the consequences of your choices, you are free to choose whatever you want.*** You cannot choose not to have done and experienced what you have up to this moment I You can choose what you will learn from this, what meaning and conclusions you will make about yourself and others. ***Notice your reactions to this truth.***

The truth is that the more you use energy hating yourself and others for what has happened up until now, the less energy you have for starting where you are starting at this moment. In the same way, if you are consumed by fears of future consequences you are robbing yourself of making healthy changes in the present. You can't do both at the same time. Share your reactions toward this truth with me in your journal. This is a difficult one for most of my clients to accept and embrace. It seems counterintuitive to most people; what are your reactions? Appreciate your resistances, learning deeply what they are saying.

Have you ever had the experience of accepting your consequences freely, with grateful humility and the desire to learn and grow from an unwanted experience? What did you notice? Powerful Vulnerability is the result of caring more about learning and growing than being right. When you shift your focus and goal toward growing, without judging, you greatly increase your ability to choose health in the present. Powerful vulnerability greatly increases your healthy power in your personal relationships.

When I accepted myself in the present, including the tantrums by ten-year-old Jimmy inside that I shared in Chapter Three, I became free to begin changing this recurrent pattern. That doesn't mean that I expect to never have another tantrum. Progress includes steps backwards with grace. Most clients start out the coaching process judging and hating themselves for the unwanted patterns that bring them to coaching. The first dozen times I suggest they "feel good about noticing" some dysfunctional pattern, they look at me like I'm crazy: "How can I possibly feel good about the fact that I have destroyed any chance of getting my wife back and some other guy will be raising my kids, in my house?"

I respond, "I'm not asking you to feel good about your starting point. I'm asking you to feel good about noticing what you can learn in your starting point, and seeing this noticing as an important step in beginning the change process." Don't expect yourself to get this truth immediately or perfectly, feel good about each step forward in your believing of this "Nugget" and learning from each step backward. Share this learning process with me in your journal. This is what makes core change possible. I believe God's Plan of Grace captures this truth perfectly and allows us real freedom to grow. Can you give yourself the freedom to grow?

Jerry came to coaching when his depression and stress threatened to cost him both his job and his marriage. He had met Janie in college and was drawn to her strength and her sense of direction in her life. When Janie became pregnant she dropped out of school and they were married. Tensions began to build over the years as Jerry felt a growing resentment for Janie's controlling ways. Their social life was directed by Janie, and any time Jerry wasn't working, she had something for him to do. He was afraid of conflict-had been since childhood. He did love Janie, and he loved his two boys, but he felt that she made it impossible for him to really connect with them.

His resentment and anger colored everything. He would hide out at work, spending longer hours away from the family. Janie would nag at Jerry for being gone all the time, and would constantly tell him all the things he was not doing for his sons. This cycle became a repetitive pattern in the marriage, causing Jerry to feel overwhelming resentment when thinking about going home.

At first Jerry was so flooded with resentment that he felt there was no hope for his marriage. He was afraid that if he ever started letting out the feelings he was holding inside, Janie would not be able to handle it and the relationship would be over. He was also afraid that she would argue with him about his feelings and convince him that he was wrong to feel this way. Just thinking that would make him boil. We spent the first two sessions helping him safely release and begin looking at all the feelings he was storing inside. He learned to use the lantern of grace rather than the judgmental flashlight both Janie and he normally used.

He began to realize that he had not been honest with Janie all along about his feelings and what he wanted in the relationship. The honest regret that he began to feel as he looked through the lantern allowed his resentment to soften. He began going to a CAIR Group and working with the CAIR Handbook to help him recognize any distorted filters that were robbing him of healthy choices.

He would listen to the Journey Podcasts with Janie, stopping and sharing frequently - www.CAIRforYou.com. This was a safe way to begin opening up a sharing process between them. The Podcasts are packed with "Nuggets" that helped them look at things differently, and create a gentle, loving tone for sharing. I role-played with Jerry how he would begin to let Janie know what he had learned. I helped him experience a model of loving honesty, with a lantern of grace. When he was ready to take the big step, he asked her to join him in his next coaching session.

Janie came to the meeting armed for bear. She assumed Jerry was going to tell her that the marriage was over and it was all her fault. We had practiced this moment several times and Jerry was able to respond in New Program rather than react in Old Program. He said, "Janie, I'm realizing that I have not been honest with either of us. I have let you control our relationship, and my life, and never really shared what I was feeling about it. I want to be honest now with you, not to blame either of us, but to work together to create a healthy relationship we can both feel good about."

After she displayed several defensive flashlight responses, I helped Janie hold up a lantern too, and begin to notice how the old relationship felt to her. She admitted that she often felt resentful too, feeling forced to make all the decisions and plans, making sure everything got done. She shared how lonely she felt in the marriage, and how scared she was that Jerry would fall in love with someone else and leave her like her dad had done when she was nine. Her defensive anger melted into tears of relief as she learned to comfort and supervise her little nine-year-old inside, who was feeling so strained by the years of pressure, trying to keep Jerry from leaving also. She had believed she must be perfect to keep the abandonment from happening again. Janie learned to create a healing relationship with little Janie, removing her from the driver's seat.

Both Jerry and Janie learned to accept the consequences of their choices up until now, and began working together, sharing more honestly with each other than at any time in their 15 + year marriage. Both chose to learn from the past, rather than use their Time Machine to keep reliving the painful scenes. Both began to use the Reaction Compass (see, "I Am Chooser In

My Life") to recognize when Old Program filters were interfering with their healthy relationship, and applying New Program tools and concepts to the situation.

They both learned to be more respectfully honest with each other, and to accept the consequences of their previous choices as a starting point for learning. Choosing to accept the consequences of their previous mistakes, rather than judging which leads to defending or blaming, allowed them the freedom to turn their marriage around. I would see them from time to time to help through rough spots. They both went to CAIR Groups to continue practicing New Program as a way of life.

My Identity

"Allow me to see myself and others
through Your eyes,
And respond to what I see
in Your nature."
Oh Lord, as I have prayed that
these last few years,
I sense that You are answering
that prayer.
I catch glimpses of myself as one held
very dear in Your eyes,
And I am amazed by Your grace;
I am who You see.
I can let go of the old self and see
accurately—though imperfectly—the real me. The past:
the pain, perfectionism, depression are not who I am.
By Your grace, I am learning to see
my true identity as new creation in Christ. And as
I learn to see others more accurately I can let go of
expectations, And allow Your grace to flow
through me to them.
Little by little this is coming to pass,
I am so grateful, Lord.
As I find my home in You,
I thank You that I am part of Your Family.

Roberta K.

THE POWER OF IDENTITY IN DRIVERS TRAINING

Can you remember getting behind the steering wheel of a car for the first time? Do you notice any difference in your identity as a driver between the first attempt at driving and driving today? I remember my first time. It was in the alley behind my house. It was a little Morris Minor pickup with standard transmission-A CLUTCH! I must have killed the engine a hundred times as I hopped down the alley, popping the clutch, grinding the gears, feeling that I could never become a driver; it was impossible. If someone had told me at that moment that I would get to a place in my identity as driver that I could adjust the side mirrors, tune the radio, and steer with my knee as I eat a sandwich, all as I'm carrying on a conversation with my passenger, I would have told them they were crazy.

My identity as driver formed through a process of practice, practice and more practice. I looked forward to opportunities to practice when I was first learning to drive. I wanted to be a driver; I wanted that identity. That is how I feel now about my ongoing adventure into becoming. I love my identity as becoming, and recognizing that what I choose really does make a significant difference in how I experience my life.

We will be exploring four "Nuggets of Wisdom" related to identity that impact Fundamental Principles of Healthy Change in your recovery: "I Am Not My Story, And My Story Affects Where I Am Starting Today!"

"Identity Leads To Perceptions!" "I Am Chooser In My Life!" and "There Is An Economy In The Giving Process!" Allow yourself to chew on these "Nuggets of Wisdom" at an experiential level of action rather than intellectually holding them at a distance. This makes change the path of least resistance.

I strongly encourage my clients to do active homework between coaching sessions. *Take the time to practice believing these truths in your daily life.*

It doesn't take any extra time, but it does require you to live consciously in the present, noticing with your lantern of No-Fault learning. See yourself and others imperfectly through the healthy "Nuggets" in this chapter, knowing that the more you practice, the deeper these healthy truths can bring the Fundamental Principles of Healthy Change into your recovery.

Nugget: I Am Not My Story, And My Story Affects Where I Am Starting Today!

As we say in the Introduction that is read at the beginning of each CAIRing Grace Group meeting, *"We are not defined by our story, and our story affects where we are starting today. We can remember that our true identity is not determined by how we are doing or what we are feeling at a given moment"* How do you define who you are, and how do you determine your identity? Is it based on your "rear view mirror" of all the things that have happened up until now in your life, or is it based on your "windshield" of becoming in the present? Which direction are you looking as you drive your bus today-rear view mirror or windshield?

This is a common trap that robs people of the ability to make changes in their lives. The truth is that your past does effect where you are starting in the present, but it does not need to define who you are, or who you can be becoming today. *This book is about learning to see yourself through your windshield.*

If you were to consider your life a movie, what words would you use to give a brief summary of the movie? As you take the long view of your life, do you begin to see patterns where the story is the same, and the content/ players are different? The same things seem to keep happening again and again, even though you hate the patterns? Begin to allow yourself to feel good about noticing any unwanted patterns. Are these patterns happening in the present? How do you feel about yourself as the star of your movie? Who are the primary supporting actors and what are the key pivotal scenes in your movie?

As the scenes unfold, make a list of any dysfunctional patterns that you notice and add to the list as you progress through the book. ***Remember that you are not your patterns, and your patterns affect your ability to exercise choice in the present.*** It can be such a relief to share what you are noticing with me in your journal. Clients look forward to sharing in our sessions. As you learn more about how I would respond, add this dimension to your journaling, building a dialogue that helps to develop your inner coach to support your recovery.

Clients often feel they have no hope because of terrible experiences growing up. They feel shame or deep resentment for their pain. They tend to live their pain over and over in their Time Machines. Their past draws them away from the present, and makes them afraid about the future. They continue to keep repeating the same patterns in the present that they are experiencing internally in their Time Machines. Or they block off all their feelings in order to avoid the pain.

The problem is that blocking off your feelings creates its own pain. ***Blocking creates a sense of "nothingness" that feeds anxiety and depression.*** Imagine a structure with ten foot walls all the way around, to keep the pain out. Imagine yourself inside those walls, safe and alone, completely alone. What do you notice? The truth is that you can learn to accept past pain and experience it differently in the present-no matter what kinds of wounds you may have experienced in the past. You can learn to have choices about your feelings as a result of living consciously, relaxing into New Program perceptions and perspectives. Practice, Practice, Practice.

This is a picture of my dad when he was eight years old. It was the first time he had been with his four brothers and father since he was four. He remembered this picture taking experience his whole life. He was given a suit to wear for the picture, and he had the chance to be with his family. Between four and eight he lived with a variety of different families, sometimes with another family member and at other times alone.

He died over 20 years ago at the age of 87. He lived his last few years with my brother and my brother's family. Prior to that he lived 35 years in a run down trailer park in a rough area of town.

Everyone in the park thought he was on welfare and knew him as grandpa Pete. They loved to visit with him.

His story has more objective trauma than most clients I have seen over the years. He was the next to youngest of five brothers, whose mother died when he was four. He grew up in abject poverty in the rural Ozarks of Arkansas. Some of the time he lived with his father; at other times he would live with whichever stranger would take him in. He was expected to work for his keep from the beginning. When I learned more about his story, I could understand why I felt older than my dad when I was four years old, and why he couldn't be the kind of father I needed him to be. He had no support to grow emotionally beyond that wounded little boy.

I did not know his background until in my 40's, when I began to have breakfast at McDonald's most Saturdays with him. Although it was difficult to "find" the time to meet with him in my busy schedule, I felt led to get to know the man who was my father. It took several years of these breakfasts before he began to share more about his life growing up.

As he got older he lived his life in very rigid habits, writing everything that happened in his day so he would be able to remember, and that helped give him a sense of structure. He would not go to another restaurant, or even another McDonald's. If I showed up on any day other than Saturday, he would say, "Why are you here? It's not Saturday." He would not go out to eat if it was not the planned day.

His ruts allowed him to live independently into his 80's. As I learned more about his story, I became amazed that he was as good a father as he ended up being. In spite of all the difficulties in his life, he was never bitter or resentful about his past. One of the most important gifts he gave me was the realization that **expectations create bitterness, not the experiences themselves.** My dad had many emotional scars from his toxic life growing up, but he never lived in the past, or recounted war stories with resentment and bitterness. He had no expectation that the world should have given him a different hand. He never asked, "Why me?"

When he was nine he was living with a farm family in Arkansas. He told me about the time he was riding along a country road in the back of the farmer's pickup when the farmer stopped to talk to another farmer going the other way. The farmer he was with commented that he liked the dog that the other farmer had in the back of his pickup. The other farmer asked if he wanted to trade for the boy, and my dad was told to get out of the truck he was in, and get into the other farmer's pickup. The story was told with no bitterness or self-pity.

He would wet the bed and get a beating most mornings when the bed was wet. He shared that when he was 11 he was living with his dad again and they had to sleep in barns. He liked the fact that the beatings stopped when he got to live with his dad. As he was telling me about sitting with his dad, eating watered down potato soup, and still feeling hungry when the food was gone, I asked him what he was experiencing at that time. He said, "I wish I had some more soup" with no resentment in his voice.

When he was 17 he was living on his own, working on a farm in Nebraska when a bull broke his back. When he got out of the hospital, he went back to work for the same farmer, who made him use a short handled shovel. This caused him to walk stooped over for the rest of his life.

Dad decided that education was important. He had not gotten much education moving around from house to house and then migrating with his father, who had a third grade education. He decided to put himself through high school. He graduated at age 21, living on practically nothing, constantly hungry and dirty. I can't imagine the strength of character he must have had to achieve graduation.

At the time I was born my mom, dad, and sister Bette lived in a small trailer with no insulation, which was moved frequently to new areas as he sold subscriptions to the Nebraska Farmer. Soon after I was born we moved out to California so he could sell the California Farmer. There wasn't a future in this, so he traded our trailer for a down payment on a house and started selling real estate in Modesto. **He never saw himself as a victim, or felt the world owed him anything. Life simply was what it was for him, and he lived his life without looking back, fully in the present.**

He seemed to naturally see the positive in people and situations. Growing up with him was difficult because his wounded little boy would feel overwhelmed with how to be a father, so he put most of his time into working (something he knew how to do). He seemed to constantly be working, and frequently reminded me how lucky I was to have a home. He would drive through the poorest areas of town and ask me how I could possibly want more of an allowance when these people didn't have enough to eat. I know now he loved me, but his woundedness never let him give me the blessing when I was a child.

I was always trying to be good enough to get his praise, and his little boy couldn't give it to me. I do remember him coaching me in baseball when I was six or seven. The overwhelming emotional memory was feeling ashamed because the other kids, and even many of the parents, laughed at him for not having any skills in baseball. He was coaching because he believed that is what loving dads do. Years later he confessed that he hated the coaching, but wanted to help me be able to play. I cried when he shared that with me, feeling flooded with love and a core shift of perceptions of my dad.

Recovery is not about blame; it is about change in the present. In Therapeutic Life Coaching I help people appreciate and respect the wounds that are filtering their choices in the present. The content related to my own wounded kids is not dramatic, but the effects have had a profound impact on my life. It is important for you to respect wounds that you find on your journey whatever they may be, bringing loving nurturing to the wounded parts of yourself, whether you understand the reason for the wounds or not. *It is not a contest; each individual's experience is real for them, deserving respect and valuing.*

Share with me what you notice as you experience this truth that you are not your story, and your story affects where you are starting today. Adding an "and" allows a different perspective of identity and change. *Accepting your history as previous learning*, gives you the ability to use that history to practice approaching past experiences differently. Using the Split-Screen Technique (see "Nugget": We Become Addicted To The Familiar) can give you a wealth of opportunities to experience New Program approaches in a safe context using past situations for practice.

Putting the original experience on the "left side" of the Split-Screen, begin to build your "right side" experience of how you choose to approach it in the present. What assumptions and patterns do you notice on the left side? Who's driving the bus? Use the tools in the book to explore these assumptions and patterns, including Power Of Mind distortions and "Nuggets" from the Fundamental Principles of Healthy Change. *The only cost involved is time and thought given to your becoming. Give it a try.*

When you realize that your true identity is actually a process of becoming, it changes everything. It allows Powerful Vulnerability. You are free to begin making healthy changes in your life today. You don't have to defend your past history, you can learn and grow from it, giving meaning to past pain. You can take healthy responsibility for pain you have caused others, apply the Prayer of Serenity to the situation, and learn from it for the present/ future.

You can choose how you interact with people who have been hurtful in the past. Protecting them from hurting you-physically or emotionally-in the present is an important first step. You can see it as applying the lantern with that person. New Program calls for Mutual Respect and Valuing in our relationships. With the support of your Higher Power, and your coach guiding you toward accuracy and choice, change is truly possible. You can parent your wounded kids inside, as you learn to be healthy in the present, shifting from survival to living. You can make amazing growth into health when you believe the truth that you are not your story.

Nugget: Identity Leads To Perceptions!

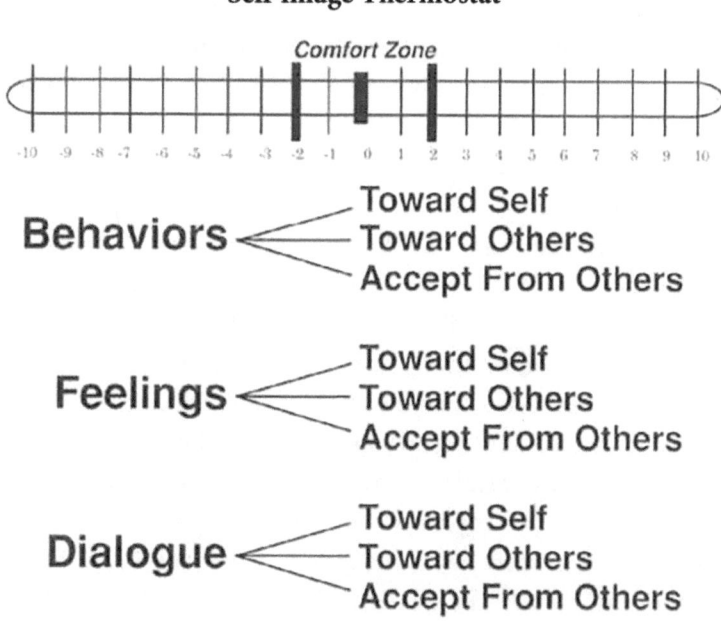

Reflect on each of the nine dimensions presented in the Self-Image Thermostat. Take the time to experience each dimension deeply, feeling good about noticing where you are starting at this moment. Under behavior, how do you see yourself behaving toward yourself? How do you treat yourself compared to how you treat others you care about? How do you treat others? What behaviors toward others fit with your Self-Image Thermostat? What behaviors do you accept from others, what behaviors are acceptable to you? Do you notice differences in different areas of your life? Do you have any problems within the three elements of behavior-behavior toward yourself, behavior toward others, and accepting behavior from others? Are there changes you want to make in the areas of behavior? Share with me in your journal what you are noticing and how you are feeling about where you are stating. Respect these feelings and notice what your resistance is saying.

Under feelings, how do you feel about yourself; what are your normal feelings toward yourself? Does it feel more familiar to be ashamed of yourself for some reason, or to feel good about how you are growing and moving forward in your recovery? How do you feel about others? What feelings do you express to others and how do you show them? Can you give honest, negative feedback when needed, or do you tend to stuff your feelings until depression, anxiety and/or rage overpower everything else? What kinds of feelings do you accept from others? What feelings tend to activate your survival reactions in Old Program? Anything out of your comfort zone will increase stress-positive or negative. Do you have any problems in the three elements of feelings-feelings toward yourself, feelings toward others, and feelings accepted from others? Are there familiar patterns regarding feelings in your life up until now? Are there changes you want to make in the areas of feelings? Again share what you are noticing.

Under Dialogue, how do you talk to yourself, what tone and attitudes do you notice when relating to yourself? You can notice core beliefs about your identity when you tune in on your internal dialogue. Do you recognize when your inner kids are talking? You can use the Split-Screen Technique to help change how you approach your self-talk. *If your commentator is very harsh, you can start by changing the voice to some comic character like Donald Duck or Mickey Mouse.* Allow the words to remain the same, but change the voice saying the words. Imagine Mickey Mouse saying, "You are such a disappointment to me," or "Why can't you be like your brother?"

Changing your commentator can have a powerful impact on your core self-esteem. How do you talk to others; what tone and attitude to you convey when communicating with others? What kinds of communication are you willing to accept from others? Are there areas of dialogue that fire off your survival reactions? Do you notice any patterns regarding dialogue-dialogue toward yourself, dialogue toward others and willingness to accept dialogue from others? Are there areas you want to change in how you communicate? What are you feeling about what you are noticing? Share with me in your journal.

These nine dimensions included in the Self-Image Thermostat give you a way of looking at different areas of identity and perception, noticing areas you like and areas you may want to change. How you see yourself at your core, the person you truly believe yourself to be, has a powerful affect on your perceptions in all areas of your life. It makes the issue of identity key to the recovery process.

Who do you truly see yourself? At your core, how would you describe your true self? You cannot avoid this key question and move forward in your recovery at the same time. *Most of my clients are Adult Children, and when they really stop to notice, "who's really driving their bus" in their lives, it is often a much younger part of them.* One of the key elements in the recovery process is helping you begin to see yourself as being in a process of becoming, learning to feel good about noticing accurately without judging as the first step in the change process.

In our culture there is significant resistance to allowing your identity to be defined as a process. We want to be able to count it, or weigh it, or measure it in some way. We feel a strong need to compare ourselves to others, and to where we think we should be. *As you read this, how do you feel about defining yourself in terms of a process? Feel what it's like to describe yourself as "becoming."*

The process of believing this new identity is uneven and multi-leveled. Most of my clients get frustrated about slipping back into old, familiar patterns. *I tell them to feel good about noticing that sometimes you believe yourself to be becoming, and other times you judge yourself and demand to know "who you really are."* The secret to change is to feel good about noticing this too, relaxing into your identity of becoming as soon a you can, releasing judging imperfectly, using this experience to practice your New Program tools.

Spirituality is at the core of my own personal identity. I will share briefly my relationship with my Higher Power and my recovery. What is most important is that you explore your relationship with your own personal Higher Power. This is just how I make sense of life for myself.

My marriage to Sonia, being a dad to Jesse and Nathan, being a coach and writer, all have their roots in my relationship with my Big Brother Jesus. I am a relational Christian, with the focus on spirituality/relationship rather than religion. I believe God has made it possible for me (along with the rest of the world) to become a new creation, and to do it imperfectly.

In 2 Corinthians 5:17, **Paul states:** "Therefore, if anyone is in Christ, he is a new creation; the old has gone, the new has come! All this is from God, who reconciled us to Himself through Christ and gave us the ministry of reconciliation: that God was reconciling the world to Himself in Christ, not counting men's sins against them. And He has committed to us the message of reconciliation. We are therefore Christ's ambassadors, as though God were making His appeal through us. We implore you on Christ's behalf: Be reconciled to God."

This has often been misunderstood and misused in the past to mean that the past should be left alone because "the old has gone, the new has come!" How can you have reconciliation without interaction? Paul makes it clear in Romans that he continued to struggle with his old nature patterns. *I believe that Paul was talking about a change of identity-freely choosing to believe himself a new creation in Christ, regardless of his human failings of feeling and action.* This ministry of reconciliation has often been applied only to reaching out to others. *I am convinced that God's call to be His ambassador in a ministry of reconciliation includes both reaching out to others and reaching in to my wounded kids inside stuck in my old nature.* What kind of representative have you been in relating to the wounded parts of you up until now?

I believe this is the heart of God's Plan for our recovery and growth-a new identity in Him. *Although His Spirit is fully formed at the point of accepting Him as Lord, learning to believe and apply this truth in our lives takes a lifetime and can never be done perfectly.* This identity in Him has allowed me to grow and develop healthy choices in my life today. I have a long way to go, and I know I'll never get there. *The meaning is in the journey.* We are given a new role/function in His Service: to be His ambassador in the reconciliation process. This is true reaching out to others and also reaching inward to the wounded parts of us, currently stuck in our old nature. He has become my own, personal Inner Coach.

When you think about "who" you really believe yourself to be, your true identity, does it reflect yourself as a new creation or your old nature? Is your identity based on the "rear view mirror" of your life story up until now, or the "windshield" of becoming, as a new creation? *Your identity will strongly shape your perceptions; what do you believe about your real identity? In CAIRing Grace Groups we embrace this special relationship:* "Because of God's loving Grace, who I am is 'becoming' in His Holy Spirit, and my recovery is the process of experiencing the adventure of becoming like the person and nature of my Big Brother Jesus."

These words capture the essence of God's Owner's Manual for our healthy living under this present covenant of Grace. Let's look more closely at Jesus as a model for our recovery from dysfunctional patterns in the present. Jesus said: *"Come to me, all you who are weary and burdened, and I will give you rest. Take my yoke upon you and learn from me, for I am gentle and humble in heart, and you will find rest for your souls. For my yoke is easy and my burden is light." (Matthew 11:28-30).* Let's look closer at how Jesus describes Himself and what he wants to offer us today. He is reaching out to those of us who feel weighted down by aspects of our lives: Addictions, depression, anxiety/panic, relationship difficulties, poor esteem, etc. In other words, He is reaching out to me. How about you?

Imagine how a yoke actually works in pulling a heavy load. On a double yoke the two pull the load together. Jesus has willingly joined me in living my life, sharing a yoke that allows Him to pull what I can't pull on my own. He always allows me to carry what is healthy for me to carry; He will carry the rest. His Spirit will draw me forward with His loving support and guidance. This perception of who I really am as a new creation has been invaluable in applying The Prayer of Serenity: "Lord, Give me the serenity to change what I can change; The freedom to release to you what I cannot change; and the growing wisdom to know the difference."

He offers me rest, and the opportunity to learn from a perfect coach how to live life to its fullest. His style is gentle and humble. He is the perfect counselor for recovery: perfectly honest, accurate, and loving. I use Him as a Model for relating to myself and to my clients in Therapeutic Life Coaching.

Modeling is the most effective learning process to gain complex abilities and changes in your life. As I borrow His eyes, I am not only keeping Him in focus, I am experiencing through Him as well. In psychology, the more you can identify with the model, the greater the learning. Jesus allows me to see God through Him, and His Nature is perfect for modeling how God wants me to be becoming. This special relationship as my loving Big Brother allows me to want to be like Him.

Many of my Christian clients feel a heavy pressure to live up to His Standard, so they can be a good witness for Him. I explain to them that when we walk His walk (imperfectly), through the power of His Spirit, we draw unbelievers unto Him. When we try to be perfect (wearing masks), attacking others for being different than we think they should be, and constantly walking in fear, we actually become a stumbling block for unbelievers coming to the Lord.

A great example of modeling was watching Jesse and Nathan when they were small. Jesse is 2 + years older than Nathan, and Nathan would constantly copy everything Jesse did, unless Jesse pressured Nathan to copy him. The moment there was a demand; there would be rebellion and resistance. *A freedom to want to be like your model allows the modeling to have the maximum power to transform. Erecting a set of rules to follow will not help create a modeling relationship.*

Paul expresses this modeling relationship in **Ephesians 5:1-2:** *"Be imitators of God, therefore, as dearly loved children and live a life of love, just as Christ loved us and gave Himself up for us as a fragrant offering and sacrifice to God."* His unconditional love allows us to want to be like Him, not because He demands it. His love takes the rebellion out of the relationship, leaving the freedom to want to be like Him-modeling at its best.

In his letter to the Galatians, Paul explained: *"Because you are sons, God sent the spirit of his Son into our hearts, the spirit who calls out, 'Abba, Father.' So you are no longer a slave, but a son; and since you are a son, God has made you also an heir." (Galatians 4:6-7)* Take a moment to experience this view of God's Plan for your recovery. What is it like to think of God as a loving Father? Notice your reactions to being free to call God "Daddy." Share your reactions with me in your journal.

Paul goes on to share, *"You, my brothers, were called to be free. But do not use your freedom to indulge the sinful nature; rather, serve one another in love. The entire law is summed up in a single command: 'love your neighbor as yourself.'" (Galatians 5:13-14)* What is your view of your

Higher Power's plan for your recovery? Is there a loving, supportive guidance for you on your journey? Can you feel the difference between imitating God as a dearly loved child, and wearing a mask to hide your fallibility?

I am impressed with God's great sense of humor. I am a very imperfect example of "becoming", with many flaws and areas of resistance to becoming. I am not what I want to be, but I am continuing to grow in His Nature. *I truly believe that His Spirit will continue to transform me into health. In spite of my fallibilities and areas of resistance to His Will, He chooses to use me for His purposes, as part of His family, as a friend. I am overwhelmed with grateful humility.* The depth of my relationship with my Father God and my Big Brother Jesus continues to grow freely, with my focus on becoming, as I receive His Grace and give that Grace to myself, and others in very imperfect ways.

The more I pour grace inside myself, as His ambassador, to help in the reconciliation process between my true identity in Him, and the wounded parts of myself, that are stuck in my old nature, and the more I pour grace outwardly to those I touch, the more room there is inside me to receive His ongoing Grace. As God's son, I will always have a Father who loves me and offers me His Home. I will always have a loving Big Brother who I can turn to and ask for guidance and direction. No problem is too great for me to handle through Him.

You need to take responsibility to choose whether or not you want/need outside help in living your life. Remember that responsibility simply means ability to respond, and has nothing to do with blame and fault. If you like the results you are getting, great. If you don't like the results you are getting, great. Feel good about recognizing that fact, and give yourself the freedom to ask your loving Higher Power to offer a hand. The Big Book of AA says that: *"Insanity is doing the same thing over and over, expecting a different outcome."* We need to accept different choices, in order to gain different results. *"If you want to know what God wants you to do, ask him, and he will gladly tell you, for he is always ready to give a bountiful supply of wisdom to all who ask him; he will not resent it."* (James 1:5) Are you free to ask for help and support from your Higher Power?

Notice how your current identity leads to your perceptions. What effect does your relationship with your Higher Power have on your sense of identity? Share with me in your journal as you reflect on this key issue.

Notice any resistance to exploring this key issue of the impact your identity has on your perceptions.

Nugget: I Am The Chooser In My Life

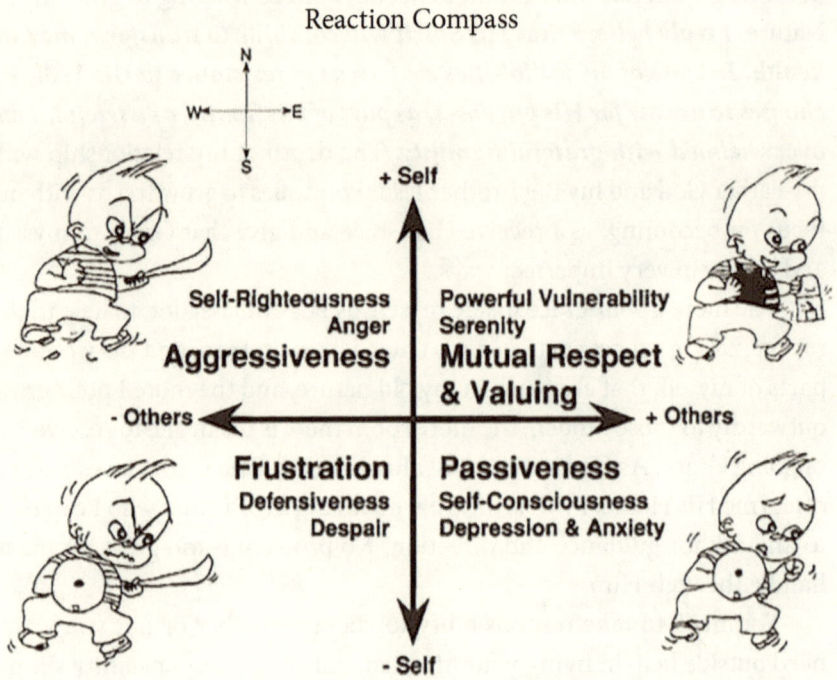

What does it mean to you to be chooser in your life today? The Reaction Compass helps you decide what direction you want your relationships to go in your recovery. Did you realize you could learn to choose the attitudes you bring to your relationships with yourself and others? You need to consciously decide what attitudes you choose to have toward yourself and toward others as you approach life. I'm not talking about an intellectual perspective, but rather a process of experiencing yourself becoming in the healthy direction of Mutual Respect and Valuing.

Deciding to respect and value yourself and others leads to Powerful Vulnerability and Serenity. Deciding to respect and value yourself while being negative and judgmental toward others leads to self-righteous anger and aggressiveness. Deciding to value and respect others while being rejecting and negative toward yourself leads to self-conscious passivity, depression, and anxiety. Deciding to be negative, judgmental and rejecting toward both yourself and others leads to frustration and despair.

Each of these four possibilities leads to a different direction on the Reaction Compass, and to different attitudes and feelings. Which position feels most familiar where you are starting? Notice consciously how often you bring these attitudes into your interactions. If you want to feel different, if you want a different outcome in your relationships, you will need to turn around and head in a healthy direction. Mutual Respect and Valuing is one of the Fundamental Principles of New Program. When you are applying New Program tools in any situation, it is important to be aware of what direction you are coming from on your Reaction Compass.

Most people, living in automatic pilot, do not see themselves as choosing these attitudes. They assume that whatever comes "naturally" is how they are. They fail to decide to decide. Do you fall for this trap? How does it feel to realize you can actually choose to foster attitudes toward yourself and others? Take several slow, deep breaths and experience acknowledging what you are deciding in your life at this moment. Notice what feelings come up as you become conscious of noticing what you are deciding. Remember Second-Order Feelings (see Introduction). Share with me in your journal.

It is a sense of identity, not a set of rules to follow. It is not a Black or white filtered dilemma of all or nothing. You can decide to be valuing and respectful toward yourself, or you can decide to be demeaning, negative, and judgmental toward yourself. You can also decide to be valuing and respectful toward others, or you can decide to be negative, defensive, demanding, and judgmental toward others. Not deciding is also a decision. Each of these decisions is really a dynamic continuum. The first step in becoming chooser in your life is learning to live consciously in the present. Share with me in your journal the different reactions you are experiencing as you embrace this "Nugget."

In Therapeutic Life Coaching I help my clients learn to recognize what is happening around them, and also what is happening within them. They learn to carry a respectful, accurate, nonjudgmental lantern of Powerful Vulnerability. They learn to care more about learning than being right in an interaction. New Program provides the tools and attitudes that make healthy change the path of least resistance.

The "Nuggets of Wisdom" regarding the Fundamental Principles of Healthy Change that saturate this book allow you to experience new ways of perceiving and reflecting on your process of change. These "Nuggets" and perceptions are a central part of Cognitive/Perceptual Reconstruction. Words have powerful perspectives attached to them that function at a subliminal level with most people. Take the word aware.

Most of my clients learned survival programs that translate being aware into being a boxer. Tension becomes an integral part of awareness. Picture a boxer in action. He keeps his muscles tight so the blows of his opponent won't hurt as much. He looks for the best opportunity to hurt the other boxer and defend himself at the same time. He needs a break after a few minutes because it is exhausting to keep the isometric tension necessary for boxing.

In Therapeutic Life Coaching I show the client how to shift to the martial art of Aikido, away from being a boxer. In Aikido the person relaxes into feeling fully in the present, noticing everything and holding on to nothing, allowing the present to be fully experienced. There is no desire to harm anyone or anything. If someone attacks, then you will use their energy to protect them from hurting you. You add nothing to the energy, but rather direct the energy away from harming you.

The more energy someone attacks you with, the more discomfort they are likely to experience as you deflect their attack. **Rather than coming from fear "trying to protect yourself from harm," you can come from the healthy desire to "protect the other person from harming you." There is a significant difference between the two approaches.** Which feels more natural for you where you are starting-being a boxer or using Aikido? You can learn to shift your perspective to increase your healthy power.

One important area of choosing is teaching your environment how to treat you as you are changing in your recovery. Your environment will often resist your changes because it is not used to them. A helpful tool in teaching others how to respond to you is called the **Four-Step Assertion Technique:**

1. Share with the other person what you are wanting from them in a respectful way;

2. Next, share with them with a firm tone what you are wanting and why you are wanting it;
3. Next, let them know with a firm voice that if they are not willing to respect your request, what your response will be. For example, "If you continue to yell at me, I will end this conversation."
4. Finally, take the action that was stated in Step 3.

People often keep saying the same thing over and over, feeling a growing resentment that the other person is ignoring them. They wait until they are very hurt and/or angry before they blow up, exploding toward the other person in a way that either drives the person away or makes them feel guilty for getting so upset. ***People unconsciously know when someone really means what they are saying; for example, children will often ignore the first five or six times their parent says something to them, waiting until that certain tone appears before responding to the parent's request.***

As chooser in your life, you are responsible for how you communicate with others and how you allow others to respond to you. ***Do you like your teaching up until now?*** Share with me in your journal your current style of communicating with key people in your life. Allow yourself to practice the Four-Step Assertion Technique and notice the changes in your relationships. You will feel awkward at first but it will become more natural with practice.

It is your responsibility to choose who you truly believe yourself to be, your core identity. ***You can choose to believe that you are defined by your mistakes and rebellions, or you can choose to see yourself as a new creation even when you are messing up and slipping into Old Program patterns.*** I choose to believe my identity in Him does not depend on how well I'm doing at any given time. I choose to believe that I will always have His loving relationship, no matter what happens in my life. The Power Of Identity In Drivers Training may fall away at any given time.

This does not mean that what I choose does not matter to God, but rather that His faith in my becoming, and His Spirit drawing me toward Him, allows me to focus my attention on making healthy changes in my life. Jesus said: *"What do you think? There was a man who had two sons. He went to the first and said, 'Son, go and work today in the vineyard.' 'I will not,' he answered, but later he changed his mind and went. Then the father went to the other son and said the same thing. He answered 'I will, sir,' but he did not go. Which of the two did what his father wanted?"* (Matthew 21:28-32)

That does not mean that God wants rebellion. Because He loves us perfectly, He wants our complete submission to Him, for our own good. The Truth is that He knows our submission will come in steps and layers.

The parable of the father with two sons makes it clear that God would rather have honest rebellion, which transforms into obedience, than the mask of obedience that leads to hidden rebellion. Share your feeling with me in your journal. Notice the different reactions to this truth, experiencing being chooser in your life. Choosing is a very imperfect process. You will often want to go north, but rebel and go south in key areas of your recovery. What is most important is not to confuse choice with blame. *Learning to supervise the wounded parts of yourself that are resisting and rebelling is a process. It is your responsibility to do the supervision.* Would it help to have New Program tools that maximize your healthy power in any given situation? Share in your journal the different reactions to this truth that you are chooser in your life.

I believe we all choose from what we believe to be true and possible at any given time. What is important to me, as your coach, is for you to be conscious and aware of what you believe, the assumptions you are bringing into a given situation. I share in this book my own personal spirituality. It is really OK to agree or disagree with anything in my beliefs. I welcome questioning and looking deeply. As your coach I want to support your spirituality. No one has the right to impose their beliefs on you.

I choose to believe that Paul's prayer is true for me personally in my own spiritual life, "I pray that out of His glorious riches He may strengthen you with power through His Spirit in your inner being, so that Christ may dwell in your heart through faith. And I pray that you, being rooted and established in love, may have power, together with all the saints, to grasp how wide and long and high and deep is the love of Christ, and to know this love that surpasses knowledge-that you may be filled to the measure of all the fullness of God (Ephesians 3:16-19)."

Dwelling means to make yourself at home, to become comfortable in a primitive setting, to plan for a long stay. I believe His Spirit is at home in the core of my being and I choose to allow that to define my identity.

Putting that into action is a lifetime process of "got it, got it, ain't got it," as I continue my adventure of becoming a new creation in Him. The impact of that choice has been profound in my recovery and in my quality of life.

I often hear clients trying to convince me they don't have time to do their homework. They see homework as something to be done in a set place and time. ***Often a major part of Therapeutic Life Coaching is helping clients make the paradigm shift that allows them to see homework as living consciously in the present, owning the truth that you are responsible at any given moment to be chooser in your life.*** You can either choose to be becoming in a healthy direction, or not choose to choose to be becoming in a healthy way.

There are several explanations for why you might end up not choosing to choose New Program and your identity as becoming. One of the most common reasons is the misperception you may have of your own identity. If you see your identity coming from your rear view mirror, then it will feel natural to believe "that's just how I am" (see **Power Of Mind Distortions** from **Chapter Two**) and not a matter of choice. ***If you see your identity as becoming, experiencing life through your windshield in the present, it is natural to be chooser.*** Another common reason for not choosing New Program comes from failing to be living your life consciously. ***Automatic Pilot will naturally lead to Old Program patterns.*** To gain access to New Program you need to be living **The Power Of Identity In Drivers Training** manually. Living consciously naturally leads to being chooser.

I choose to embrace the paradox that allows abundance in my life-to live each day as if it could be my last, while living each day as if I was going to be around for a long, long time. This is an intentional choice to live consciously, deliberately looking for opportunities to grow and learn on my life's adventure. ***What are you choosing in your life? Notice your reactions to being able to choose abundant living in your life today. Reflect deeply and share what you discover with me in your journal.***

Nugget: There Is An Economy In Your Giving!

An important dimension of identity is how you see yourself in the area of giving and receiving. The saying, "It is more blessed to give than receive" is only true when the giving is done freely. There are attitudes and perceptions that transform free giving into "begrudging" giving. Notice what's going on inside when you are giving to important people in your life. Do you find yourself giving with a feeling of obligation and duty, feeling that you should give? Do you notice yourself anticipating the other person's reactions and responses to your giving? In your mind are you playing "Let's Make A Deal" with the other person, without them even being aware of the agreement? These "Hidden Agendas" suddenly rupture into consciousness when the other person fails to deliver on the "deal" they were not even a part of.

Do you notice an underlying feeling of fear in your giving, a sense of being coerced in your giving? Are you afraid not to give? Do you keep detailed score of the giving and receiving in your life? Do you find yourself giving simply because you don't know how to say "no?" Are you giving because you don't know how not to give in the situation, even though you are feeling resentful about feeling trapped into giving? **The truth is that you are not really free to give unless you are also free not to give in a particular situation.** These are some of the sources of "begrudgingly giving."

Free giving comes from an attitude of abundance, and the desire to share the giving for its own sake. There are no strings attached to the giving. There is a dramatic difference between the economy of giving freely and the economy of begrudgingly giving. In begrudgingly giving a gift that has an intrinsic value of five dollars will cost you 20 dollars due to the hidden cost inherent in begrudgingly giving. When you give your gift begrudgingly, the person receives a ten-cent gift, again affected by the attitude behind the giving.

By contrast, that same gift, when given freely, costs you only a dollar, and comes with a ten-dollar rebate. Freely given, the person receives a 50-dollar gift, the value again affected by the underlying attitude in the giving. **The attitude of begrudgingly giving can make giving an expensive, draining process leading to a feeling of bankruptcy that causes even more of a begrudging attitude.** Free giving leads to such a feeling of abundance that there is a natural desire to even give more. No one can force this free giving attitude. Learning to give freely comes from an attitude of grateful humility.

When you think about how generous you are naturally, the answer will be dependant on the underlying attitudes in your giving. This is particularly true in sexual giving. When you are free to be sexual, your desires grow. When you feel obliged, coerced, expected to be sexual, there will be a natural dampening of your sexual feelings. When you are free to use your Time Machine to experience positive sexual encounters from the past, it increases your current desires. ***Reflect deeply on this truth as it applies to you personally.***

Learning to move away from begrudging giving and looking for opportunities to give freely, will make you naturally a more generous person. Most people think of their giving style as "that's just how I am" and not something they have a choice to change. How does it feel to realize you can have a significant impact on your self-image of generosity? Notice your reactions to this truth and share with me what you find in your journal.

ADVANCED DRIVING TIPS FOR HEALTHY CHANGE

We will be exploring four "Nuggets of Wisdom" related to attitude, which effect the Fundamental Principles of Healthy Change in your life today: "Believing Is Seeing!" "Judging And Defending Prevents Change!" "It Is Wise To See Your Glass Half Full, Rather Than Half Empty" and "Forgiveness Is Letting Go Of Holding On!" Take the time to experience believing each of these truths in your life today.

Nugget: Believing Is Seeing!

When I was eight years old I had a powerful experience of this truth. I had recently seen the movie "The Tingler," about a creature that grows along your spine when you are afraid. The Tingler would crush your spine if you didn't scream as loud as you could. The end of the movie showed all of the people running out of the theater screaming, with a voice saying, "The Tingler is coming, scream, scream!" The setting for this intense experience of "believing is seeing" was my bedroom a few days after the movie. My mom kept her salon-style hair drier in my room, in front of the window. I have always been fairly messy, and would hang clothes on the drier to keep them off the floor.

This particular night I was suffering from croup, and woke up coughing and having trouble breathing. I looked toward my window and saw a weird monster in my room, silhouetted by light outside the window. I became overwhelmed with panic and tried to scream. I couldn't make a sound because of the croup. All of a sudden I remembered the Tingler, and to my terror, realized that even if the monster didn't get me, the Tingler was going to crush my spine! I was defenseless to stop the Tingler because I couldn't scream.

This panic seemed to last forever until, all of a sudden, out of nowhere, my mom came into my room and turned on the light. The relief flooded over me as I saw that the monster was really the hair drier, and that the Tingler had not gotten me. I shared with my mom about the Tingler, and she assured me that it was only a movie, not reality. I had blocked the experience out of my mind until it came up during a coaching session with a client many years later.

Are there areas of your life where distorted beliefs are causing you tremendous pain and suffering? Begin to explore and examine the fears that are currently robbing you of healthy choices. Treat your fears very respectfully. Notice what happens when you turn the light of truth on your fears, like my mom did with me. Feel the resistance to turning on the light. What is your resistance saying? Write what you notice as you explore the truth that "believing is seeing." Share in your journal thoughts and feelings about your reactions and assumptions, and about what it is like for you as you learn that Believing Is Seeing.

A powerful example of "Believing Is Seeing" comes in perceiving the differences in communication styles between men and women. I was at a men's retreat several years ago, a huge room filled with men wanting to learn how to be more successful in their relationship with their wives. The speaker was nationally known, and was sharing his perceptions of how men and women are different. He concluded that women speak in "spider webs" of "unnecessary" information that has no real value. Women go on and on while men get to the point, e.g., tie a knot in the rope of the conversation. What is important for men is getting to the bottom line, fix it, solve it, or forget it.

The speaker used the example of how his wife would weave a spider web of different things into her conversation, often driving him nuts trying to understand what her "point" really was. The room full of men broke out in laughter as they agreed with his example. Everyone but me seemed to join in the laughing. I felt deep sadness. Spider webbing is an intimate process, whether done with a group of guys watching football, talking about plays made at previous games, comparing players, getting excited when their team is winning, getting upset when things go badly, or a free-flowing time of sharing at a personal level, as women are known to do.

The process itself is what is valued in spider webbing. **When the focus is on getting to the point, it takes the intimacy out of the process.** Because so many men believe this faulty filter, they never even try to learn to spider web personal sharing with their partners. The result of this false belief is that men often don't even see the possibilities of communication with their partners, and therefore marriages die of emotional starvation.

I spend many hours a day dealing with toxic notions like the one that made everyone else laugh. The fact is that men are just as capable of sharing with spider webs as women. What is sad is that men often exercise their ability to spider web in important areas like sports, business, hobbies, etc; while their wives beg them to spider web about their relationship, the kids, future plans, growing transparency, etc. Many men believe they can't spider web with their wives about "all that personal stuff."

The truth is that men can learn to share at a personal, feeling level with their partners. The real question is their willingness to start where they are starting, and begin learning how to share at that personal level through awkward practice. Learning emotional spider webbing is like learning any sport or activity: practice, practice, and more practice. Skill comes from the desire to learn.

The real issue is the gift of thought, and the willingness to give thought freely in these areas. I can't tell you how many times over the years I have seen men frantically, desperately willing to learn to be intimate with spider web sharing, after their partners has given up. It is tragic when they wait too long. Share your reactions with me in your journal. Take several deep breaths, noticing deeply the feelings activated.

Marital dysfunction is a great example of the power of "Believing Is Seeing." Each marital partner has their own unique movie of what is going on in the relationship, filtering everything they see.

David and Julie had been married 12 years before coming to a Therapeutic Life Coaching session. They had three young children, two boys and a girl. David had become interested in a woman at his work. The woman had been going through some personal difficulties and had reached out to David. There had not been any overt sexual behavior, but both felt an intense attraction for the other. Julie had become overwhelmed with being a mom and trying to work part-time. Sex and communication had dropped off between Julie and David over the past two years. It had been several months since they had gotten together sexually.

Both were feeling intense resentment and fear toward the other. Because of his beliefs, David saw Julie as withdrawing from him and wanting to be with the kids rather than with him. He felt she didn't care about him, and was letting herself go in terms of getting dressed up and taking care of herself, because she didn't care about him. Julie saw David as getting to escape to work, and live an interesting life. She felt fat and ugly, undesirable, and definitely not sexy. She resented doing things for him and he seemed to expect that she wait on him since she didn't "work."

Each felt the injured party in the marriage. Each felt the other one should change and make things better. Each was waiting for the other to change things, and feeling a growing resentment as things got worse over time. In the first session I shared with them that I sensed the two of them sitting in the back of a big old '52 Ford, feeling very upset at how reckless the other one was driving, and feeling totally powerless to change how the car was being driven from their back seat position.

The early sessions focused on helping both David and Julie learn to use a lantern to see what was going on at any given moment. Both had come to use very judgmental flashlights toward the other, and at times, toward themselves causing even more defensiveness. Each tended to be judgmental and perfectionist (each showed it differently). The Economy Of Giving in their relationship was leaving them both feeling near bankruptcy (see more **Advanced Driving Tips For Healthy Change** on this in the "Nugget": There Is An Economy In Your Giving).

Learning to share their individual movies with each other was awkward, and they both felt self-conscious at first. At first they would try to use the New Program tools to make their points, but would call each other on Old Program patterns, making the other partner defensive. They had to learn to apply what they were learning to themselves and to understand the partner, not to use it as a weapon.

They went through the CAIR Handbook together, page-by-page, and each went to a CAIR Group each week for months. They learned to enjoy each other rather than judge and resent. David came to realize that because he had crossed the line with the woman at work, he needed to release that relationship completely. He went through a feeling of loss, which allowed both David and Julie to understand their own relationship more deeply. They both worked actively to bring healthy New Program into their marriage, allowing themselves to have fun practicing. They both listened to Journey and Grace Podcasts from www.CAIRforYou.com.

There are many "Nuggets" that I share with each Therapeutic Life Coaching client. I will share them in many different ways and use a variety of different examples to help the client understand a "Nugget" at the level of believing-in-action. I can't tell you how many times a client will suddenly sit forward in their chair and say, "I finally get it!" regarding some core "Nugget." Understanding intellectually, and believing at the level of action are different. A person's beliefs effect what they see at a subliminal level. What beliefs are coloring your ability to see accurately? Reflect on the different areas of your life, noticing any patterns that you would like to change. Share these with me in your journal.

"Believing Is Seeing" also applies to being able to see yourself growing and becoming. The following is a brief conversation between Les and me regarding her difficulty believing that God could love her unconditionally, and wondering what the catch would be that would make it end up a painful joke. She was also wrestling with an ongoing addiction to taking pills:

Jim: And when your wounded girls inside say, "We've got to have drugs to stop this pain. We can't do it ourselves; we need something else," what do you choose to say; how do you choose to respond to them?

Les: I want to be able to tell them everything is going to be all right...but I don't know that myself. I feel overwhelmed as the Adult too. I keep seeing the image of myself as an old bag lady, homeless and alone. When I see that picture I feel overwhelmed.

Jim: So you believe that picture, and therefore can see yourself as that lonely bag lady? You try hard not to think about becoming a bag lady, try to push down the painful feelings of being a bag lady in your Time Machine?

Les: Yeah…Oh, that's the Self-fulfilling Prophecy filter from the Handbook…(deep sigh)… so I'm actually making my fear come true… my life has continued to get worse, making my fear even stronger…what a circle! (Both laugh)

Jim: Are you interested in how God sees you, or do you trust your own perceptions more than His? How much of you believes that you are a new creation in a loving relationship with an amazing Big Brother, Jesus?

Les: I know that is true, but I can't feel it…(tears and deep sighs)

Jim: Take several deep breaths and bring your inner girls together on the right side of your Split-Screen. Feel what it's like to care about them and the pain they are experiencing. From the right side of your Split-Screen, comforting your girls inside, feel what it's like to believe that your Big Brother truly loves all of you and cares deeply about how you choose to live your life. How much of you can believe this at a core level?

Les: I have had that experience several times, but I can't keep it. A little of me believes it at the core.

Jim: **Cool!** It only takes a mustard seed of believing to grow into an amazing life in Him. ***Feel that mustard seed of believing, allow yourself to experience believing as much as you truly do right now, at this moment, and share this experience with the girls on the right side. Breathe deeply.***

Les: Yeah. There's a sense of awe. That sounds strange.

Jim: Awe? So relax into the awe and feel the humility and freedom to move toward the awe…feeling His loving hand on your shoulder as you comfort and nurture your wounded girls inside. You are His ambassador to them. You get to have His Spirit flow through you to them, giving them the love and healing they so desperately need. Notice your resistance to believing this truth more with each breath.

Les: The girls are afraid to trust me, and I'm afraid my adult will disappear again.

Jim: Leslie, you are the Adult. The wounded parts of you are all parts, but you are the Adult, whether you believe it or not. The problem is the camera angle that you perceive through. When you see the New Program Adult in your imagery, comforting your wounded girls, where is your perspective?

Les: I'm not sure.

Jim: Are you seeing the Adult and the wounded girls on the screen, with you sitting on the fence, feeling powerless to affect what happens on the screen? Seeing the Adult as separate than you? Are you looking through your Adult eyes and seeing *your* wounded girls in front of you, with you actually in the scene with them? Are you looking through the eyes of one of your wounded girls inside?

Les: I don't know (deep sigh). I guess most of the time I don't have a clue...I guess I'm looking through the eyes of one of my girls, often the twelve-year-old who wasn't adopted after being promised that she would be. She's afraid He will change His mind at the very last moment. After she allows herself to really believe Him, He will reject her and she will feel like a fool for believing that anyone would ever really want her. (Tears flowing)

Jim: As you see her through your Adult eyes, borrowing the Lord's perspective to see her through Him, as His ambassador of reconciliation, see her as truly precious and worth adopting. Allow your mustard seed of believing to grow in a loving atmosphere of Grace. Let His love flow through you to her, and to all the wounded girls inside.

Les: It sounds strange but I'm noticing a struggle from the girls. They want to believe this, but are so afraid, too...I just realized that I could do something right now to help them feel more comfortable and safe...This sounds weird but I just had the experience of seeing us all through His Eyes and suddenly it's as if...strange but it's like He was actually connecting with them through me.

Jim: When you choose to believe imperfectly, like your mustard seed, and allow yourself to see from this perspective, allowing His Spirit to flow through you, you are using His Plan. ***Identity is at the heart of the healing process. When you believe the truth, the truth sets you free.***

Les: I feel more relaxed than I can ever remember...I've got to remember this.

Jim: You don't have to remember so much as allow yourself to believe the truth of this experience. Carry that believing into your future. Live consciously, feel the truth of your identity, and be His ambassador to those wounded kids inside. Feel yourself always in relationship with Him; let Him guide and support you as you take care of those precious girls inside.

What did you notice in this conversation with Les? What feelings and reactions came up as you experienced the exchange? Reflect deeply and share with me in your journal. Does her pattern feel familiar to you personally? Notice how her beliefs had a profound affect on her ability to see accurately. Once she began to believe experientially what she had held onto intellectually, she was able to see the right side of her Split-Screen more accurately.

Paul shows us how to approach the experience of believing as a new creation when he says in ***Galatians 5:5 "But by faith we eagerly await through the Spirit the righteousness for which we hope."*** When you try on your own, you generate isometric tension in the form of resistance. Your role is to want to be transformed, to eagerly look forward to becoming more like Him, seeing yourself and others through His reflection, as becoming.

It is your responsibility to choose to believe imperfectly so that you can begin to see what is possible. How would you describe your attitude toward where you are starting and where you want to be becoming in the present? Are you feeling relaxed and enjoying the adventure, or are you feeling terrible about where you are starting? Share your reactions to Believing Is Seeing with me in your journal.

Nugget: Judging and Defending Prevent Change!

Take a moment to reflect on your life up to this moment. It is important to let yourself notice accurately, without judging what you see. How would you describe your life up to this point? As a whole, how do you feel about your life up until now? As you begin to experience this reflection, how are you feeling about what you are noticing? Most people are not aware of this Second-Order process in their feelings. They tend to lump all their feelings together under a single label. They then assume their "feelings" are the direct result of the situation they are struggling with. Judging has a very negative impact on your ability to make changes because of the impact judging has at the level of Second-Order feelings.

If you stop and think about it, it makes perfect sense. If you begin to feel very bad about noticing an unhealthy pattern in your life today, it is only natural that you will begin to avoid noticing. When you stop noticing a pattern, change becomes impossible.

The reason that your Old Program filters are able to continue, in spite of the fact that you would reject many of the fundamental principles and assumptions that form your Old Program, is because you are not consciously aware of your filters. ***Judging interferes with noticing, and greatly increases your subjective feeling of pain. It also increases the chances that you will push away your awareness, in order to avoid the painful feelings associated with judgmental awareness.***

Notice what happens if you let yourself "feel good about noticing" the things in your life that have negative feelings attached to them. ***One trap that many people fall into is feeling bad about what they see, rather than feeling good about noticing the unwanted situation.*** When you let yourself feel good about noticing accurately, as the first step in the change process, it affects your entire experience, by creating a new perceptual filter. For now, let yourself begin using "no fault learning" imperfectly as you begin applying what you are learning in this book.

To live consciously, aware of proactively seeking to borrow the Lord's Eyes and His Nature, to respond through His Spirit to what you see, makes recovery a very different process. It becomes an allowing rather than a forcing. ***You need to accept any dysfunctional elements from your past, and take the responsibility to learn healthy attitudes and assumptions to deal with these problems in the present, as a new creation.***

We need to remember that God has given us His Holy Spirit to illuminate our path, share His Wisdom, and draw us closer to Him. Change and growth are possible. ***The way you approach change will determine how successful you will be.*** God knows that an attitude of grateful humility will help you in your process of growth and change. The Spirit's light is a lantern, not a flashlight. It illuminates in all directions with loving Truth and Grace, not with a harsh, judgmental light shining in only one direction.

The following conversation between Les and myself shows the toxic power of judging and shame to keep a person stuck in dysfunctional patterns of defending:

Les: sigh, tears flowing down her face.

Jim: Take a deep breath. Feel good about noticing what the tension is saying inside.

Les: It hadn't dawned on me that I was still holding on to such a fear of getting my hopes up, afraid it will go away. And I feel sad about that.

Jim: Feel sad...Feel sad. Respect that honest feeling...Feel good about feeling sad and feel the regret.

Les: Yeah...Yeah!

Jim: What's it like to honor the truth with an appropriate feeling of sadness?

Les: Les breathing...there's kind of a peace that comes withthat.

Jim: But I thought sadness was a bad thing.

Les: No. (Defensive tone)

Jim: You seem to try to avoid sadness and push it away...you seem to try to avoid sadness at all cost.

Les: Pause...Yeah I know I do that because it scares me too.

Jim: I see, so you have a Second-Order feeling huh?

Les: Yes.

Jim: You feel sad and you feel scared about feeling sad.

Les: Yeah.

Jim: Who inside feels afraid of the sadness, Les?

Les: Les breathing…my kids inside, because sadness before **Who's Really Driving Your Bus?** has always been so overwhelming.

Jim: So their life experience has taught them that sadness is just the beginning of lots of bad stuff?

Les: Yeah.(tears streaming down her face)

Jim: So if they don't shut down it's going to hurt even worse?

Les: Yeah!

Jim: What are you feeling?

Les: I jumped to the left side I guess. (Split-Screen Technique)

Jim: You guess?

Les: I did. And I was feeling disgusted.

Jim: Ok, so what's it like to move back?

Les: (breathing deeply).good.

Jim: Then feel the good feeling.

Les: OK…There's a warm feeling that comes with that. Just kind of a warm comfortable feeling that comes with that.

Jim: With what?

Les: With feeling the good feeling.

Jim: But aren't the kids afraid? Haven't they been hurt every time they got their hopes up? Doesn't their fear make sense?

Les: If I don't tell them otherwise.(heavy sighs and frustration in her voice)

Jim: And at least so far you haven't been willing to commit yourself to caring for them, have you? Notice what you are say-ing to yourself?

Les: OK, I guess I'm judging myself for being so defensive. Boy that's a good circle of Second-Order feelings (both laugh)…I haven't been consistent…I don't seem to notice them until it's too late.

Jim: What does it mean to be too late…and because of that you don't get consistent positive results?

Les: I'm always ending up stuck on the left side. (Deep sighs, tears)

Jim: And therefore you're afraid to let your hopes really rest in the process because you don't get consistent results? And the fear of getting your hopes up causes you to shut down?

Les: (sigh). Yeah.

Jim: Out loud.

Les: I'm just sick of it…I hate it!

Jim: Umm, you're sick of it, you hate it, you're feeling disgusted? What side are you on Les?

Les: Yeah…the left side again.

Jim: Hum. So even as we're talking about it.

Les: Well, I just went back, that's all.

Jim: That's all?

Les: Well, I mean I went back…I didn't realize that I went back…I don't always realize when I go back (whine in her voice).

Jim: Do you ever realize when you go back to the Left Side?

Les: Yeah.

Jim: So what's the difference between the times you realize it and the times you don't?

Les: Breathing…I guess how much attention I'm paying.

Jim: You guess? So how do you make the decision as to how much attention you're going to pay at any given time?

Les: Right now a lot of it has to do with my concentration because of the headache (defensive tone in her voice).

Jim: I see.

Les: And it's harder to pay attention because of the headache.

Jim: How does the headache make it harder to pay attention?

Les: The pain. It hurts…my head hurts.

Jim: And doesn't the pain remind you of the pain that the kids are feeling inside?

Les: Yeah? I guess it does, now that you mention it. I never thought about connecting my headache pain and the pain they might be feeling at the same time. It could be a signal.

Jim: Exactly! Way to go girl! Imagine that the headaches can just as easily remind you to go inside and to nurture and to love your girls inside, and comfort them? You could almost look forward to headaches as opportunities for further healing.

Les: I did that driving home from the CAIR meeting; I comforted them.

Jim: I see.

Les: I did! (Defensively)

Jim: I believe you. Is there a limit as to how many times you can do that?

Les: No. (Both laugh)

Jim: And what happened when you did that nurturing?

Les: I felt better.

Jim: So coming home from the CAIR meeting you spent some loving time with your wounded girls inside, and you felt better? And then..

Les: A little bit.

Jim: Not totally…so you stopped?

Les: Yes…I feel so stupid. Why do I keep going through these circles again and again? (Disgust in her voice)

Jim: So the rule is if it doesn't work perfectly-stop doing it.

Les: No!

Jim: No what?

Les: I know that's not the way it's supposed to work.(frustrated)

Jim: We're not talking about "supposed to" anything, Leslie. We're talking about accuracy here. The truth will set you free…not what your "supposed to" do or feel. The truth seen in a loving, grace-filled way…is what sets you free.

Les: Yeah!

Jim: Take a deep breath. And you'll never be perfectly free because you're human like the rest of us. When you add judging to the equation, you go into a circle of defending yourself while judging yourself. I get dizzy even thinking about it. (Both laugh)

Les: Breathing…I've been fighting not to take a Fiorinal with Codeine because I held out this far and haven't gone in for a shot.

Jim: I couldn't understand you.

Les: I said I've been fighting not to take a Fiorinal with Codeine because I went this far where I didn't go in for a shot that I didn't want to take that either, But.

Jim: How do you fight taking Fiorinal with Codeine? How do you do that? What does that mean?

Les: I'm holding on tight so I won't have to get a shot or take the pills.

Jim: You're holding on tight so you won't have to take the Codeine?

Les: Yeah.

Jim: So what happens when you hold on tight, Leslie?

Les: The headache gets worse. (Whine, defeated sounding)

Jim: So how does getting the headache worse keep you from taking the Codeine?

Les: It doesn't! (Defensive tone)

Jim: Now is this something you already knew?

Les: (sigh) Yeah. (Tears flow)

Jim: So how did you keep this a secret from yourself? How do you keep this important information away from yourself when you need it the most?

Les: How did I keep it a secret?

Jim: Uh hum? You knew because of previous experiences with this exact pattern. How did you keep this pattern a secret while you were doing it today?

Les: I didn't look at it I guess.

Jim: You didn't look at it?

Les: I didn't...I didn't think about it until you mentioned it.

Jim: Why bother because nothing's going to really work...I keep trying and I keep ending up back on the left side, again and again. Is that what you were thinking?

Les: It's not that I'm thinking that staying on the right side isn't helpful and isn't going to work too...but...it's that I...I guess you're right, maybe I'm expecting to do it perfectly.

Jim: So you're expecting more of yourself than I expect of myself? I don't expect myself to do my recovery perfectly, I don't expect my Christian walk to be perfect, so you think you should be able to do what I can't, and don't even try to do? Not only that, but then you hate yourself for failing. **Judging what you see keeps you in your circle, because you will naturally defend when attacked. This is true even when you are attacking yourself.** What would it feel like to be free to notice accurately without judging what you see?

    What did you notice as you were reading the exchange between Les and me? Do you see how her strong need to judge herself was feeding into a vicious circle of defending? It ends up being very costly for Les to be aware consciously and accurately.

Judging causes her to tune out, and not notice much of anything, thus avoiding the pain of judging. This makes her blind to unrealistic expectations of perfect change; she would only be aware consciously of the feelings of failure and defeat coming from the toxic expectations.

Without being aware of what is happening inside, she has no quality control to help her be a healthy chooser in her life. This pattern robs her of the fruits of her efforts in her recovery up until now. I believe Les will grow as she learns to accept herself "in transit" imperfectly, and begins to have fun with the adventure of healthy growth. We have come to call the destructive pattern that has made her growth so elusive, **"The Embarrassment Cycle."**

The Embarrassment Cycle works as follows: When Les becomes aware of something that is unhealthy; her first reaction is to judge herself for what she notices. When the intensity of the judging reaches a certain level, she reacts to the feeling of pressure that comes from her judging with a sense of defensiveness. She begins to defensively feel that she can't be perfect. The fact that it is herself that demands the perfection does not stop her from feeling defensive. Noticing causes such tension and pain, as a result of her judging, that it becomes too painful to notice. When she tunes out her inner feelings there is a feeling of relief. This feeling of relief reinforces her tendency to tune out and ignore her inner signals.

The problem with the Embarrassment Cycle is that Les cannot make healthy changes in her life as long as she continues to live unconsciously. Automatic pilot will generate Old Program, and her painful life of survival will continue. Her hope lies in consciously choosing a different path, in choosing to live consciously. Reflect deeply on the Embarrassment Cycle and share what you notice with me in your journal. Remember to feel good about noticing any toxic patterns as the first step in the change process.

It is important to understand that Les has put a tremendous amount of time and effort in her recovery; it is sad that she will continue to undermine her recovery as long as she continues her toxic cycles. This change is possible, and I have faith that Les will ultimately choose to believe the truth of her identity, taking loving care of her wounded girls inside, and believing-in-action that New Program applies to her personally. Her openness has given us many important patterns that have helped thousands. I can't wait until she can benefit from what she has given to so many others.

We need to understand deeply before we judge, either ourselves or others. Jesus said, *"Do not judge, or you too will be judged. For in the same way you judge others, you will be judged, and with the measure you use, it will be measured to you." (Matthew 7:1-2)* It is partly for this reason that I choose not to judge anyone, but rather notice as accurately as possible through His loving eyes. God wants us to notice accurately, choose according to His Word, and leave the judging up to Him.

Defending robs you of healthy power in your relationships. For example, if John begins to yell at me and attack me for being a terrible coach, my first reflex is to hold up my lantern of curiosity and Powerful Vulnerability (It has only taken me 40+ years of active practice). *I always handle things in New Program, except when I don't. It never gets better than that!* It can never be done perfectly. The truth is that most of the time I have no need to defend against John's attack.

When I do slip back into defending, I get tired of the costs involved in defending fairly quickly and shift back to New Program as I remember that "who" I really am is really becoming. I am deeply committed to Powerful Vulnerability, as a new creation, growing in His Nature by living consciously with Him. It is important information for me when I begin to feel defensive.

When I feel defensive, I try to notice what part of me is feeling the reaction and what assumptions I am making at this moment. *Again, this is not intellectual, but rather allowing the defensive feelings to become a useful signal to help me understand and grow.* Go back and review several perceptual filters in Chapter Two including Who Defines Your Reality and Powerful Words. Understanding and believing these perceptual filters gives you a whole new set of choices in this situation.

Defending is a powerful "Nugget." I want to share a paradox of defending that comes from the Fundamental Principles of Healthy Change. When you defend yourself against a verbal attack from someone, and the validity of the attack is fundamentally false, by defending you make the false attack effectively true. When you respond to a false attack with Powerful Vulnerability, you effectively show it to be false.

On the other hand, when you receive an attack that is fundamentally true, and you defend yourself, you make the true attack even more intense and the exchange will tend to escalate in proportion to the amount of defending. If you receive a valid attack and respond with Powerful Vulnerability, you effectively take the power out of it. Notice my response to John in the next paragraph.

I can say to John, "Wow, you are really feeling some strong feelings about my coaching and are feeling very mad at me right now. Can you tell me what specifically I have done so I can correct it and become more successful in coaching you?" The fact is that I am being truthful with John. The truth is that I would like to be successful with everyone I coach-including you as you read this book. If John is mad at me, I want to understand what he is mad about because I want to improve our coaching relationship.

After John has deescalated and we are reflecting on what happened between us, I will let John know that I respond much better when he can share his feelings with me more respectfully. I will also help John notice early signs when he is beginning to get angry in the future, with me or with anyone else. I will explore with John if he experiences these anger outbursts in other situations and with other people.

The original "attack" has been turned into another "Nugget" to help us both grow and learn. You cannot fake this response, but you can shift consciously into New Program and allow these attitudes to help you have increasing healthy power. *I promise you that it will feel very unnatural at first.* Seeing accurately is like a muscle, the more you work it out, the stronger it becomes.

What comes naturally is usually Old Program and may rob you of important choices in your life.

Look for opportunities to spot "Nuggets" that will help your recovery. I have given you many examples of what I consider "Nuggets," and the many forms and different types of "Nuggets" you can learn to recognize in your daily life. Writing this book has greatly heightened my experience of "Nuggets," and I find myself frequently sharing them with my clients in our coaching sessions. The easiest way to transform yourself in healthy directions is to learn to appreciate the "Nuggets" that will help you peel the layers of onion regarding your different issues. Wisdom comes in "Nugget" form. Would you like a chew?

"*Cheap grace*" is the notion that our choices do not really matter. It assumes that what we do and how we live our lives has no real affect on our relationship with our Higher Power. It tries to remove personal responsibility from our choices and actions. Cheap grace cannot create an attitude of grateful humility, and therefore can never transform.

Paul shows us how to approach the experience of being a new creation when he says in **Galatians 5:5 "But by faith we eagerly await through the Spirit the righteousness for which we hope."** When we try on our own power we generate isometric tension in the form of resistance. **Our role is to want to be transformed,** to eagerly look forward to becoming more like Him, seeing ourselves and others through His reflection, as becoming. It is our responsibility to imperfectly choose to embrace Powerful Vulnerability and put our energy into learning and growing. Judging and defending prevent Powerful Vulnerability.

His Word calls for us to keep our eyes on Him: **"Let us fix our eyes on Jesus, the author and perfecter of our faith." (Hebrews 12:2)** There is a pattern in this approach. Modeling is the most effective learning process to gain complex abilities and changes in your life. As you borrow His eyes, you are not only keeping Him in focus, you are experiencing through Him as well. In psychology, the more you can identify with the model, the greater the learning. Jesus allows you to see God through Him and His Nature is perfect for modeling how God wants you to be becoming.

This special relationship as your loving Big Brother allows you to want to be like Him, welcoming Him to be your Inner Coach. When we walk His walk (imperfectly), through the power of His Spirit, we will draw unbelievers unto Him. When we try to be perfect (wearing masks), attacking others for being different than we think they should be, and constantly walking in fear, we actually become a stumbling block for unbelievers coming to the Lord. Fear is the opposite of curiosity. Share your reactions to this "Nugget" with me in your journal. Notice the areas of your life where you are actually defending against the very things that you are wanting to change.

JAMES O. HENMAN, PH.D.

Nugget: It Is Wise To See Your Glass Half Full Rather Than Half Empty!

I am a child of the '60's, Peace Corp., Head Start, and Migrant Education. The Peace Corp had a saying: "Do you see the glass half full or half empty? If the answer is half full, you may be cut out for the Peace Corp." The truth is that there is a real impact, depending on which perspective you choose.

If you see the glass half empty, there are several natural reactions you are likely to have-feeling bad about what is missing, resenting what is missing, getting defensive about what isn't there. These reactions make it harder to enjoy what is in your glass. On the other hand, when you see your glass half full, there is a natural tendency to value what is in your glass, thus increasing the chances of enjoying it. This reaction naturally enhances your pleasure with what is in your glass.

The extreme of this difference comes when you see the glass that is filled to the half point as if it was totally full or totally empty. Some try so hard to be positive that they deny reality and focus only on the positive. I find most of these people have a strong, underlying fearful child inside, afraid to acknowledge any negative feelings for fear of breaking the dam, and starting a flood that may never end. At the other end of the continuum are those who see the half-filled glass as empty. If it isn't perfect, forget it! It's all or nothing for these folks. What feels most familiar to you? Notice deeply and share with me in your journal.

Some people take the stand that to be most realistic, you must adopt the half empty perspective as coming to grips with what has been lost. They say, "Take off your rose colored glasses and face facts!" The truth is that either describing the glass as half full or half empty is equally accurate. The real question is the cost/benefit of each perspective. Which generates contentment? Which works best? Do you recognize either of these patterns as being familiar? Share your reactions with me in your journal.

One subtle but powerful cost of **survival mentality** is the core feeling of scarcity that comes with this perspective. This core sense of scarcity filters everything. From this survival mentality it is natural to see your glass as half empty. It is also natural to feel anxious when things are going well (Second-Order feeling), because of previous experiences of getting your hopes up, only to be disappointed. It is very difficult to relax into becoming when everything feels like a test. These assumptions are affecting your ability to be chooser in your life.

The truth is that you can learn to develop a more constructive perspective by **consciously attending to positive aspects of your daily experience.** Think of it as building a muscle. Habits form from repeated experience, so practice, practice and more practice. Savoring what is in your glass not only allows you to increase your pleasure, others will tend to be drawn to you.

This is not about faking it or wearing masks! It is about applying the Fundamental Principle of New Program: A growing commitment to the acceptance (acknowledgement) of Reality in the present. By giving yourself the permission to start where you are starting in the present, you can relax into enjoying the adventure of learning and growing. You can have fun with the clumsy, awkward feelings that are natural when learning something new, living consciously with your glass half full.

As you practice this perspective it comes more easily and feels more natural. Don't fall for the trap of believing the filter **"That's Just How I Am" (See Chapter Two).** Some people are more naturally positive while others are more naturally negative. Both physiology and early conditioning play a part in where you are starting regarding your "normal" perspective of half full or half empty. Practice and a willingness to develop this perspective determine your future. *It is not written in ink, but in pencil. What do you choose for your future?*

People suffering from depression often develop a half-empty perspective toward life. They focus on what they don't have, sure that things will turn out badly. They concentrate on the flaws in themselves and others, feeling robbed by life and resentful for what is missing in their lives. This attitude/perspective tends to be a turn-off to others, and damages their relationships. It actually keeps them from risking and taking chances to make healthy changes in their lives. Imagine what it would be like to come home from school with a report card of five "A's" and one "B." Many clients suffering from debilitating perfectionism share the experience of bringing such a report card home and having a parent say, "Why do you have this B," with no acknowledgment of the A's.

Although life experiences have affected your perspective up until now, from this point forward, you get to choose which elements you are going to notice. This is just like working any muscle to get it into shape. It is the process of developing a habit. The truth is that you can choose to begin noticing what is in your glass, and can choose to feel good about what you have at this moment.

This is not a denial of what is missing or painful about this moment, but rather a chance to apply the Prayer of Serenity to the unwanted things, at the same time, appreciating and valuing the positive things. ***In the Prayer of Serenity you are asking for the serenity to change what you can change, the freedom to release what you can't change, and a growing wisdom to know the difference.***

This is where spirituality really comes alive. What is important and what is not? What are needs and what are wants? What assumptions are you bringing into your life? Reflect deeply on your ability to learn to see your glass half full, and share what you notice with me in your journal.

Paul presented God's Plan for contentment in Philippians 4: 11-13, "...I have learned to be content whatever the circumstances. I know what it is to be in need, and I know what it is to have plenty. I can do everything through Him who gives me strength. I have learned the secret of being content in any and every situation, whether well fed or hungry, whether living in plenty or in want."

Paul presented the heart of what he had learned to create such contentment in verses 4-7, "Rejoice in the Lord Always. I will say it again: Rejoice! Let your gentleness be evident to all. The Lord is near. Do not be anxious about anything, but in everything, by prayer and petition, with thanksgiving, present your requests to God. And the peace of God, which transcends all understanding, will guard your heart and your mind in Christ Jesus."

When I first read Paul's words, I felt that I could never develop that kind of attitude, and felt that his plan was something I could never achieve. What I realize now is that Paul is telling us how to do it the easy way; he is describing a perspective/attitude that fills us naturally with contentment. When Paul says he has learned to be content, he uses the Greek word ***"autarkes"*** which means "self-sufficient." This is a key point-how does Paul define self? He makes it clear that his self, his identity, is in Christ as a new creation. Therefore Paul is really saying that he believes his sufficiency is in Jesus, who supports everything Paul does as a new creation.

It is clear that God's Plan calls for us to see the glass half full, with God at the center of everything. It also is clear that His Plan calls for intimate interaction with Him, sharing with Him, asking Him for what we want/need, and feeling good about sharing what we do have with Him, from Him, and for His purposes. Having that intimate relationship with God is what makes His Plan naturally generate contentment. What is your relationship with your Higher Power? Start where you are starting, and allow yourself to build a growing freedom and identity in your Higher Power relationship.

There is a relationship that God offers us, that allows us to begin healing the wounded parts of ourselves stuck in Tupperware in our old nature. He offers to stand as our loving Parent, to guide us into health and growth. We can learn to parent our wounded inner kids the way He parents us. We are no longer "stuck" withthe programming we have had up to the present.

The key is the relational/spiritual connection at the level of experience. This is not an intellectual exercise; it is core believing that your identity comes from the depths of your relationship with your Higher Power. This believing grows with practice, practice and more practice.

Paul shares the process of God's Plan: **"This being so, I want to remind you to stir into flame the strength and boldness that is in you, that entered into you when I laid my hand upon your head and blessed you. For God hath not given us the spirit of fear; but of power, and of love, and of a sound mind." (2 Timothy 1:7).** God's Plan involves our accepting His free gift of Healing Grace, and accepting the reality of the present, without shame, self-hatred, or blame toward others. We are His ambassadors of reconciliation. Looking with a lantern through His Eyes at your current circumstance, allows you to see the possibilities, rather than being distracted by what is missing. Notice deeply your reactions and share them with me in your journal.

Nugget: Forgiveness Is Letting Go Of Holding On!

Forgiveness is often misunderstood, or misused, and we need to be clear about what is meant by the term. Forgiveness simply means that we are allowing ourselves to be free to learn from the past, without dragging the past into the present. It means the process of 'letting go of holding on.' It does not mean that the past events were O.K., or that we need to forget that they happened. The problem with holding on to the past is, it makes it difficult to make changes in the present. We are all controlled by the things we do not forgive!

How does this definition fit your beliefs about forgiveness? Look at areas of your life where forgiveness is an issue. How have you been looking at forgiveness up until now? Does this perspective of forgiveness involving "letting go of holding on," give you any new choices? Share your feelings about forgiveness with me in your journal.

You cannot force yourself to forgive without generating resistance that makes the whole situation worse. You can sometimes only want to want to forgive, through the power of your Higher Power. Sometimes you don't want to forgive at all! Respect the resistance and use these signals to bring into focus what the resistance is trying to say. I often find that there is a good reason for the resistance. If you are keeping the wounded parts of you in solitary confinement, ignored and rejected, stuck in the painful scenes needing forgiveness, then forgiveness is like leaving fallen comrades behind enemy lines to rot.

While your inner kid (who can be any age-including adult) continues drowning in shame, experiencing the painful scene over and over, forgiveness does not make healthy sense. Forgiving the perpetrator in the scene and closing the "books" on the situation is an outrage to that wounded kid left behind. If you are ready to forgive the perpetrator, you need to also be ready to reconcile and begin a healing relationship with that wounded inner kid.

Look at any areas of unforgiveness in your life. Have you begun a reconciliation process with the wounded parts of you? If not, noticing is a healthy starting place in the forgiveness process. What do the wounded kids need from you in order for forgiveness to work? Share your reactions to this attitude toward forgiveness in your journal. Notice the different feeling reactions, and the feelings about those feelings. Forgiveness is a complex process.

In truth, forgiveness is really a gift to you, not to the person or situation you are resisting forgiving. You become freed from the original situation when you forgive freely. You can forgive and learn from the same situations. The Time Machine is often involved when issues of forgiveness are activated. When you go in your Time Machine, you become who you were in the original scene again and feel the flood of feelings that were in the original experience. This flood of emotions makes learning most difficult.

Keeping out of your Time Machine allows you to put your focus on learning, and growing, and healing, when dealing with forgiveness issues.

If you put on a mask of forgiveness, because you "should" forgive, or you are getting pressure to forgive, it will simply push the "unforgiveness" deeper into subliminal storage. You will then be at risk for feeling guilty when the "unforgiveness" resurfaces in the future. You need to accept yourself where you are in your forgiveness process-Grace makes this all possible. ***Remember that one of the Fundamental Principles of New Program is "A growing commitment to the acceptance (acknowledgement) of Reality in the present."***

There is also the issue of forgiving yourself for things that you have done and not done in the past. Many of my clients have things they resist forgiving themselves for when they enter Therapeutic Life Coaching. We will start by accepting where the client is starting regarding hating and rejecting parts of themselves. We will work with the resistances to embracing the rejected parts of the client. As is often true, your resistances can help you make the most significant growth and change. Experience your resistance to becoming respectful toward wounded parts of yourself, parts you have not forgiven yet. Anxiety and depression are directly related to the lack of forgiveness of self and others. Share with me your reactions to the whole issue of forgiveness. Share in your journal what you notice as you reflect deeply into how forgiveness is affecting your life today.

The truth is that your choices and decisions do matter. They affect the quality of your life and your ability to be happy and healthy. When you live your life as if your choices don't matter, it is difficult for your life to really matter to you. ***Reflect deeply, and share with me your reactions to this concept.***

Final Thoughts From Your Coach

As you come to the end of this book, it is important to realize that you are just beginning a lifetime adventure of growth and change. You have the right and responsibility to choose how you approach this unfolding process-as a painful struggle/test where you condemn and judge yourself for needed areas of growth, or as a chance to relax into noticing areas of needed change. *Feeling good about noticing needed changes can make all the difference in how you experience the journey, and how successful you will be in making the desired changes.* Practice is the key to successful change, and the more you practice the more natural your New Program responses become, as you learn to live consciously. *Practice, practice, and more practice.* You will never be able to do it perfectly.

This book is designed to be read over and over again. Each time you experience the material, you can get something new out of it. It is like peeling an onion, each layer adds to the total experience. Bring the issues you are currently facing to the book, as a client would bring them to a coaching session. Let this book come alive as you share with me in your journal, and share with at least one other person what you are experiencing in the process.

It is imperative to apply what you are learning by putting it into action. You will be awkward at first, and feel unnatural, but this will pass as you continue living consciously, allowing me to join you on your adventure into becoming. *It works when you work it; so let yourself work it because you are worth it!* Now that you have come to the end of the book, notice how much more you can understand and apply the material as you start over again from the beginning. Allow yourself to read it again and again for the first time. Listen to the Journey and Grace Podcasts, pausing to allow time for the nuggets to sink in. www.CAIRforYou.com.

It is true that you only have so many hours in your day. It is my experience that most people feel their lives are filled and there is no extra time to set aside to practice learning New Program tools and applying "Nuggets" in daily life. The truth is that when you choose to live consciously with grace, you tend to generate more meaningful time. When you are more aware of choices you can reach your goals more effectively.

Seeing everything as an opportunity to practice "believing your identity as becoming," creates a powerful perception. Wondering how New Program tools and principles can help you at this moment allows you a mindset of open curiosity, which is the opposite of fearful defensiveness.

Embracing this attitude allows your entire life to be one big practice. This perspective has the best possible chance for you to continue making healthy changes in your life. You will never perfectly fathom the depth of the wisdom shared in this book. I learn something new each time I read it, and I wrote it. Allow His Wisdom to come alive in your recovery. Change really is possible!

EPILOGUE

A Deeper Look at How Faith Impacts Healthy Change

Why does God let bad things happen? Why won't He help me? Why didn't He answer my prayers? God wants us to have a faith that allows us the freedom to question and doubt Him, to be angry and upset with Him, and to bring our struggles to Him. This concept may appear paradoxical at first. The fact is that freedom to doubt and question is what allows faith to grow and develop, which is why He desires us to interact with Him in this honest, transparent way. **A growing faith is what allows relationships to come alive – with God, with ourselves, and with others.**

Religion has to do with the questions of salvation and the name we give our Higher Power. **Spirituality** has to do with the <u>relational qualities</u> we see in our Higher Power. This paper will focus on how faith & spirituality impact healthy change - sharing my own personal spiritual faith with the reader.

I have faith that God wants to be in a living relationship with us. **God does not expect or demand "blind" faith from us; a mustard seed is more than enough to start an adventure with Him.** He wants to help us make healthy changes in our lives today <u>because</u> He loves us. He also desires us to love Him. It is this mutual loving, sharing, accepting, and experiencing that allows God's Plan to come alive in us. It has to go both ways for a living relationship to grow and develop. He created us in His image to be one with Him through His Holy Spirit.

"Faith is the process of perceiving from a perspective, 'as if' particular beliefs are true, which cannot be proven or disproven." It is fundamentally experiential not just intellectual. The more deeply the beliefs are experienced, the more they will be reflected in daily life. Faith must be seen as a verb, not a noun. It is inherently an imperfect process. Demanding perfect faith is unrealistic, considering the fact that we live in an imperfect world. Such demands actually prevent a healthy, growing faith.

Developing **faith can be the conscious act of choosing to believe** in something that is intangible and difficult to support logically or scientifically; e.g. many religious beliefs. What we often fail to realize is that some key elements of our **faith can be formed out of conscious awareness; through a process of believing in "perceptual filters" resulting from childhood experiences,** where the adoption of distorted and flawed perceptions may have been a means of emotional survival.

We all experience our world through **perceptual filters** that have a profound effect on how we feel, what we believe possible and where we put our faith. These perceptual filters are made up of our underlying assumptions and beliefs about reality, our attitudes toward ourselves and others, our experiences from the past, and our current expectations. **The way in which we process all of this information forms our "survival software".**

There is a profound difference between following survival software and living software. Survival software has, at the core, a belief that there is something profoundly wrong with us at the level of identity – the essence of who we are. What's really wrong at our core is that we were created to be in loving relationship with God. We spend a lifetime trying to make up for it – creating a SURVIVAL mentality, which filters everything we experience. We try to hide or get rid of unwanted parts of ourselves, preventing healing of those wounded parts.

We all have some survival software growing up in a very imperfect world. **Faith will be manifested in the life of the believer, whether consciously chosen from living software or unconsciously developed from survival software.** Conflicts between conscious faith and unconscious faith cause cognitive dissonance/tension and low esteem which feeds the gamut of emotional and addictive problems. **Expectations arising out of conscious faith, combined with the impact of unconscious faith in survival software, leave us feeling shame and guilt. Expectations, not experiences create resentment and bitterness.**

This survival software has a profound impact at how we perceive God, often seeing Him as having the nature and style of our parents. I have faith that **God is deep and simple; unfortunately we often try to make Him superficial and complex,** with a million rules, with Him judging and being ashamed of our flaws, expecting perfection from us. We feel crushed trying to live up to His Perfection – yet He describes His load as light.

Following rules is a substitute for relationship. The harder we try to follow the rules, the more burdened we feel, and the less "grateful humility" we experience in our relationship with God. **As His ambassador, we can bring His Nature and His Style to help us heal our wounded inner parts in the present.** Through us, God can love our inner wounds into healing. It is this "living software" that makes healthy change possible as we see ourselves and others through His Eyes.

In reality, the only thing really wrong with most of us is this fundamental fear/belief that there is something terribly wrong with us at the core. This toxic circle feeds on itself, and grows over time. The more we fear being fundamentally "damaged goods", the more that fear causes emotional distress which proves there is something wrong. This is a belief worth challenging and replacing with healthy truth.

The truth is that we are all fallible human beings, falling incredibly short of a Perfect God who I believe loves us perfectly. **We can all develop faith in our ability to be becoming in Him – learning and experiencing "living software" imperfectly. "But by faith we eagerly await through His Spirit the righteousness for which we hope." (Galatians 5:5)**

If we look at life through a pair of eyeglasses that have dirty lenses or a faulty prescription, we cannot see clearly. If we want to see accurately, we would choose glasses that correct our vision as close to 20/20 as possible. If we want to make healthy changes in our lives, we need to develop **"living software" that makes the process of healthy change the path of least resistance. Grace is at the heart of God's living software for healthy change.**

Grace is God's desire for an intimate relationship with us, even though we can never merit the loving relationship He offers. **He cares about our**

suffering and wants to supply healthy living software to neutralize the toxic impact of survival software from a flawed world. We can learn to recognize and change toxic perceptual filters robbing us of healthy living. We can learn to develop our own **inner coach** to help in difficult areas of our lives.

God's **living software** for making healthy changes in our lives is dependent on us allowing Him to share His Loving Grace and Guidance with us. **God's living software is integrated and freely given. He wants to live with us, through us, and for us.** We provide the willingness; **He provides the rest:**

- The Adventure of living consciously with Him in the present, with **Grateful Humility** - the attitude and perception that naturally comes from deeply accepting that His Loving Grace is given to each of us personally and freely. We can never earn it! It is His Loving Goodness, not ours!
- Experiencing life through our lanterns of grace with **Powerful Vulnerability** – the attitude and perception that it is more important to learn and grow than be right!
- Relaxing into becoming who we truly are – **God's ambassadors**, as new creations, as His Spirit draws us deeper and deeper into His Nature, and into our healthiness.
- Applying **The Serenity Prayer** imperfectly: "God grant me the serenity to change what I can change, the freedom to release to You what I can't change, and a growing wisdom to know the difference."

God's **living software** for healthy change does not include airtight submarine compartments to protect ourselves from pain and shame. When we block pain and store it in a timeless Tupperware container, we create fractures in our core self, leaving an *Adult Child Character*. He wants to join us in our airtight compartments, supporting our opening up by drawing us toward Him, through His Loving Spirit and Guidance. His loving us is a reflection of His Nature, not our lovability!

Grace allows us to begin exploring the roots of our faith in survival software in a different light. With our grace filled lanterns we can learn to feel good about noticing perceptual filters, which drive toxic patterns in our lives as the first step in healthy change. **The truth is that we are not our "story" and our "story" affects where we are starting in the present.** It can never be done perfectly!

God freely pours His Loving Grace into us. The more we pour His Grace inside ourselves, as His ambassador, to help in the reconciliation process between our true identity in Him, **and** the wounded parts of ourselves, that are stuck in our old nature; **and** the more we pour His Grace outwardly to those we touch, the more room there is inside us to receive His ongoing Grace. **Being transformed as a new creation is instantaneous when we accept His free gift; experiencing this truth in our daily lives is a lifetime process of "becoming in Him".**

We often misunderstand **"dying to the old self"** to mean hating and judging our wounded parts. I believe "dying to the old self" as Paul reflects, is about our **identity** at the core. Christians often suffer from **"Identity Alzheimer's"** as we enter recovery – **where as new creations we believe ourselves to still be our old nature.** We continue to believe at our core we are still "damaged goods" needing to hide and make up for being ourselves, feeding shame and self-condemnation. This is our old nature identity, but not our new nature identity.

As Christians we are in fact born again at the level of identity, at the core, with God living in our heart. **Unfortunately this Identity Alzheimer's causes us to define ourselves, not by who we really are in God, but by our past and present life experiences. This often causes us to allow our old nature to drive the bus in our recovery – leading to an emphasis on performance and rules to follow, needing to earn God's free gift of Grace, trying to do things perfectly.** This is often an exhausting process. **Old nature "seemingly" gets healthier, but is still old nature; feeling crushed trying to be justified through our actions.**

As God's sons and daughters, we will always have a Father who loves us perfectly and offers us His Home. We will always have a **loving Big Brother Jesus** who we can turn to and ask for guidance and direction. No problem is too great for us to handle through Him. **I have faith that being His** ambassador, both inward to me and outward to others, defines me at the core - becoming in Him; faith that we can all be becoming in Him imperfectly together. There are free audio, video and written materials on **www.CAIRforYou.com** that explore this in more depth.

Additional "Nuggets of Wisdom" For Further Reflection

Each of the following "Nuggets" captures a significant piece of wisdom about the process of healthy change and is an opportunity for you to chew on and digest each bite. Share with me in your journal as you reflect on each "Nugget", taking the time to look deeply into each one. These "Nuggets" will add additional healthy power to your recovery:

Nugget: Beware the power of your questions!

Nugget: We All Have A Commentator Inside Defining And Filtering Our Reality!

Nugget: Understanding Is Not Changing!

Nugget: Change Is An Integrated Process!

Nugget: Trying To Convince Prevents Believing!

Nugget: Change Can Never Be Done Perfectly!

Nugget: An Attitude Of Entitlement Prevents Appreciation And Satisfaction!

Nugget: Feelings Are Like Waves-You Can Learn To Safely Ride Them!

Nugget: Freedom Is The Ability To Do What You Want To Do, Even When Someone Tells You To Do It!

Nugget: It Is Difficult For Victims To See Themselves As Perpetrators!

Nugget: Positive Intentions Can Blind You To Negative Effects!

Nugget: You Can't Not Think About Purple!

Nugget: Learn To Protect Others From Hurting You!

Nugget: Embracing The Paradox Of Powerful Vulnerability!

Nugget: Thought Is One Of The Most Precious Gifts You Can Give!

Nugget: Transparency Is The Only Way To Really Feel Accepted!

Nugget: Expectations Create Bitterness, Not The Experiences Themselves!

Nugget: Life Simply Is; The Key Is How You Live It!

COGNITIVE / PERCEPTUAL RECONSTRUCTION: APPLIED MINDFULNESS

Dr. Henman has spent the past 40+ years in full time practice as a Psychologist, counseling & educating in areas of self-esteem, addictions, relationship dysfunction, depression & anxiety. He is currently in full time practice with Psychological Associates in Modesto, CA as a Therapeutic LifeCoach, author, & lecturer. Dr. Henman developed Cognitive/Perceptual Reconstruction as a integrated Coaching approach to the treatment of Adult Children of Dysfunction in 1985. He wrote "Changing Attitudes In Recovery - A Handbook On Esteem" in 1990, & "Who's REALLY Driving Your Bus?" in 2003.

He has shared presentations over the years to help listeners learn how to approach the process of healthy change & build their own "Inner Coach". His style of sharing combines humor & sensitive self-disclosure in a deep, thought provoking, impactful way.

THE JOURNEY SERIES PODCASTS

In "The Journey Series," Dr. Henman uses examples from daily life to illustrate various aspects of recovery in a way that makes them come alive. Each presentation can be experienced over & over, gaining something new each time. Each presentation addresses specific issues common to most people wanting to explore recovery & gives useful tools to help in the recovery process. He shares his unique views on self-esteem & how to produce healthy change in these podcasts.

Understanding The Wounded Child Within, Part 1 and Part 2
"Understanding The Wounded Child Within" will give you a deeper appreciation of how to recognize and begin a healing, supervising relationship with the wounded parts of yourself.

> **Part 1**: 48 min
> **Part 2**: 36 min

A Developmental View of Addiction, Part 1 and Part 2
"A Developmental View Of Addiction" gives you an overview of how to approach your sobriety and recovery differently. It will help you understand the emotional causes of addiction.

> **Part 1**: 57 min
> **Part 2**: 31 min

Exploring "New Program" - A Blueprint For Recovery, Part 1 and Part 2
"Exploring "New Program" - A Blueprint For Recovery" will give you an overview of how to integrate Twelve-Step and New Program wisdom into a path of sobriety and recovery. You will learn how "New Program" fits into Steps II & III of the Twelve-Steps.

> **Part 1**: 53 min
> **Part 2**: 36 min

Roadblocks to Recovery, Part 1 and Part 2
"Road Blocks To Recovery" will give you an overview of how to approach your depression/anxiety/relationships/addictions differently.

    Part 1: 49 min
    Part 2: 45 min

Building Recovering Relationships, Part 1 and Part 2
"Building Recovering Relationships," gives you a way of approaching the important relationships in your life that helps create healthy change.

    Part 1: 57 min
    Part 2: 34 min

Building Heathy Self-Esteem - Relaxing Into Change, Part 1 and Part 2
"Building Healthy Self-esteem – Relaxing Into Change" helps you understand the real sources of esteem and the building blocks that make healthy esteem possible.

    Part 1: 37 min
    Part 2: 70 min

The Role of Feelings In Recovery
The Role of Feelings In Recovery.

    Part 1: 61 min

THE GRACE SERIES PODCASTS

In the Grace Series, Dr. Henman applies the Wisdom of Scripture to the process of making changes in our daily lives. He makes an important distinction between religion & relationship with God. Dr. Henman presents God's no-fault plan for growth & healthy esteem, which allows us to relax into His loving Nature. Embracing God's Plan of Grace makes change & growth the path of least resistance. He shares from his own personal relationship with his loving "Big Brother" Jesus & how this relationship affects his own personal recovery. Website: http://CAIRforYou.com/

Transforming Grace - Healing The Wounds That Bind, Part 1 and Part 2
"Transforming Grace – Healing The Wounds That Bind," will help you see God's Plan for healthy change and the building blocks of spirituality.

    Part 1: 51 min
    Part 2: 47 min

God's Grace and Our Freedom to Obey, Part 1 and Part 2
"God's Grace and Our Freedom To Obey," explores deeply how our perceptions and attitudes affect our relationship with our Higher Power.

    Part 1: 48 min
    Part 2: 46 min

The Truth Can Set You Free, Part 1 and Part 2
"The Truth Can Set You Free," helps you explore deeply the assumptions and blind spots that rob you of healthy choice in your spirituality.

    Part 1: 50 min
    Part 2: 44 min

Willing to be a Fool for God, Part 1 and Part 2
"Willing To Be A Fool For God," will explore where God is during painful, difficult times, and how our assumptions color our relationship with God. It will also help you discern when God is guiding you and when it is your old nature.

    Part 1: 45 min
    Part 2: 47 min

ABOUT THE AUTHOR

Dr. Henman began his professional career working in Head Start and Migrant Education preschool programs in central California in 1968. He has spent the last 40+ years in full time practice coaching and educating in areas of self-esteem, addictions, relationship dysfunction, depression and anxiety. He earned his Ph.D. in Psychology from the California School Of Professional Psychology-Fresno in 1978, and received his California license for Psychology in 1980. He is currently in full time practice with Psychological Associates in Modesto, California.

He developed Cognitive/Perceptual Reconstruction (CPR) as an integrated approach to Therapeutic Life Coaching in the early 1980's. The focus of CPR is learning to create a loving, supervising relationship with the wounded parts of self, associated with addictions and emotional problems, and building healthy self-esteem in the present.

With the help of a steering committee of recovering individuals, he wrote ***Changing Attitudes In Recovery-A Handbook On Esteem (CAIR)*** and founded free CAIR Self-Help Groups in 1990. The CAIR Handbook provided the format and structure, which allowed people from a variety of different problem backgrounds to come together and develop healthy self-esteem. The CAIR Handbook supplied the tools and resources for the support groups. He wrote Who's REALLY Driving Your Bus? in 2003, and publishing Who's REALLY Driving Your Bus Today? In 2022, reflecting the changes over the past 20 years. For more information on Dr. Henman and his therapeutic approach, please contact his web site at www.CAIRforYou.com.

www.ingramcontent.com/pod-product-compliance
Lightning Source LLC
LaVergne TN
LVHW041759060526
838201LV00046B/1059